WINNING ON HR ANALYTICS

Leveraging Data for Competitive Advantage

RAMESH SOUNDARARAJAN
KULDEEP SINGH

ATLANTIC
PUBLISHERS & DISTRIBUTORS (P) LTD

ATLANTIC
PUBLISHERS & DISTRIBUTORS (P) LTD

7/22, Ansari Road, Darya Ganj, New Delhi
Tel.: +91-11-4077 5252, 2327 3880
E-mail: orders@atlanticbooks.com
Web: www.atlanticbooks.com

This edition published in 2024 by Atlantic Publishers & Distributors (P) Ltd.

Previous edition published by Sage Publications in 2017

Printed & bound in India by Atlantic Print Services

Advance Praise

This book provides HR Analytics techniques and very practical set of action oriented recommendations to leverage human talent.

Srinivas Kandula,
CEO, Capgemini, India

Ramesh and Kuldeep have filled this book with helpful and timely examples of leveraging analytics in Human Resources today. Analysts, benefit from their research and help your organization further its goals.

Jeremy Shapiro, Executive Director,
HR, Morgan Stanley

This book provides broad insights to this emerging field and practical guidance and advice for every HR practitioner.

Marc Effron, President,
The Talent Strategy Group, New York

HR is one of the fastest-growing areas for analytics, and this is an invaluable guide to the subject. If you want to hire, retain, and motivate the best people, you need to read this book and follow its advice.

Thomas H. Davenport, Distinguished Professor,
Babson College, Author of Competing on
Analytics and No Humans Need Apply

In a rapidly moving and advanced field like HR Analytics, there is always a need for new and useful up-to-date content and learning. This book adequately and provocatively fills this space bringing new perspectives and practical ideas for HR and analytics professionals.

Max Blumberg, PhD, Analytics Advisor to the CIPD, Management Consultant, and Visiting Researcher, Goldsmiths, University of London

We often miss the strategic and financial value of insights into our organization's workforce. This book provides a framework for extracting and putting them to use.

John Cunnell, Serial Entrepreneur

Dedicated to objectivity and transparency in people management

Contents

Foreword

It has been a half century since HR was known as the personnel function, and two decades since Dave Ulrich challenged HR to get a seat at the table. As part of the evolution of the function toward being more strategic, we have moved away from an emphasis on basic measurement to scorecards, engagement surveys, and strategic workforce planning. Today, these activities are all grouped under the umbrella of HR analytics.

Despite the enormous attention being paid to HR analytics today, there is a good deal of confusion regarding where people should be focusing their attention and what they should be doing. As Soundararajan and Singh note in the Preface, a lot of what exists in HR today can be traced back to scientific research that occurred at some point in the past. And what is not explicitly based on research usually has a strong measurement component. Data and analysis have been a part of HR for as long as the function has existed. So what is new about the current emphasis on HR analytics?

I see the current excitement and energy arising from converging trends in strategic HR, computing/technology innovation, and an appreciation for the benefits of learning from proven practice (evidence-based HR).

On the strategic front, HR has been searching for the longest time for the secret sauce that will enable it to be more strategic. There has been quite a bit of progress, but at the same time, there have been a lot of frustrations as well. The survey of the state of the HR function conducted by my colleagues, Ed Lawler and John Boudreau, at the Center for Effective Organizations over the past 20 years has shown surprising little change in the amount of time people in HR spend on strategic versus transactional activities.

It's possible to read this as a lack of progress in becoming more strategic, but I have a different take on this.

There is a lot of basic work that has always been and will always be part of the work of HR, most of which does not seem particularly strategic at first glance: making sure that people are paid properly, open positions are filled, performance reviews are conducted, development planning takes place, and much more. Under certain circumstances, these activities *can be* strategic, yet most of the time they are more about "keeping the lights on"—enabling the business to do its work by ensuring that people are in place to do the work when and where it needs to happen. Sometimes, when there is a critical business need best served by these traditional HR practices, doing this everyday work of HR is strategic. So, whether traditional HR is truly strategic or not often depends on the context. One job for HR analytics is to understanding when and where that is the case.

The second trend is the rapid development and deployment of technology that makes it easier to collect and warehouse data in easily accessible formats. This includes both the proliferation of survey vendors and do-it-yourself Internet-based survey tools. It also includes the widespread installation of enterprise resource planning (ERP) and other business IT systems that link together for joint analysis of previously disparate data systems that were hard to integrate.

On the employee side, the now widespread ability to survey people has easily led to an explosion of surveys conducted both internally and by outside consultants. It seems that everyone wants to measure as much as possible related to people, in the hopes that something will emerge that will be useful. Yet the often-cited problem of survey fatigue is a telling sign that we have too much measurement that is not being guided by the right questions and models.

On the business IT side, there has been an enormous shifting of priorities for many HR functions, with the cart too often being placed before the horse. The promise of the ERP systems, along with their outrageous price tags, creates a set of "facts on the ground": warehoused data that is expected to be analyzed first and foremost before turning to other data sources. This happens for two reasons. One, because the data is readily available, it is very tempting to dive right into mining it for interesting patterns, a temptation that most data scientists know can be very hard to resist. Second, the obscene sums spent in installing the systems create enormous pressure on the HR function to do *something* with the data to justify at least part of the sunk costs, which usually were authorized outside the HR function in the first place. Rather than question the wisdom of focusing on that data, HR dutifully falls in line and dives right into mining it for interesting patterns, even when there is no strategic compass to guide the work.

The third trend is the increased awareness of the importance of practicing evidence-based HR. In truth, this trend is more aspirational than widespread, getting more attention in the academic and research communities than within the HR function itself. Yet the growing number of data scientists and people working in HR with advanced degrees in industrial-organizational psychology and other fields has provided a good deal of internal momentum toward taking a more scientifically valid approach to defining and analyzing HR issues.

The good news is that there's a lot of evidence to draw upon to improve management practices such as goal setting, allocating rewards, doing employee selection, allocating training investments and more. Yet the information on the evidence is usually not communicated in ways that make it widely accessible to a broad management audience, and, even worse, little to no guidance is provided on how to prioritize what HR and the business should focus on. Consequently, the messages that emerge from the scientific community about how analytics can improve HR and management practice are disjoint and not focused directly on pressing business issues.

Even worse, many of the data scientists and social scientists with advanced degrees who work in and consult with organizations do not take enough of a systems perspective when approaching the analysis of HR issues. They too often settle for incrementally better (more scientifically valid) measurement approaches without first ensuring that the most important, pressing business issues are being addressed.

Today there are tons of data available that measure the execution of HR processes: headcount, vacancies, time to fill, completion of performance reviews, distribution of performance ratings, details on individual development plans, and so on. The problem with the current practice is that HR analytics is used to describe these processes without embedding the inquiry in a strategic context. This means that the analysis often reveals data patterns that can seem interesting but more often than not elicit a "so what" response: What is the value in looking at the data? Where are the insights that can help the business to function more effectively?

To address these questions and ensure that HR analytics adds maximum value, there are three steps to follow: (a) ask the right questions, (b) do the right analysis, and (c) lead the change. Of these three, only the second is done today in HR analytics with any regularity, but even then common practice falls short of the ideal. This book and other contributions make important advances in this area, but with some critical caveats because common practice is not changing fast enough. On the other two fronts, there has been very little progress except in rare instances, with the exceptions proving the rule.

Start with asking the right questions. For me, the most important place to start for any HR analytics inquiry is the hypotheses being tested. What is the main purpose in doing the analysis? What business problems are you trying to solve? Are you trying to improve the current HR practice to make it more efficient and effective? Are you trying to help the business to improve strategy execution?

Asking the right questions often requires looking beyond the specific request that is made regarding HR analytics to get at what's really at the heart of the matter. For example, "how do we improve employee engagement" at face value can sound like "how do we improve employee morale" or "how do we get our people more actively involved in providing discretionary effort?" Faced with that request, most HR analytics practitioners will charge ahead and look only at how people feel about the work they are doing and search for ways to improve their attitudes and motivation. Such a pursuit is worthwhile—if indeed employee engagement is the ultimate end result that the business needs. Yet in most cases, engagement is not the end result but instead, one of the contributors to performance, and it is performance that is the real target. As detailed in my book *Strategic Analytics*, to answer such a question, you need to take a more systematic look at the factors driving performance at the individual level, and broaden the scope of the HR analytics inquiry to include the work design and the competencies of the people in the role.

Soundararajan and Singh set the stage the right way by putting the discussion of how to link HR analytics to business outcomes at the beginning of this book. What the reader should know as you dive into the content is that there are multiple ways to frame and address business impact. Whether it's the approach taken in this book, in my book, or any of a number of other ways, choose the one that works for you and makes the most sense to your stakeholders and business partners. It's the destination that matters more than the path chosen to get there.

When it comes to doing the right analysis, there are more different types of analytics that can be conducted. Trying to sort through them all is very daunting if you start from the perspective that you need to have a good grasp of all the different types of ways HR analytics has been applied—and especially if you feel like you need an advanced degree in statistics to make sense of it all. My advice here is (a) stick closely to the questions at the core of your inquiry, (b) find the right data to answer them, and (c) don't choose elegance of the analytical method over a laser-like focus on answering the questions. For example, many of the analyses presented in this book are very simple, consisting of calculating ratios or showing data patterns in a table or graph. If you are asking the right question and have the right data to answer it, those types of analysis are often all that you need to do. And to that toolkit I would add diagnostic interviews which often are the only way of analyzing issues like organization design and alignment, cross-functional effectiveness, and strategy execution at the business unit level.

The last key for doing HR analytics the right way is integrating the analysis with organizational change processes. To be most effective, this means starting with the end in mind: no HR analytics analysis should ever be undertaken without a clear understanding of how the analysis will be used, including knowing how the relevant stakeholders will react when presented with the information. This means that the business case for doing the analysis needs to be already known ahead of time, or needs to be established jointly with the relevant stakeholders. This last foundation for doing HR analytics the right way is usually the one least followed, leading many, many analyses to fall on deaf ears: they can generate some interest but often little to no action that makes a difference. If this sounds to you like I am promoting good old-fashioned organization development (OD) and change management, you are correct: the most effective HR analytics processes incorporate those core OD principles.

The journey to more effective HR analytics will not be completed in a day, month or even year. And the tools and resources needed cannot ever be contained in one volume. This book can be a very useful contributor as you make your way on that journey, so long as you keep in mind the big picture of what you're trying to accomplish, how you can best serve the organization's larger strategic needs, and how your work in HR analytics fits in.

Alec Levenson,
author of *Strategic Analytics: Advancing Strategy Execution and Organizational Effectiveness*,
Senior Research Scientist,
Center for Effective Organizations,
Marshall School of Business,
University of Southern California,
Los Angeles, CA, USA

Preface

You see things; and you say "Why?" But I dream things that never were; and I say "Why not?"

—George Bernard Shaw

HR analytics is in the hype cycle today. There are conferences around this emerging field. Cool new technology is evolving that can help organizations visualize their existing data into sparkling charts. There seem to be only two kinds of companies: Ones that use predictive analytics in HR and the ones that are planning to! Some gurus even hope that HR analytics is the latest tool that can take the function to the next level.

Are analytics really that new in HR? Unlike many other functions, HR is based on behavioral research. Right from the pioneering Hawthorne experiments to Theory Y, solid behavioral research underpins HR challenges such as training and motivation.

Geert Hofstede had set up a personnel research department in IBM around 50 years back. He arrived at the cultural dimensions theory based on more than 100,000 surveys. Jac Fitz-enz initiated his outstanding work on HR metrics and measurement in the 1970s. Gallup's Q12 was based on researching millions of survey responses in the 1990s. HR scorecard by Brian Becker and Dave Ulrich was published in 2001.

Taken that way, HR analytics is more an evolution than a revolution. If it is an evolution, what is the need for a book at this point in time?

When observed with intent, two patterns emerge in HR. First is the rush to adapt best practices without enquiry. Around the turn of the millennium, General Electric (GE) emerged as the benchmark for HR practices. Irrespective of the maturity of business, companies started setting up leadership development programs. Competencies were identified, leaders were assessed, and development plans put in place. Yet, even after all these years, one cannot correlate with certainty whether having a dedicated leadership development program produces better leaders.

The adaption of Bell Curve is a classic illustration. Every company had a performance appraisal process and a compensation review process. Based on their culture and business needs, companies had different levels of interconnect between the two. Many had a public appraisal rating and a more secretive compensation decision. Just then everyone read about the great impact of normalization on GE's performance. HR heads cheered on by CEOs embraced normalization without really taking a deep breath and exploring the intended business results. In a sense, if you are not normalizing, you are not one of us!

Let us flash forward to 2016. While it could have helped GE with streamlining its workforce, the benefits of using the normal curve have not been equally visible across the board. Murmurs had started 7–8 years back on the negative impact of normalization on employee morale. However, companies kept going with normalization till one of them pulled the plug and announced that it is not working for them. Adobe, Microsoft, and Deloitte are some of the high-profile trendsetters. Suddenly traffic is jammed with companies moving away from normalization!

These are just two examples of how HR organizations have been adapting practices not based on their own insights, but due to a bandwagon effect!

This brings us back to HR analytics. Unlike other practices, analytics is not about identifying a few people, buying some technology, and making some presentations, though it involves all the three. This book does not follow the path that you are being left behind every day if you are not using predictive analytics.

In our personal experience at work, we have been fascinated to see that:

- College, percentage marks, and performance in aptitude test have no correlation with on-the-job performance of graduate engineers, but performance during training has.

- There is no correlation between percentage salary increase and retention.
- Employees undergo training programs and their competency scores actually decline!
- Pride of association with a successful company has a strong correlation with employee satisfaction.
- There is a correlation between employee satisfaction and customer satisfaction for a given business group.

Most of this analysis was carried out using the advanced functions of spreadsheets and simple presentations. Since then, the analytical and presentation capabilities have improved manifold. At the same time, it is not a surprise to see even large and successful companies struggle for reliable data on which they can form their hypothesis.

Hypothesis is the operating word here. The classic PDCA cycle emphasizes plan, do, check, and act. You set goals, plan strategies to achieve them, measure outcomes, and take corrective actions where required. Analytics can help ask the right questions and align all the four.

This book is based on our experiences and insights gained from a cumulative experience of 50 years. It is our conviction that companies can win with analytics. However, that needs a structured approach based on:

- Planning HR strategy around hypothesis,
- Setting up goals for the strategy implementation,
- Review using metrics,
- Make course corrections based on what metrics say.

For ease, the book is organized into three parts:

- Evolution of HR analytics and establishing the business case for HR programs using analytics.
- Focus on each talent management process: acquisition, development, engagement, performance management, etc.
- Summarize with an implementation strategy.

Some of the processes and implementation are supported with insights and case studies.

This book should be handy if you are starting off your career and would like to get a perspective on taking an analytic view to HR. It would be handy if you are heading an HR function and would like to improve your performance. Even if you have a sophisticated analytics operation, we hope you can find some insights that are relevant.

Again, this is not about the latest and greatest things happening in the world of analytics. While we have expanded the scope to include subjects such as network analysis, contextual search, and text-based analytics, there could be better resources if your interest is solely in leading edge work. However, this is more around developing an analytical view of the function that leads to an effective use of what is out there.

Just a question in closing: We had mentioned that authors have a cumulative experience of 50 years. What exactly does it indicate? Is it better than 40 years' experience? Would someone with 60 years be better? Or it is five times as valuable as 10 years' experience?

If you have been asking such questions, we are sure you would find this relevant! To go back to the famous quote at the beginning, whether "Why" or "Why not," curiosity to question is where analytics begins.

Acknowledgments

This book may not have been written but for sports and politics—especially cricket with its focus on statistics and unending debates on who is really great across different eras. Both sports and HR are about people, talent, and contribution. Nevertheless, one has the database for meaningful debates, while the other is still evolving. This book owes to all the statistical research studies on Gavaskar versus Tendulkar and so on.

We would also like to acknowledge the opportunities presented by two of the organizations we had been associated in individual capacities—Infosys and Indian Institute of Management (IIM). The People Capability Maturity Model (P-CMM) framework and the analytical rigor it called for in parallel with the HR scorecard created enough opportunities to develop unique analyses. IIM, Kashipur, offered an opportunity to connect the topic to the HR community. Ramesh had worked with Sasken Communication Technologies Ltd, where people were very receptive to use analytics to review HR strategy.

We would like to thank our editor Sachin Sharma for staying the long course, supporting the evolution across nearly three years from a blind message on the website to a published book. While one Sachin (Tendulkar) contributed to the causes, the other Sachin (Sharma) enabled fleshing it out! We also thank Priya Arora and her editorial team for diligently reviewing the book and converting it into a final product.

The following people helped with their case studies, without which this book would have been half done.

- Mr Richard Lobo and Mr Vinu Sekhar from Infosys
- Mr Saurabh Jain and Mr Neeraj Sanan from Spire2grow

- Mr Tej Mehta and his team from iCube Consulting Services
- Ms Tracey Smith
- Mr Mark Berry
- Ms Stela Lupushor
- Mr Srinath Thirumalai
- Mr Andrew Marritt
- Mr Steven Huang
- Ms Alexis Croswell
- Mr Ranjan Dutta
- Mr Eric Olesen
- Ms Gia D. Graham

Before we close, our thanks and acknowledgments to our families. Hope their tolerance and unstinting support have been worth the while!

1

It Is the Right Time for Analytics in HR

CEO: Let us invest more in our people.
CFO: That is a risk! Their marketability will increase. What if they quit?
CEO: What if we don't invest in them and they don't quit? Is it not a bigger risk?

Often when HR asks for more strategic involvement, it is asked to show the evidence linking investments in human resources of the organization to either top-line or bottom-line performance or gaining competitive advantage. And this is where HR struggles to find an answer. HR and corporate strategists are like proverbial rail tracks which have been struggling to find a meeting point. While strategists are concerned about competition in the industry and competitive challenges such as innovation, productivity, scalability, customer centricity, etc., HR is more focused on ensuring right talent at right time and right cost. Organizations repeat year after year that people are their "key assets." However, articulating this asset value and appreciation tangibly has been tough even for those organizations with best HR setups.

HR's Tryst with Competitive Advantage

- In 1950s, Peter Drucker wrote, "Some wit once said maliciously that [personnel management comprises] all those things that do not deal with the work of people and that are not management." (Drucker, 1954). And since then HR has been struggling to be accepted as part of management (or seat at the table). An article published by J. Barney, in *Journal of Management* (1991), for the first time articulated clearly on the resources an organization has and their link to competitive advantage. The article built on resource-based view (RBV) theory by E.T. Penrose (1959). RBV theory has been seen as key in bridging the link between human resource management (HRM) and business strategy. As per RBV theory, any organization has tangible and intangible resources. Tangible resources are land, machinery, or money and intangible are goodwill, patents, or human capital pool. Barney elaborated that resources can be sources of competitive advantage only if they satisfy four criteria, namely the VRIO framework:

- Valuable,
- Rare,
- Inimitable, and
- Organized.

Any resource—tangible or intangible—satisfying all the four criteria can be a source of competitive advantage. A simple analysis reveals that human capital pool is one resource which cannot be easily imitated or may be unique (rare) to the organization and, hence, has a huge potential to be the source of sustained competitive advantage.

Human Capital Alone is Not Sufficient

Critics of RBV theory argue that having human capital alone is not sufficient for competitive advantage. What is needed is a *path* which facilitates interactions in the form of collaboration among the human capital that leads to uniqueness and inimitability resulting in competitive advantage. In layman's language, behaviors, and actions displayed by human capital at workplace are critical to capitalize on this valuable resource. HR's role becomes critical in designing policies and procedures to encourage right behaviors and actions delivering business performance.

HR Policies Are Critical Too

Human capital coupled with appropriate behaviors and supported by HR policies creates a potent mix for sustained competitive advantage. HR policies have not only to be aligned with the organization life cycle stage and business challenges such as productivity, innovation, scalability, etc., but also have an *inter se* alignment. While the first type of alignment is called *vertical alignment* or *fit*, the second type is called *horizontal alignment* or *fit*, which was popularized by Lloyd Baird and Ilan Meshoulam (1988). Presence of both the fits also ensures that the HR function becomes complementary to other business functions in achieving organizational performance. Vertical fit ensures cross-functional collaboration between HR and other functions leading to better appreciation of how HR contributes at the business strategy level in solving key business challenges. Horizontal fit ensures collaboration between various HR subfunctions so that their synergy helps HR contribute in achieving business objectives.

EVOLUTION OF HR APPROACHES TO MEASUREMENT CHALLENGE

All the preceding arguments make one understand that human capital plays a critical role in achieving business results. The challenge then is to demonstrate a link between the HR, business strategy, and performance using data. HR function's tryst with data is very old. Ever since the organized way of doing business started, managers have been concerned with this cliché question—"How to find the right person for the right job at the right time and cost." And answer to this is still evading managers.

Back in the early 20th century, a Philadelphia-based manufacturing company used a novel method to find the right people for its various positions. This company would ask the potential job seekers to assemble as a group outside the company premises and then the manager would toss the apple in the air. Whosoever caught the apple amongst the group was offered the job!

Later on, after World War II, due to the acute shortage of skilled employees, US Army started using skill tests to find the people having right attributes and this was adopted by AT&T in the corporate world. Subsequently more tests such as 16PF, TAT, MBTI, and host of others were designed by various psychologists to find the right people. With time, companies moved towards competency-based practices that are based on attributes related to workplace. Personality tests provided an optional supplement to talent management processes.

Mid-1990s onwards company executives and HR function started generating their own questions to find the right people, and these included: Why manholes are round? How many triangles can fit in a square of a particular size? etc.; these were more popularized by product companies like Microsoft and Google which used these questions while selecting people in 9–10 rounds of candidate interviews.

HR measurement attempts so far have been confined to find the right people for the right job and people who can deliver high performance. However, in 1978, Jac Fitz-enz published an article in *Personnel Journal* (the predecessor to *Workforce Management*) titled "The Measurement Imperative." In it, he proposed a radical, anti-establishment idea: that human resources activities and their impact on the bottom line could be measured. The response received by Fitz-enz from HR practitioners was at best lukewarm and cynical. However, this article had triggered debate and interest by some other scholars leading to more publications on measuring HR. This led to the beginning of data capturing for key HR activities such as employee turnover, recruitment, compensation, and training by the HR function followed by comparing data with similar organizations in the same industry giving birth to what is called "benchmarking."

Thus began an era of benchmarking key HR measures against the best practices which reached its peak in the 1990s and early 2000. But soon it was found that benchmarking was not providing any insights for action and the only benefit was a solace how the company was doing compared to others. Also during the 1990s, there was emergence of human resources accounting and utility analysis approaches to quantify human resources, but that had limited impact.

However, in 2002 Oakland A's use of metrics by its general manager, Billy Beane, in the selection of team members and subsequent publication *Moneyball—The Art of Winning an Unfair Game* by Michael Lewis (2003) emerged as a path-breaking strategy in the selection space. Oakland A's with a paltry budget of USD 41 Million were competitive with teams with much larger budgets like the New York Yankees. How A's did this is very simple—it extensively used *sabermetrics* (player data based on extensive analysis of baseball) in the selection of players. The A's found that players with strong sabermetrics correlated to winning games than those players who were strong in traditional metrics like batting average used in the selection of baseball players. Also A's found that sabermetrics also offered an opportunity to put together the match-winning team which was far less expensive. And traditional metrics were used heavily by others while selecting their teams. A's challenged the established convention in selecting baseball players and discovered that by using sabermetrics to measure the player value, it got cheaper talent which delivered the results!

Extension of the *Moneyball* concept to the corporate world happened in 2006; Billy Beane gave a talk on 'Moneyball Approach to Talent Management' at an HR Conference in Texas, Austin, and it caught the eye of corporate America. In 2009, Google started "Project Oxygen" to find out "what makes a good manager." In year 2010, Davenport, Harris, and Shapiro (2010) published an article in *Harvard Business Review* titled "Competing on talent analytics," thereby creating buzz in the corporate world. In 2011, Google shared the results of Project Oxygen highlighting data-based findings on what makes a "good manager"—forcing the corporate world to take note of Google's data-driven approach to find attributes of a good manager. Soon thereafter there were series of publications focusing on benefits of using analytics in workforce or people management in *Wall Street Journal*, *Forbes*, *Harvard Business Review*, *Fortune*, etc., including findings from

Project Oxygen of Google (Garvin, Wagonfel, & Kind, 2013) that showed that academic grades and types of questions it asks during selection have no correlation to employee performance.

Corporate world saw a new hope and the possible answer to the question of finding the "right people" by using a data-based approach to workforce management which got labeled as "workforce analytics" or "people analytics" or even "workforce science," while metrics-based HR analytics had been in use for a long time in the corporate world. What workforce analytics promised was a step beyond metric-based analysis to "predictive analysis" using an algorithm-based model relying on huge volumes of data (internal or external or often called big data) to make the data-based people management decisions. In an interview to *The Atlantic*, John Hausknecht, a professor at Cornell University School of Industrial and Labor Relations, said,

> In recent years the economy has witnessed a huge surge in demand for workforce-analytics roles. You can now find dedicated analytics teams in the human-resources departments of not only huge corporations such as Google, HP, Intel, General Motors, and Procter & Gamble, to name just a few, but also companies like McKee Foods, the Tennessee-based maker of Little Debbie snack cakes. (Hausknecht, 2013)

What Is HR or People Analytics?

HR or people management has been traditionally seen as an "art," relying on the use of gut or intuition while making people- or HR-related decisions in organizations. However, recent developments, as mentioned earlier, have highlighted the benefits of using data while making people decisions and thereby giving a semblance of data-based objectivity (scientific basis) in people decisions. This scientific approach to HRM in organizations has given birth to a new field called HR analytics or people analytics or workforce science, which uses a mix of understanding patterns based on data algorithms and intuition in making people decisions across an employee life cycle; typically, 80% data-based analysis and 20% intuition seem to be the rule of thumb. It is generally

Figure 1.1 HR Analytics Continuum

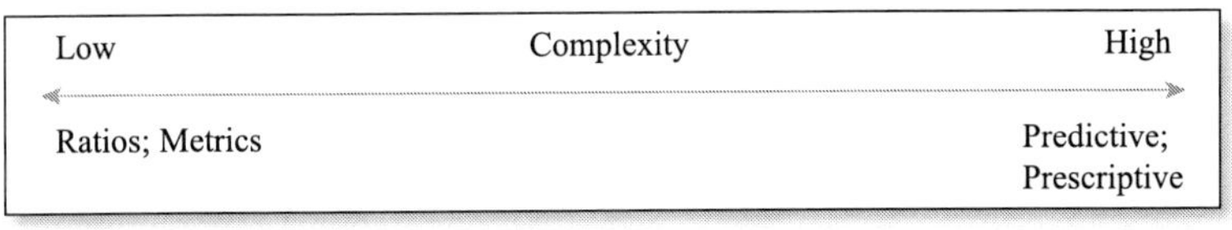

Source: Authors.

defined as a systematic collection, analysis, and interpretation of data to improve talent management decisions.

It is equally important to know what is *not* HR analytics or workforce science. One view is that generally it does not include metrics or dashboards, or reports of simple headcount or employee engagement score or attrition data. Other view is that HR analytics includes only predictive and prescriptive analytics. However, truth lies in between. HR analytics is like a "continuum," and on one end it can be basic ratios and metrics and on the other it will be complex algorithm-based predictive and prescriptive analytics. So an organization can be anywhere on the spectrum based on the maturity of HR processes, data quality, and capabilities available (Figure 1.1).

With the dawn of data era, information is available in abundance and low cost. Technological advances have facilitated the capture of information across employee life cycle events, thus making available humungous volume of employee data.

Why This Sudden Interest in HR Analytics?

For a long period, HR has been striving to get a seat *on the table* along with finance, operations, and sales and marketing functions to become a strategic function in any organization. In its quest to become "strategic," at the basic level, it has been demonstrating its value-add to business by showcasing metrics focusing on "efficiency," such as lowering HR cost per employee or reducing cost of per hire, etc.

Some other organizations have gone a step ahead and showcased "effectiveness metrics" such as employee engagement, satisfaction increase, or employee retention increase to highlight HR's value-add to business.

However, the C-level has been skeptical of these metrics and these have been generally labeled as metrics for justifying the existence of HR without any tangible link to either top-line or bottom-line performance. So this gap of showing how HR metrics link to business metrics has always remained. HR needs to move up the "measurement or metrics value chain" (Figure 1.2) from efficiency–effectiveness metrics to "business impact" metrics to demonstrate the link between HR metrics and business metrics. These impact level metrics require the use of advanced statistical modeling techniques and complex algorithms to perform key types of analysis including predictive analytics, prescriptive analytics, and cognitive analytics.

Predictive analytics will inform the C-level about "what will happen," for example, who will quit next, while prescriptive analytics will inform the C-level about "what can be done to prevent that attrition." New generation of analytics like cognitive analytics can identify patterns form large and complex data using multiple hypotheses to identify patterns and insights which could not have been seen earlier due to human limitations to construct models. For example, cognitive analytics can convert a simple hypothesis into a relationship between hiring channel and employee performance into multiple patterns worth considering, which otherwise would have required creating a hypothesis and analysis of data each time, making the process akin to finding needle in the haystack. So this kind of HR analytics, purely based on data, catches the attention of the C-Level and, hence, provides an opportunity for HR to become truly strategic, and this, in turn, will transform how HR is practiced.

Google leads in the use of predictive and prescriptive analytics and lot of other large companies such as Shell, Procter & Gamble, Morgan Stanley, Xerox, and General Motors have started using these analytics. However, the number of companies globally using these advanced HR analytics is very small. Latest study done by Bersin by Deloitte in September 2013 shows that only 10% of Fortune 500 companies are using these advanced analytics and

Figure 1.2 HR Analytics Value Chain

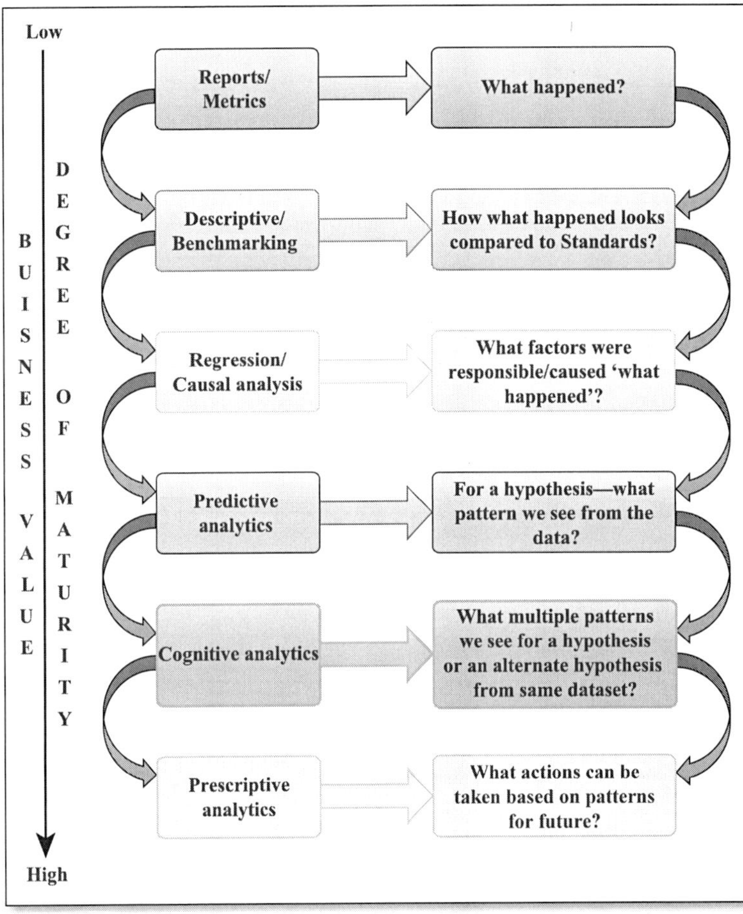

Source: Authors.

out of this 10%, only 4% are using predictive and prescriptive analytics, while other 10% are using basic statistical techniques for HR analytics (Bersin, Leonard, & Wang-Audia, 2013). According to Bersin (*Fortune Magazine*, March 21, 2016), the number of companies using predictive analytics has risen to 8%. The major reason why only a small number of Fortune 500 companies are using HR analytics is because HR faces big challenges to scale up for using HR analytics.

Big Data Era and HR Analytics

Everything which is connected today to Internet is generating volumes of data in one form or another from various sources such as handheld devices, laptops, and machines. This generation of voluminous data was characterized by Laney (2001) as "3D data" meaning data volume, data velocity, and data variety. Later on, some organizations added "data veracity" to it, making it 4 Vs. More Vs such as value, variability, and visualization have been added by some organizations to enhance the character of big data.

Big data is positioned as equivalent of telescope and microscope in terms of revolutionary ideas. As telescope helped to see stars and galaxies never visible to naked eye in the universe, similarly microscope made it possible to capture the life at cell level. In the same manner, big data is helping businesses to capture unseen patterns and trends, find answers to unanswered questions, and deal with uncertainty.

Today big data is being used in sports, politics, retail, insurance, healthcare, public departments like police, etc., for making decisions which earlier were made on the basis of intuition. Within an organization, functions such as marketing, finance, procurement, etc., are using volumes of data to streamline business processes and increase organization's efficiency and effectiveness. However, there is a limit up to which factors of production, like machine, can be maximized for efficiency while there are several blocks related to another key factor of production—human factor—which prevent any efficiency and effectiveness optimization. And "human factor" is the key driver of business in service and other people-intensive organizations. There have always been attempts to align human factor of production with organization performance through various methods such as better training, rewards and recognition, work redesign, etc., but with limited success. As it is said that organizations do not produce business, it is the people or humans working in an organization that do so.

Traditionally, HR has always been collecting volumes of data on various dimensions of human resources, such as:

- Demographic
- Performance management
- Compensation/benefits
- Educational history
- Job location
- Training
- Talent movement

However, this data has been used so far to compute metrics or ratios and do benchmarking. As highlighted earlier, benchmarking helped an organization to compare its status of HR practices vis-à-vis others in the industry and get an idea about various best practices followed by the industry. For example, if an organization had an attrition rate of 17% and the industry attrition rate was 19%, the comparison only gave solace to the organization that it is doing better than the industry but did not inform it about who is leaving, why they are leaving, and what can be done to prevent attrition. Thus, organizations were merely using available data to justify its existence by comparing with industry, whereas board and CEO wanted HR to show evidence of HR investments impacting the top-line and bottom-line.

Cascio and Boudreau (2011) pointed out that HR faced "big wall" in moving beyond benchmarks and scorecards to demonstrate evidence-based HR's impact on revenue and profitability (Figure 1.3). In Figure 1.3, the vertical column is the "wall" sometimes called *china wall for HR,* which HR has been attempting to cross to demonstrate its "strategic impact" in terms of causation and organization effectiveness.

Big data's HR promise is to help cross this wall and demonstrate its impact on top-line and bottom-line by showing with data how various elements of employee life cycle can drive revenue and profits and make "people" as a source of competitive advantage and become truly strategic like other business functions. In the next few chapters, we will explore how data-driven HR can help demonstrate its business value and become truly strategic.

Figure 1.3 Scope HR Measurement Approaches

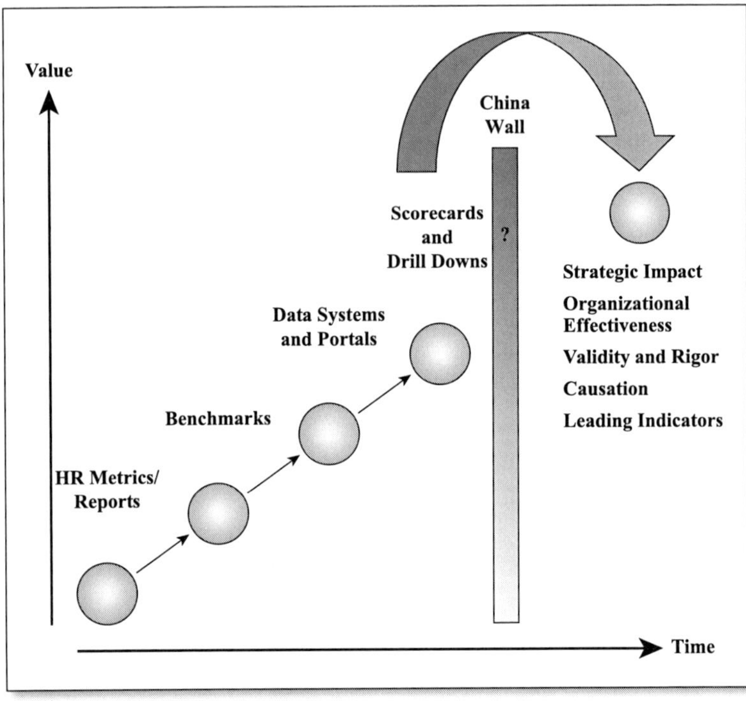

Source: Cascio and Boudreau, 2011.

Business Strategy–HR Analytics–Competitive Advantage Integration

A 2011 MIT study on analytics found that top performing organizations use analytics five times more than the lower performing organizations (LaValle, 2011). HR analytics can help organizations to deal with competitive landscape at tactical and strategic levels. At strategic level, typical competitive challenges faced by any organization include productivity, innovation, global scaling, lean delivery, etc. The HR function can align vertically and horizontally using a data-based approach to help an organization deal with these competitive challenges and gain competitive advantage. Figure 1.4 provides an overview of business challenges and HR analytics linkage. In Chapters 2–9 of this book, we will cover how HR analytics and right metrics can help HR to provide evidence of contributing to organization performance at the strategic level.

Figure 1.4 Competitive Challenges–Business Strategy–HR Analytics Integration

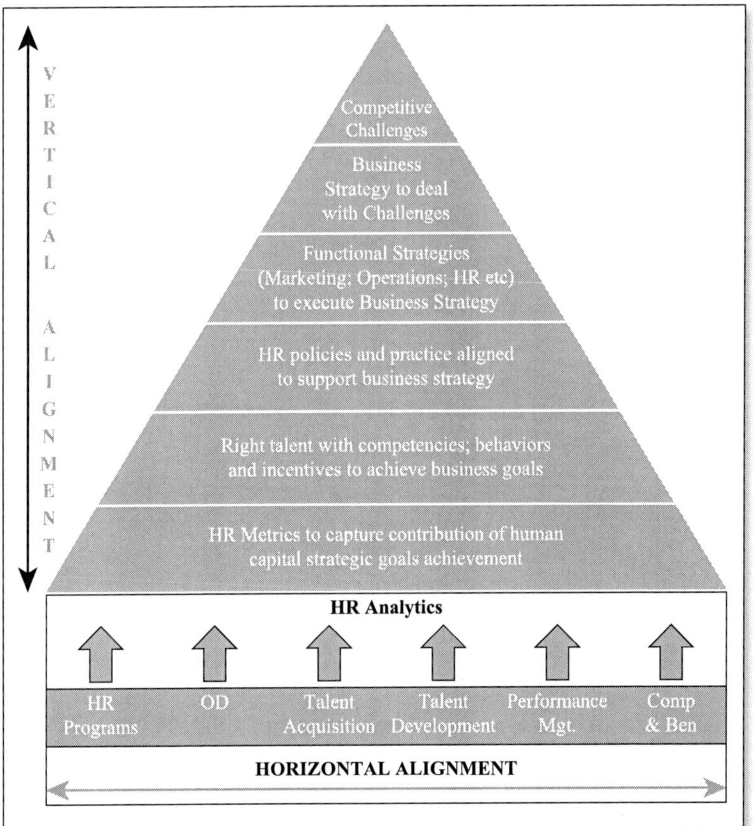

Source: Authors.

2

Articulating Business Value of HR Programs

Economy has evolved from purely agrarian based to industrial to information and now to idea or intelligence based. In keeping with this, HR has shifted from a pure policing–administration role to personnel to business partner and now to key player at the strategic level. This shift has been largely due to recognition of people as resource with a pair of hands to people with ideas as key players in execution of business strategy and source of competitive advantage. Publications like McKinsey's classic *War for Talent* and series of research studies in the last two decades have contributed in highlighting the role of HR in business strategy.

In many organizations, cost of payroll and running various HR programs amount to as high as 50% to 75% of organization's total costs. Hence, it is no surprise that a reduction of 10% in HR costs results in significant uptick in net profits, while cutting cost is the easiest way to shore up profits with the other option being for HR to showcase how investments made in various HR programs create business value and can even create greater value by increased investments.

In a predominantly knowledge- and idea-based economy, studies have shown that intangibles have 30% to 40% impact on market capitalization of the company.

- A study by Ernst & Young Center for Business Innovation (Mavrinac & Siesfeld, 1998) found that intangible factors (e.g., strategy execution, managerial credibility, strategy quality, attracting and retaining talent, management experience, and compensation strategy) explain much of the variance in the market value of companies. The impact of these factors varies across industry; for example, in the technology industry, the quality of management explains as much as 13% of the total variance in market capitalization.
- A large study by Huselid (1995) found that companies with sophisticated HR programs/systems (also known as "high-performance work systems") have a significant financial impact on profits per employee, sales per employee, and market value per employee. Findings of this and other similar studies have gained the attention of executives interested in measurement of HR programs as well as in redesigning employee programs like appraisals to ensure that HR is held accountable for enhancing their workforce's contribution to the bottom-line.

A Conference Board survey (Gates, 2002) found that HR's efforts to showcase its business contribution have been facing challenges on the measurement front as the C-level was not convinced of the measurement effectiveness as compared to marketing, finance, or operations. However, with the advancement of technology, falling cost of data storage has come as boon to HR to tide over the measurement challenge. In the last decade, IT applications have linked dispersed data in HR subfunctions to get data insights into various HR subfunctions. This emerging field of HR analytics has bridged the gap of reliability in HR measurements. Today, it is no longer question of having no faith in HR measurement effectiveness but of where, what, and how much should be measured which shows HR's impact on business outcomes.

HR Analytics Linkage to Business Outcomes

HR analytics can impact business outcomes such as sales, productivity, profitability, customer satisfaction, etc., either by adopting an HR measurement system covering all HR practices or by focusing on a single HR practice, like recruitment, without a full measurement system.

1. Adoption of HR analytics as a model or framework using technology/tool: Here, the focus is on how the implementation of technology- or system-based HR analytics as a cogent model or framework of some maturity level by any organization impacts business outcomes, for example, use of a human capital management (HCM) reporting and analysis system.
2. Adoption of a HR program/practice: Here, the focus is on how the use of various HR programs such as employee engagement surveys, workforce planning, succession planning, compensation management, performance management, learning and development, etc., based on analysis link to business outcomes. For example, based on recruitment data analysis, an organization identifies certain attributes linked to high performers and then hires those who have those attributes. Some of the programs will be covered in this chapter while others are covered in subsequent chapters.

Measuring Use of HR Analytics Impact on Business Outcomes

HR function has been collecting various types of employee data for many decades now. Much of this data by any organization has been used to gather inputs on what has happened in the last year and what is happening at the moment on HR metrics, such as headcount, attrition rates, absence rate, cost per hire, training hours per employee, etc., primarily to get a sense of the current HR temperature in the organization. Increasing adoption of HCM suites by organizations enabled them to play with core HR data and HCM suite's data and, thus, marked the beginning of use of HR analytics at the organization level. Now an organization is able to track which units or projects are having more usage of training resources or where performance appraisal quality is better than other units or projects. As acquisition of HCM suites came with a substantial cost, management became interested to know how the use is impacting business outcomes.

Aberdeen Group published a study in 2012, based on an extensive study, to find out the impact of deployment of HR analytics on business outcomes by comparing data of organizations which had adopted HR analytics to support business strategy versus those which were not using it (Lombardi & Laurano, 2012). The study found that the use of HR analytics helped companies to achieve higher results in the range of 8%–15% for customer satisfaction, customer retention, and revenue per employee as shown in Figure 2.1.

Another study done by CedarCrestone in 2014 again found that those companies which had adopted HR analytics technologies outperformed on profit and revenue per employee parameters all those which had not adopted the same (Figure 2.2). The

Figure 2.1 Business Impact of HR Analytics

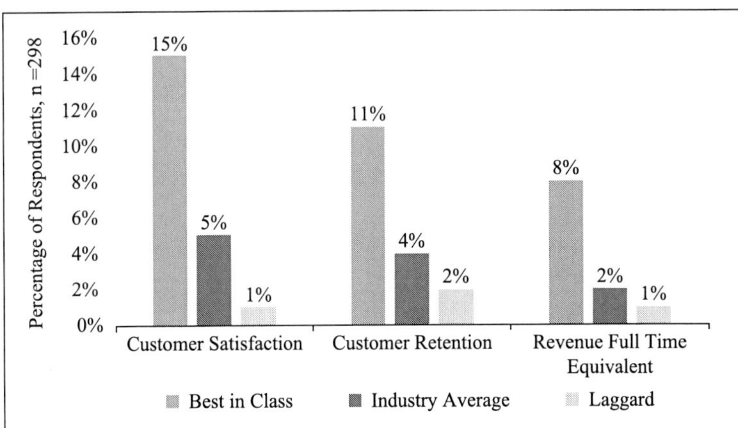

Source: Aberdeen Group (Lombardi & Laurano, 2012).

Figure 2.2 Financial Performance Growth by Talent Management Technology Adoption

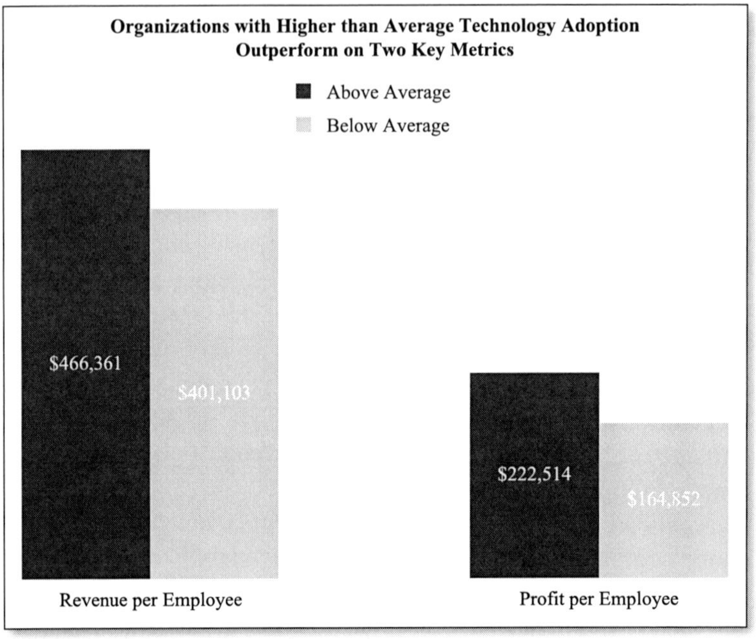

Source: CedarCrestone HR Systems Survey (CedarCrestone, 2014).

difference is 16% on revenue per employee and 35% on profit per employee.

Hence, consistent results by the above-mentioned two studies indicate that the use of HCM reporting in some manner or performing analytics in some form results in better business outcomes than those organizations which do not use it.

Measuring HR Programs for Business Results Linkages

Companies often wonder to find an answer to the question "what makes a successful company? Is it buildings or perks or infrastructure or culture or people?" And this quest for answer has resulted in many studies pointing out that everything being equal, people are the key differentiators. Almost all the organizations deploy variety of HR programs across the employee life cycle starting from attracting talent to exit of talent and even in post-exit situations through alumni programs. All of these programs cost millions of dollars to companies. For example, companies are spending close to USD 1.5 billion in employee engagement program/survey (Kowske, 2012) and yet employee engagement across the globe is mere 13% based on a 142-country survey of employee engagement levels (Gallup, 2012). Hence, it makes sense for managements to demand contribution of investments in HR programs like those for employee engagement, for better business outcomes.

Let us explore with the help of a hypothetical case. If an IT company decides to spend ₹10,000 per employee per annum on various HR programs, the total spend for different sized companies will be as shown in Table 2.1.

Let us look at HR programs investments from management's lens with a focus on net profits/earnings before interest, taxes, depreciation, and amortization (EBITDA) (Table 2.2).

Now let us assume that the CEO and CFO of Company A tell the HR head that they are doing away with the HR spend on training worth ₹10 crores for this year to increase earnings per share (EPS) so that it increases stock price to attract investors for more investment for future expansion plans. Alternatively the HR Head

Table 2.1 Sample Spends for HR Programs

Company	Headcount	Revenue (approx.) (₹)	Total HR program spend	HR program spend as percentage of revenue
A	10,000	2,500 crores	10 crores	0.40
B	20,000	5,000 crores	20 crores	0.40
C	50,000	12,500 crores	50 crores	0.40

Source: Authors.

Table 2.2 HR Programs Spend and EBITDA Linkage Analysis

Company	Headcount	Revenue (approx.) (₹)	Net Profit/ EBITDA @ 20% of revenue	Total HR program spend	HR program spend as percentage of revenue	HR program spend as percentage of EBITDA
A	10,000	2,500 crores	500 crores	10 crores	0.40	2.00
B	20,000	5,000 crores	1,000 crores	20 crores	0.40	2.00
C	50,000	12,500 crores	2,500 crores	50 crores	0.40	2.00

Source: Authors.

can continue the training spend if there is an evidence that such a training investment has an impact on business outcomes (increased sales or profits).

Company A is listed on Bombay Stock Exchange (BSE) and National Stock Exchange (NSE) and has an outstanding share capital of ₹200 crores with ₹10 face value share and the total outstanding shares as 20 crores. Assuming that the current market price of share is ₹250 and with 500 crores EBITDA, the EPS will be ₹25 giving a price to earnings (P/E) multiple of 10 (250/25).

Assuming if CEO and CFO do away with the HR training spend of 10 crores per annum, new EBITDA will be 510 crores and new EPS will be ₹25.50. Assuming that P/E remains 10, new stock price will be 255, representing an increase of 2%.

Continuing with Company A, the typical total employee cost will be 60% revenue or 1,500 crores. Assuming that the management of Company A decides to reduce the overall HR budget/employee cost by 5%, then this reduction of 5% in 1,500 crores can make the EBITDA 575 crores, and assuming that the training spend of 10 crores continues, new EPS with 5% overall reduction will be 28.75, and assuming P/E of 10, new stock price will be 287.5, an increase of 15% over 250.

The above-mentioned simple case study explains the point that reducing cost or cutting HR cost by either reducing the number of employees or reducing the training spend, etc., is the easiest way for HR to show proof of impact on the bottom-line. However, there are other cost levers too apart from HR budget or workforce/employee cost reduction which can impact business outcomes like profitability, and the HR function can play an important role in driving those cost levers to impact business outcomes. And that is what the HR function should focus on—using data to showcase how it impacted business.

For example, cost of production can be reduced by capacity expansion to impact business outcomes, and the HR function can facilitate this. In a manufacturing setup, it means increasing the current operating capacity closer to the installed capacity without increase in labor/manpower, leading to increased output with the same labor inputs. It can be easily measured to show impact on business outcomes. In a service or IT company, capacity expansion is possible by increasing the utilization rate of deployable or billable employees, again thereby increasing revenue with the same resources at the same cost. These are some of the easier ways to link HR programs, like training investments resulting in capacity expansion and, hence, higher revenue. And majority of companies employ these methods to increase revenues. However, the HR function needs to articulate its role in such methods of increasing revenues rather than easily accepting reduction in HR budget or headcount to reduce costs and increase profits.

Another measureable tactic, other than cost reduction, which HR can use is to boost profitability through use of technology. Many companies are using technology to provide self-service to employees enabling them to pursue e-learning, get answers to queries like compensation, manage benefits and performance, etc. On an average, efficient deployment of technology for HR administrative processes can reduce cost up to 30%, which is quite substantial and measurable also.

There are other ways of showcasing impact or contribution of HR on business outcomes by increasing revenue or sales. This can be illustrated with the help of an example as below.

Let us assume that company A grows by 20% and new revenue is 3,000 crores, which increases wages by 5% and continues with 10 crore HR training investments; EBITDA at 20% will be 600 crores and EPS will be 30 and with P/E of 10, new stock price will be 300, an increase of 20% of over 250.

So in the second case, if HR can show evidence that the increased revenue is due to increased investments in training of people of the company, then reduction in such investments becomes agnostic to the market price of the share for a listed company.

Let us take another illustration to explain the difference between cost levers and engaged and developed people as a lever for impacting business outcomes. Take two companies A and B with below data points as shown in Table 2.3.

Company A has a high engagement score and higher revenue per employee, but higher cost per hire. Company B has lower engagement score, low revenue per employee, and lower cost per hire. Here, company B's HR is very efficient by keeping hiring costs low while company A has a higher hiring cost. Comparison shows that HR is saving money and adding to profits in company B while people/talent is driving higher revenue per employee in Company A through high engaged and developed employees. In both the situations value gets created, though through different methods, but higher revenue per employee has more competitive advantage than the cost reduction approach. If a company can do both, then there will be a multiplier impact on outcomes.

Like employee engagement, HR has lot of levers to pull for impacting revenue or profitability through investments in HR programs which can help in building value over time and provide

Table 2.3 Sample Employee Engagement and Revenue Link

Company	Employee engagement score	Cost per hire	Revenue per employee
A	37	50,000	11,00,000
B	31	34,000	9,50,000

Source: Authors.

sustainable competitive advantage. These include building a culture or work environment which helps in attracting the right talent, developing and rewarding it, and facilitating the employees to perform at their best. This is where HR needs to invest time and money, and measurement can help in identifying where maximum investment can provide maximum returns.

However, challenge still remains in measuring the impact of a large number of HR programs on business outcomes. Some research evidence is there which has attempted to find evidence of HR program's impact on business outcomes.

Research Evidence on Impact of HR Programs

Cantrell and her team conducted a study of several companies in 2006 to find out the linkage between specific HR programs in business organizations (Cantrell, Benton, Laudal, & Thomas, 2006). Study found that companies which had a focused approach towards the following HR processes had achieved greater economic success than those which had lesser focus on these processes (Figure 2.3):

1. Process aligning people strategy with business strategy,
2. Process providing supportive work environment to employees, and
3. Process for developing employees by giving them ample opportunity to learn and grow.

Analysis showed that improvement of one quartile in these processes resulted in 10%–15% increase in capital efficiency (ratio of total annual sales to invested capital).

Another study done by Conference Board (Gates, 2008) on use of HR analytics by Marriott Vacation Club found that sales executives with higher engagement score in the top quartile had delivered higher performance on parameters like sales volume per guest and percentage of tours losing on time-share contracts (Figure 2.4).

Figure 2.3 Superior HR Processes and Financial Performance

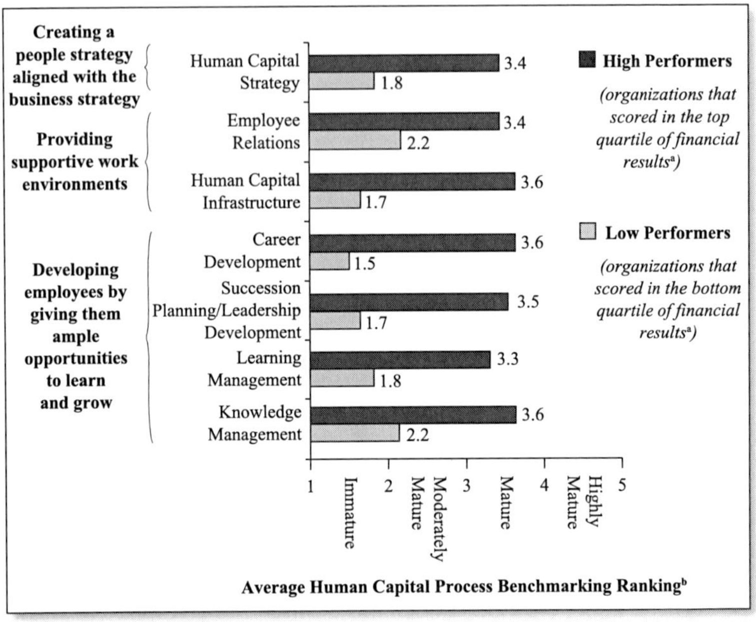

Source: Cantrell et al. (2006).

Notes: [a] *Financial results are represented by the two year average of organization's capital efficiency, or the ratio of total annual sales to the capital invested in the operations of the business by shareholders and creditors.*

[b] *Human capital process benchmarking rankings are based on relative performance of effectiveness scores compare to other scores in the database. Ranking reflect quartiles of performance (4–5 = top quartile, 3–4 = second quartile, 2–3 = third quartile, and 1–2 = bottom quartile).*

How to Measure Linkage of HR Programs to Business Outcomes?

HR practitioners know the value of measuring how HR programs are contributing to business outcomes, yet often struggle with the "how" part. Let us use some illustrations to get the understanding of the "how" part.

Engagement survey or job satisfaction survey is one of the major employee initiative or program for any company. It is done largely on annual basis and covers large number of job variables impacting

Figure 2.4 Highly Engaged Sales Executives Result in High Productivity

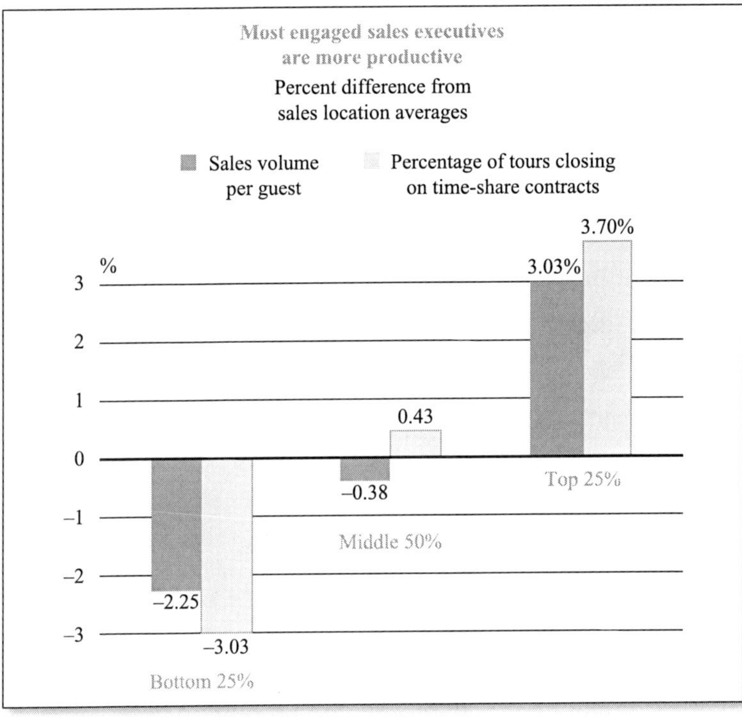

Source: Stephen Gates (2008).

employee performance and associated factors such as culture, leadership quality, company brand, etc. Data collected through such survey are large and rich and subjected to all possible ways of data dissection and bisection. Analysis of data is done in a very detailed manner but unfortunately such an analysis does not result in any meaningful actions after the survey to address employee engagement issues. And this lack of impactful action based on survey has led to it becoming a ritual affair and also employees not giving much credence to it. There are several reasons why analysis ends up in "action paralysis," but one of the major reasons is no attempts made by HR leadership of the company to survey findings with business challenges or to explain how survey provides insights for action based on the data analysis.

There are many ways in which the HR team can play with engagement survey data and link it to business outcomes, for example, in the case of an IT company which wants to know how the survey data can help in finding out the impact of software developer engagement and attrition on business outcomes. For doing this linkage analysis, the following easy steps can be followed:

1. Create a model showing linkages between dependent and independent variables/factors (Figure 2.5). Authors have created this model based on review of the literature on employee engagement and employee attrition.
2. Identify sources and types of data required for performing such an analysis.

Figure 2.5 Measuring Impact of Software Developer Engagement on Business Outcomes

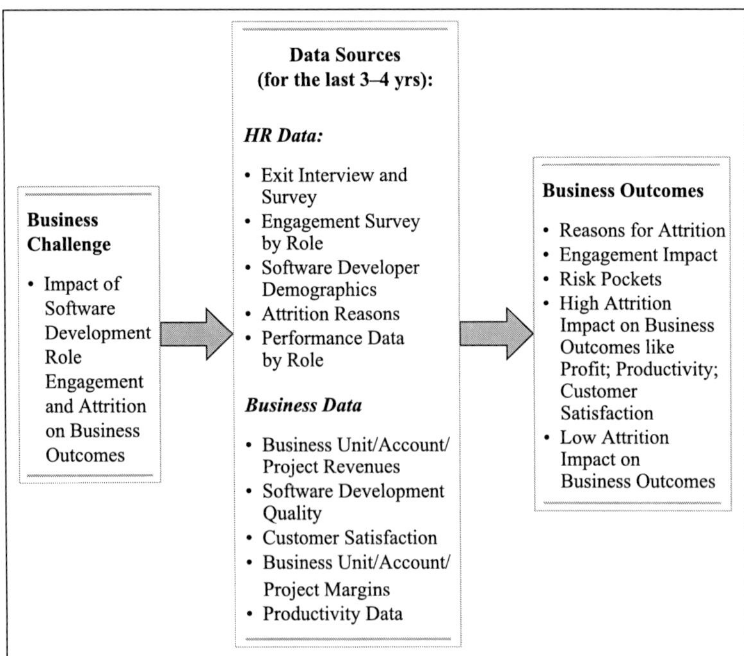

3. Perform statistical analysis based either on regression analysis or structural equation method (SEM).
4. Identify the patterns based on data analysis.
5. Draw insights based on patterns.
6. Finally, identify actionable steps.

Another key HR program/initiative is learning and development as this is a large component of the operational budget. Often questions are raised on what is the return on investment (RoI) of training programs and why not to do away with these. Measurement of training programs for business impact has been a challenge primarily due to the nature of data used in measurement. So far training measurement has been done well at two levels—efficiency and effectiveness. Typical measures used to capture efficiency have been attendance rate, cost per participant, etc. Similarly, effectiveness measures used include knowledge acquired test, knowledge applied on the job, etc. However, both these types of metrics, though relevant, fail to provide evidence of business impact.

Let us take the case of a large automobile company in the passenger car business with 1,000+ dealers across the country and about 1,000+ sales managers (SMs). On the basis of dealer sales analysis, it found that 30% of SMs working with dealers are performing at an average level. Further internal studies showed that these SMs not performing as desired were lacking in key skills related to the SM role. Company decided to roll out a 2 day sales training program for 300+ SMs across the country. At the same time, the company wanted clear evidence of training program impact on business outcomes from HR.

So how should HR go about showing business impact of training in the above case? To begin with, HR will have to identify what data is available within HR, and this will include employee demographics, annual performance review data, employee education, and training history data for SMs. Other data needed by HR will be related to business outcomes or key performance indicators (KPIs) for SM covering car sales volume, gross profit, inventory turn, productivity, and dealer satisfaction score (DSS). For KPIs-related data, HR will have to work with business managers, finance function, production function, marketing function, etc., as they are the custodians of business data. The data in possession of HR will not suffice for actionable analytics work. The model for linking training to business outcomes will look as follows:

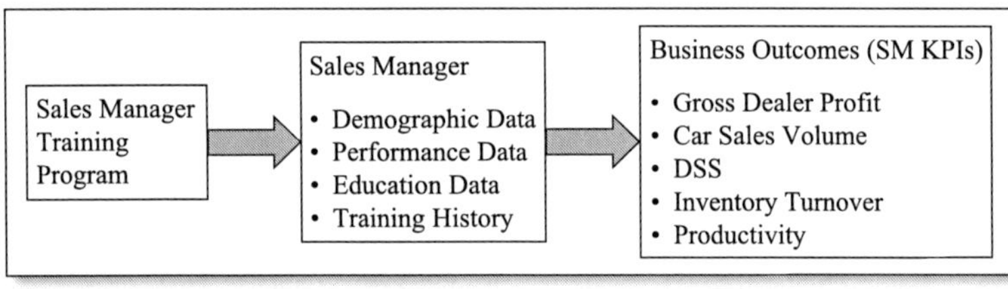

Next step will be of identifying SMs who should go for training based on SM data using criteria such as tenure, performance ratings, training history, etc. Along with this data, business outcome data for each SM before training participation needs to be collected. After going through the training program, business outcome data needs to be collected again after a period of 2–3 months to capture training impact on business outcomes. At the same time, the company can compare this data with performance data of SMs not covered by training program. Improved business outcomes for those who completed their training over the non-trained SMs clearly provides evidence of impact on business outcomes. As all the business outcomes can be quantified, it is easy to add monetary value to improvement in business outcomes due to SM training.

Similarly, actionable HR analytics for linking other HR programs such as attrition management program, retention program, incentives programs, etc., can be done with the help of data available within HR and other business functions. As HR professionals are increasingly being asked to demonstrate HR programs on business outcomes, the criticality of HR analytics becomes more important.

Industry Examples of Measuring HR Programs Impact

Sears Inc. measures impact of retail store employees' engagement on store performance. It captures data on "Moodrings" which shows how the mood of an employee changes through the day and impacts customer interaction and experience. It has crunched 1 million data points and found that an employee in good mood results in better customer experience leading to higher customer sales and repeat sales. As a next step, Sears is identifying the factors related to employee "good mood" and is focusing on those to enhance store performance.

Disneyland measures impact of "smile" on customer satisfaction and repeat visits by customers.

ConAgra used HR analytics software to predict which key employees are most likely to leave the company and why. The company scrutinized operations with high turnover and those with low attrition, and mined data looking at over 200 factors that might contribute to employees leaving. Employees' relationship with their supervisor and whether or not they were recognized for their work were two of the stronger predictors.

Xerox services HR analytics for hiring its call center employees as it was facing 60% attrition rate. Data analysis of online personality testing for selection showed that previous experience, one of the few criteria that Xerox had explicitly screened for in the past, turns out to have no bearing on either productivity or retention, while distance between home and work is strongly associated with employee engagement and retention. Using these parameters, Xerox reduced its attrition from 50% to 40% resulting in savings of millions of dollars.

Human Dynamics Laboratory at MIT in recent years has pioneered a concept called *Sociometry* with the use of specialized electronic "badges" that transmit data about employees' interactions as they go about their days. The badges capture all sorts of information about formal and informal conversations: their length; the tone of voice and gestures of the people involved; how much those people talk, listen, and interrupt; the degree to which they demonstrate empathy and extroversion; and more. Each badge generates about 100 data points a minute. Badge usage was tried out on about 2,500 people in 21 different organizations, and a number of interesting findings were discovered. Study found that about a third of team performance can be predicted merely by the number of face-to-face exchanges among team members. Using data gathered by the badges, it can be predicted which teams would win a business-plan contest, and which workers would (rightly) say they had a "productive" or "creative" day.

All of above examples indicate that every organization wants to improve efficiency and effectiveness of factors of production with special focus on human as a key factor of production. Organization's eternal quest for data-based efficiency and effectiveness for driving business results resulted in the birth of Taylorism and Fordism at the early part of the 20th century, pioneering the use of stop watches on shop floor. This was followed by assessment methods to find the right employee for the right job based on data rather than intuition around the mid-20th century. With the advancement of technology and simultaneous growth in data to zeta bite levels making easier for organization to deep dive inside the organizations and individuals to draw insights on what works best for employees to give better business results and competitive advantage. And this use of "data intelligence" in people management is likely to grow in the coming years as organizations realize increased business value by making people decisions based on data insights.

3

Analytical Problem Solving

We have seen different frameworks for analysis in Chapter 1. At the same time, when the business needs to solve a problem, we cannot say that "We are in level 2 maturity and that is a level 4 problem. We will solve it when we get there." We need to follow some approaches for solving problems using analytics.

Deep and Wide Approach

Let there be two companies. Company A has an attrition of 16% and company B has 18%. They are in the same business and have a similar size. In this situation, who is doing better?

One would, on the basis of data, say that A is doing better. However, let us examine the following graph.

It is apparent from the graph on the next page that taking the rates from a point in time alone may not be adequate. One needs to take the trend across a longer period of time. A is showing a downward trend, while B is showing a rising trend. Timeframe becomes a factor too.

We also need a frame of reference. Let us consider two companies with attrition rates as in the table on page 32.

It is evident that company 1 is having an attrition rate that is less than half of company 2. Is company 2 doing something wrong?

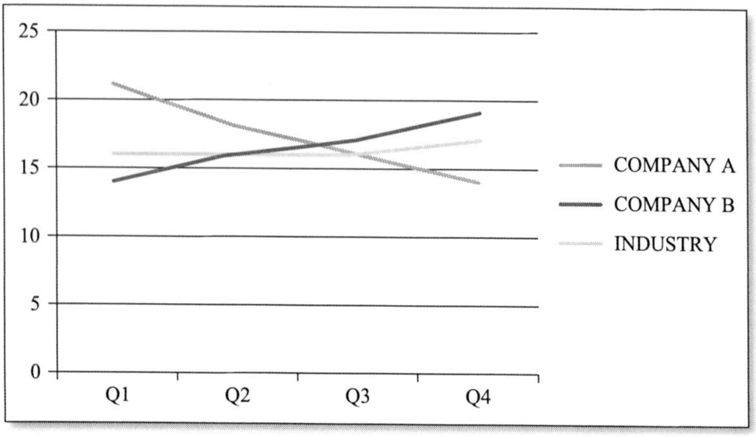

	2013–14	2014–15
Company 1	16%	18%
Company 2	42%	37%

Now, let us add another comparator. What is the attrition rate in the industry in which the company is operating?

	2013–14	2013–14 Industry	2014–15	2014–15 Industry
Company 1	16%	13%	18%	12%
Company 2	42%	65%	37%	70%

This table changes our viewpoint completely. While in the absolute, company 1 is much better than company 2, when we add industry number, it is company 2 which seems to be doing better!

Company 1 is not only having attrition rates higher than the industry, but the rate is also increasing when it is coming down for the industry. On the other hand, company 2 has lower than industry rates and it is showing a declining trend, while the industry is moving up.

One might be surprised with such high rates of attrition. However, very high attrition rates are common in industries where the hours are irregular and working conditions can be difficult (such as call centers and retail). A product development company might collapse if it loses people at 40% as the institutional knowledge would be lost irrevocably. So their retention needs to be far stronger. On the other hand, the processes are standardized and anyone can do the job with some training when it comes to stacking groceries in a shop. The cost of attrition is more manageable.

Industry benchmarks are sufficient to say how well one is doing. What about setting the direction? What if the company is already doing well against the industry?

Companies aspire to become employers of choice. To achieve this, they need a benchmark. Pan-industry surveys come in handy in this. There are different studies, such as "Great Places to Work," and "Best Employers". Participants in each of this not only are able to compare themselves to a norm but also can see if they are best in class or what improvements are needed to become best in class.

Company attrition rate	Industry attrition rate	Company engagement score	Average engagement score	Engagement score for employers of choice
13%	15%	67%	67%	78%

The data shows that the company is doing a good job of retaining more people when compared to competition. The engagement levels of the company are comparable to the participants in the employer of choice study. However, there is an 11% gap with the companies rated as "Employers of Choice." So, there is more to be done by the company in the engagement space and that would, in turn, improve its retention.

Summarizing, a company can compare its performance using the following:

- Historical trends
- Internal benchmarking across business units

- Industry benchmarking
- Pan-industry benchmarking data using workplace surveys
- Global benchmarking using surveys, benchmarking exchanges, and best practices sharing.

Now, let us look at a different challenge. Your company has an offer conversion rate of 70%. The benchmark for the industry is 85%. You would like to improve it to industry levels. Your recruitment team feels that having a sign-on bonus would help improve the conversion rates. How would you go about deciding on a course of action?

First of all, it would help to identify the problem. Is the join rate 70% across the board? Unlikely. First step would be to split into two categories—entry level and experienced. You might get a figure as follows.

Entry level conversion rate: 90%
Lateral hire conversion rate: 64%

It is obvious that the join rate is impacted by having only 2 out of 3 people who were offered actually taking up the offer. It makes sense to focus on increasing the conversion rate of laterals.

How do you analyze the lateral join rate? You could do it on the basis of the following:

- Functions,
- Job levels/experience levels,
- Roles,
- Locations.

Let us go one by one.

Function	**R&D**	**Operations**	**HR**	**Infrastructure**
% lateral hire	55	25	3	2
Offer conversion	60	75	50	90

Note: The highlighted columns indicate the segment where the conversion is below 64%.

HR has the lowest offer conversion rate. It is something that one needs to take an action on. However, only 3% of all offers are made for HR. Even a join rate of 100% in HR may not make a dent on the company's number.

The focus areas then are operations and R&D. Especially the latter, as it has the highest proportion of new joins and a lower rate of conversion. To begin with, let us take R&D. Is the joining rate different for different locations?

Location	**Bangalore**	**Pune**	**Gurgaon**
% offers	40	30	30
Join rate	55	65	60

There are some variations based on the location. At the same time, the differences are not marked across locations. Just focusing on Bangalore may not bump up the conversion rate. We then look at the next dimension—experience levels.

Experience level years	2–4	5–7	8–10	11+
% offers	55	30	10	5
Join rate	60	55	90	90

Note: The highlighted columns indicate the lower end of the comparable demographic.

There is nothing unusual in this. Conversion rates are typically lower for the levels where competition for talent is highest. Let us drill it down a further level and see if there is a need for a sign-on bonus, at least for the 2–4 year experience bracket.

Compensation quartile	Q1	Q2	Q3	Q4
% offers made	35	35	20	10
Offer conversion rate	35	50	75	90

Note: The highlighted columns indicate the lower end of the comparable demographic.

Finally, we have been able to drill down the problem. One-third of the offers being made for people in the 2–4 year experience bracket are in the first quartile of the compensation band. The conversion rate here is only 35%. This pulls down the conversion for people in this experience category who constitute 55% of all offers made for R&D, which in turn accounts for 55% of all lateral hiring.

The company has been making offers at the lower end of the pay range. While this is a cost-effective solution, it has resulted in offers being made but not having commensurate impact on the joining. A sign-on, like what is recommended by the recruitment team, may just be a band aid. HR needs to relook and come out with a better way of assessing and fitting new hires equitably. The distribution is skewed towards the lower half; 70% of offers are made below the median and only 30% above. Given that conversion rates are higher in the upper half, the company can analyze the reason for low salary and explore ways to make an equal distribution across the board. That is simplistic, but suffices for the purposes of this illustration!

In the first situation, we explored the width of benchmarking, standards, etc. In the second, we drilled deep into the numbers to arrive at the solution. Analytical problem solving involves both width and depth. Effective problem solving needs a judicious use of both.

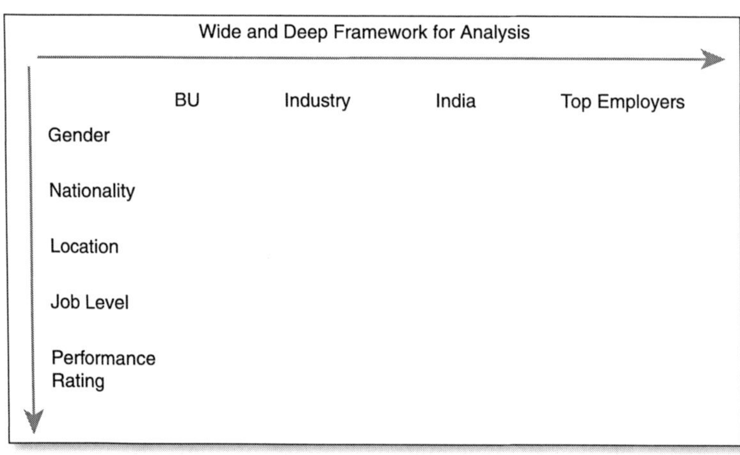

Building the Cube

We have used the deep and wide framework for visualizing analytics. This is composed of multiple scenarios of two-dimensional analysis. As the example shows, we have taken the attrition levels of two companies and compared them; this analysis is useful and a great starting point.

Now, let us consider two divisions of a same company and track their headcount growth.

Division	Headcount 2014	Headcount 2015
Division 1	1,500	1,700
Division 2	1,800	2,500

The inference is clear. Division 1 has grown its headcount by 13%, which is a decent number. On the other hand, division 2 has registered an impressive growth of 38%.

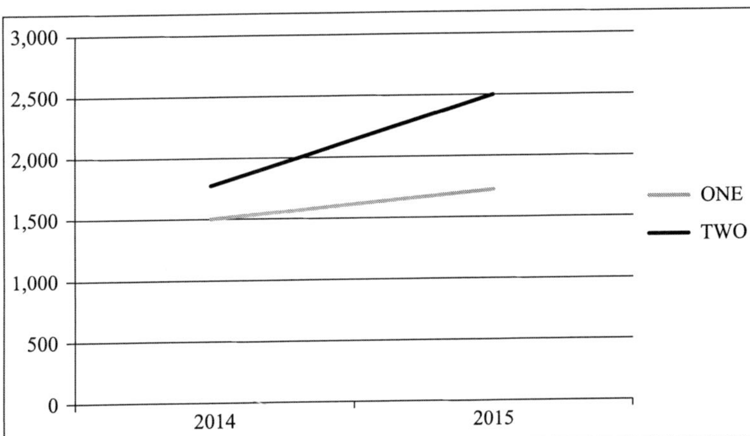

Let us pose the next question. Has there been a difference in terms of how the two divisions have grown their headcounts? In which case, we need to look at their structures. Let us have a simple structure of four levels, namely engineer, designer, manager, and general manager. Let the composition before and after be as follows:

Level	Division 1 2014	Division 1 2015	Division 2 2014	Division 2 2015
Engineer	1,200	1,275	1,435	2,000
Designer	200	280	240	330
Manager	80	115	100	135
General Manager	20	30	25	35

Our first level of drill-down showed differential rates of growth. However, one would also need to understand the quality of headcount growth. As the enclosed graph shows, the staffing pyramid has remained constant for division 2, while for division 1 the number of GMs and managers has shown disproportionate growth. It is possible that while division 2 is business growth as usual, division 1 is actually looking to expand business, hiring more senior people to seed/grow new businesses.

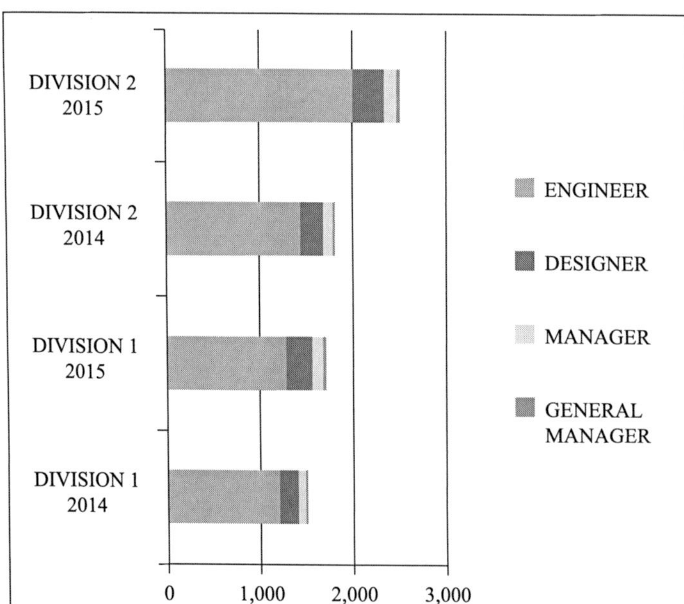

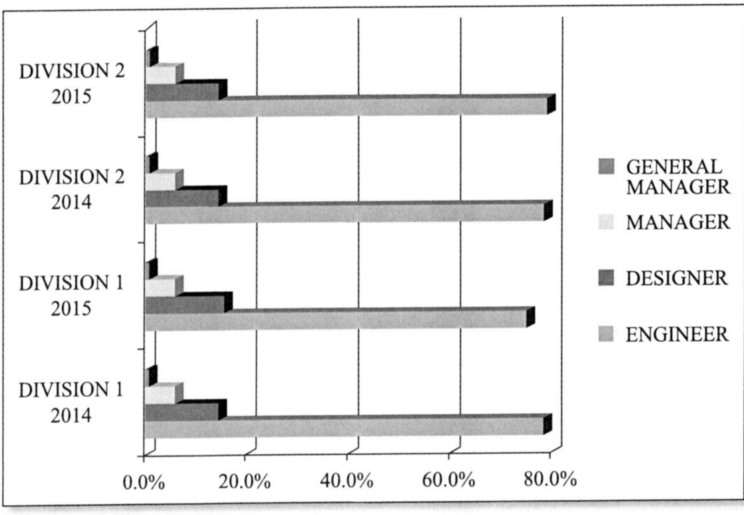

A graph based on relative percentage lays it out a little more clearly. The proportion of engineers has come down from nearly 80% to 75% for division 1. Immediately, we are able to grasp that something fundamentally different is happening there, which would not have been visible with the two-dimensional graphs.

This three-dimensional analysis of building the cube helps in the following illustrative scenarios.

- Assessing effectiveness of recruitment: Let us look at the interview offer conversion rates. Typically, it is felt that the higher the conversion rate, the more productive the talent acquisition. A company may be having a conversion rate of 75% and another having 85%. Next question would be the trend. Let us say both have improved by 5% in the last 12 months. Both have made 1,000 offers each. So who is doing better?

  Let us examine the data further, by breaking it into offers made for "freshers" and offers made for "laterals". We find that the company having a conversion rate of 75% actually has a 60/40 ratio of selection. 40% of their offers are for laterals. The second company has a ratio of 85%/15%. In general, the conversion rates for freshers are much higher compared to lateral joins. So, even though the first company makes 25% more lateral offers (40% compared to 15%) their overall conversion is reduced only by 15%. For an equal number of offers and other things being equal, the first company is doing a better job of acquiring talent. The three dimensions we have used are:

- Conversion rate,
- Breakdown into lateral and fresher conversion rate,
- Performance across 2 years on the conversion rate measure.

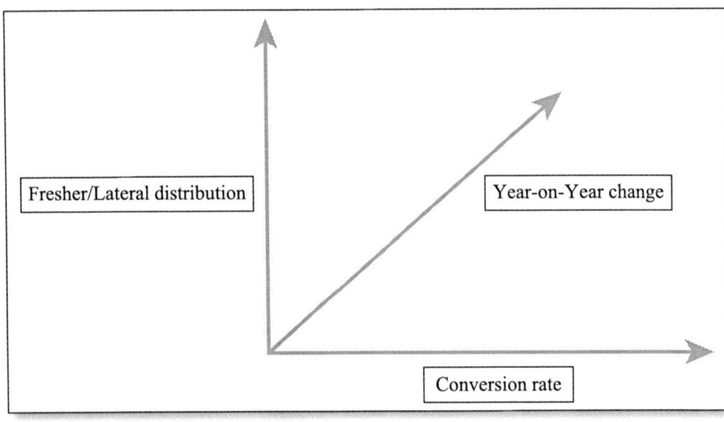

Visualizing the required information in different dimensions helps us get to the solution faster, when using analytics.

GOING FROM OPINION TO INSIGHT

The deep and wide framework acts as a reference for any analysis that we do. However, the human mind does not follow logic always. As the example discussed above shows, often we arrive at possible options for decision making based on intuition. But decisions cannot be always taken on the basis of experience and intuition alone. One needs to validate the opinion using a structured approach and arrive at the right insight.

Let us take a simple example. HR teams are always looking for ways to improve employee engagement. This in turn drives what are called "fun events." At the same time, one does not really know at what frequency the fun events improve engagement levels and at what level do they stop having an impact.

Opinion

We start with an opinion that says "fun events improve employee engagement." To validate this, we need to collect data.

Data

What is the kind of data one would need to collect? It has to be around fun events on the one hand and engagement numbers, on the other. We widen the scope of data collection.

- Employee engagement scores at two different points in time,
- Number of fun events preceding each engagement survey/dipstick,
- Count of all fun events,
- Division of fun events into major/minor, across different locations, across different business units,
- Number of people participating in different fun events,
- Retention rates of people participating in engagement programs,
- Attrition on a monthly basis.

Once we have collected all this data, we organize it based on metrics.

Metrics

The broad areas of metrics for analyzing would be as follows:

- Engagement levels; absolute and movement
- Frequency and number of events; absolute and movement
- Retention of employees.

With these, we move onto analysis.

Analysis

We now need to analyze to get insights. Some threads can be:

- Does retention increase with increase in fun events?
- Is there a correlation between participation in fun events and retention?
- Does engagement increase with more number of fun events?
- Does the same set of people participate in all programs? If so, do they stay more?
- What about the engagement levels of people who lead the programs? What about their retention levels?
- Is there a critical threshold of programs beyond which participation drops?

Our analysis leads us to insight. These could be as follows:

Insight

a) There is little correlation between number of engagement programs and engagement level.
b) There is a recency effect of big engagement programs. After big programs, engagement increases for a short time.
c) There is little correlation between participating in fun activities and engagement.
d) People who anchor cultural programs are highly engaged. Attrition levels are less.
e) A minimum threshold of fun events is required. If it is zero for a quarter, engagement drops marginally.

These and others could be insights. The insights not only validate our assumptions but also help to frame strategy and take actions.

Action

1. Have not more than two fun events a month. Have one big event every two months.

2. Identify and recognize the employees who volunteer and anchor such events of their own interest. Consider such behavior as well when identifying high potentials.
3. Create more opportunities for employee volunteering in more areas including technology, CSR, referral programs, etc. Validate whether ownership drives retention.

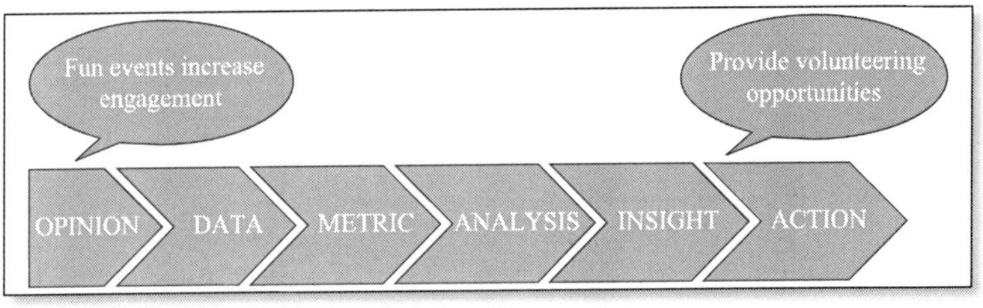

Chennai based Zoho corp has been able to develop a competitive product without resorting to hiring engineers from premier colleges. They have been successful in hiring for attitude from high school pass students, training them in computers and programming, and building productivity suites that are competitive with the best companies like Google can offer (Shobna, 2015). This is an example of a company using a contra strategy and being able to pull it off by execution.

STRATEGY VALIDATION

While the articulation can be different, every company has a talent strategy. The strategy, in turn, is based on a set of assumptions. It is not always that the assumption is based on insight from analytics. Analytics may or may not validate the assumptions. That should not come in the way of companies actually validating their assumptions based on data (Figure 3.1).

Let us take a very simple illustration. Most companies say that they create a "high performance culture." On drilling down, companies strive for high performance across different areas.

Figure 3.1 Strategy Validation Framework

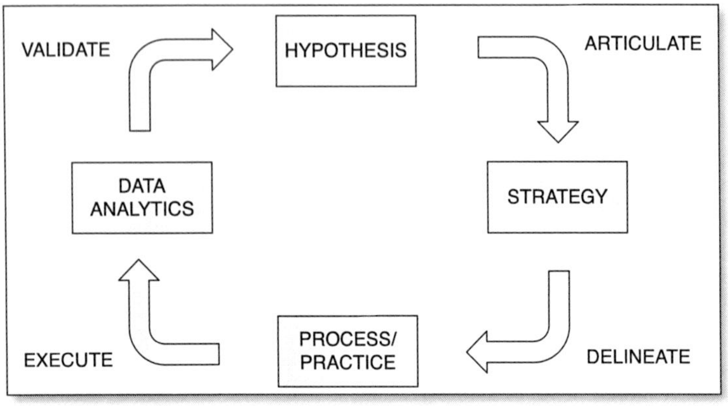

Source: Authors.

1. Hiring
   a. Hire from the best colleges and universities.
   b. Hire on the basis of consistently superior academic performance.
   c. Hire on the basis of a threshold performance on entrance exams.
2. Performance management
   a. Normalize employee performance.
   b. Take action on the bottom 5%.
   c. Align salary increases and rewards to performance ratings.
   d. Align promotions to performance ratings.
3. Development
   a. Design competency framework based on superior performers.
   b. Select on the basis of competencies.
   c. Train on the basis of competencies.

These are a few ways by which the company articulates a culture that reinforces high performance. If we need to validate, the questions should be at different levels. What are the questions?

1. In general, do people who scored more than 75% in college perform better than those who scored 70%?
2. What does a plot of performance ratings versus percentage marks look like?
3. Do employees from tier-1 colleges perform better than those from tier-2 colleges?
4. What is the normal distribution for each college/company? Does it show an abnormal pattern?
5. Does performance rating in one year predict the rating for the next year?
6. Does an improvement in competencies lead to improvement in workforce productivity?

Such questions throw up interesting answers that help validate long held assumptions, some of which had become mythical. Using a structured framework, companies have busted myths in the following way:

- Sysco Corp., a S32 billion wholesale food distributor based in Houston, found that its compensation system for drivers—paying them by hours worked—did not provide as much value to the organization as it could. "The model didn't necessarily provide better customer satisfaction or profitability," says Ken Carrig, executive vice president of administration and head of HR. Instead, Sysco changed to a reward structure it calls activity-based compensation. Drivers earn a base pay that is supplemented with incentives for more deliveries, fewer mistakes, and good safety records. Four metrics were targeted: satisfaction level, retention, efficiency (delivering more cases in less time), and delivery expense. Under the new compensation structure, Sysco found that drivers were not only more efficient, they were also more satisfied. The company's retention rates for drivers improved by 8%, and expenses as a percent of sales went down. (Schneider, 2006)
- Using analytics, Google was able to identify the following from a hiring perspective (Friedman, 2014):
  a. Grade point scores have no correlation to on-the-job performance. People who have a high grade point

average (GPA) are good in taking tests in a structured environment. This does not translate into real life.

b. Asking puzzles like "How many white cars are there in Bangalore" actually do not result in better quality interviews! Rather, using a specific behavioral interviewing technique delivers more consistent results. Even when using such interviews, one gets more insight when asking about a situation the candidate has handled, instead of a hypothetical "how would you" question.

c. The company has even started hiring people with no college qualification and it is working out well so far.

4

Competing Through Workforce Analytics

Organization structure is unique to every organization. Unlike HR processes, it does not easily allow itself to be measured for efficacy. However, improving a process produces benefits that are much localized. On the other hand, any improvement using analytics in the organization structure has greater leverage across the organization. There are different facets to an organization:

- The number of levels/layers it has, which can also be called an organization hierarchy,
- The number of functions/departments,
- Organization complexity. More the products/services offered by the company across countries, greater the fragmentation of specialization and the need for people to integrate across.
- Size: Larger companies often have more than one manager per employee, through matrix organization structures.

Business Levers of Organization Structure

Textbooks have been written on how the organization structure is one of the 7 Ss, with strategy, structure, style, etc. In a well-structured organization, there are no superfluous roles or layers, and jobs are done at the right level of competency and expenditure. For example,

- An organization looking to optimize its speed of decision making reviews the number of layers it has in the structure and reduces the unnecessary layers. Flat organizations are supposed to have not more than 4–5 levels from the entry level person to the CEO. Every additional layer adds to the timeline for decision making.
- A well-structured organization typically is organized like a pyramid, where the headcount decreases as responsibility increases.
- In any organization, the individual contributors create value while managers enhance the value by effective administration. To be effective, an organization needs to have the right ratio between the managers and the managed: too high and the work outputs are not coordinated well enough, too low and we have managers breathing down the necks of employees.
- In matrix management systems, more than one manager vies for an employee's time. This in turn influences the social and political system of the organization, impacting the culture.

Traditional Measures of Organization Structure

Traditionally, organizations have been using two measures for assessing the health of their organization. Manager span of control is the most popular measure. Quite simply put, it is the average number of employees managed by a manager. We can arrive at this by simply dividing the total headcount by the number of people designated as managers. If a company has 100 employees and 10 managers, the manager span of control is 100/10 = 10.

Companies arrive at this ratio and set goals to improve it on an ongoing basis. For example, if the ratio is 1:6.4 today, it should become 1:7 tomorrow. This is based on the underlying assumption that there is a good range for the ratio and one should strive to be within that range.

In the 1930s, V.A. Graicunas created a formula to identify a desirable span of control. He estimated the span of control based on relationships; every manager not only has to manage the direct relationship with each team member but also the relationships between themselves and the group. When all these are added up, the manager would find it difficult to handle more than six direct reports.

With time, attempts have been made to recalibrate this approach. However, given the variety in operating models, one single formula may not hold good, especially when we consider tasks to be as important as relationships.

Obviously, any action cannot be taken on the basis of average alone. The level of management and supervision required varies on the basis of task complexity and team maturity. Consider an assembly-line manufacturing. The supervisor has to maintain discipline and communicate the goals. The assembly line keeps them occupied without any need for management. In such a situation, one could even look at a management span of 1:20 or more.

On the other hand, in an R&D setup, there is a higher degree of task complexity and the manager needs to work collaboratively with the team. It would often be challenging for a manager to aspire for a team size in excess of 4–5 associates.

Even within the same industry, the management span can vary. In an ITES company, the span of control is very different for voice-based processes and data analytics.

Studies have shown that the CEO span of control in the US has increased from five direct reports in 1986 to 10 in 2006 (Neilson & Wulf, 2012). Some seem to believe that 7–8 is a magic number of optimal direct reports.

The manager span of control is a measure that every organization needs to track, identify pockets of stretch as well as inefficiency, and act accordingly. Span of control is also a requisite input to workforce planning and helps a company arrive at the right number of promotions.

TOOTH-TO-TAIL RATIO

Tooth-to-tail ratio is used in the armed forces to arrive at staffing levels. Combat personnel are the "tooth" and noncombatants like telecommunications, intelligence etc. are considered as "tail". A McKinsey study of 2012 estimates 26% as the tooth to tail ratio, on an average 26% of the armed forces across different countries are combatants. The figure ranges from 16% to 54%. (Gebicke & Magid, 2012)

In corporates also, we have the frontline staff as well as the back-office functions; we call them business functions and enabling functions. Business functions are where the value is created for the customer and delivered. Enablers assist the business functions and support the requirements of the organization overall.

Typical business functions: Sales, manufacturing, customer support
Typical enabler functions: Finance, legal, and HR

A simple way of deriving this ratio is by generating the percentage of business functions (sales + production + customer support) as well as that of enabler functions on the overall headcount.

Fighting a battle calls for far greater preparation than manufacturing and selling cars, for example. In comparison to a battlefield, the parameters in business are more known and static. As such, a 65 to 100 ratio would be an unimaginable luxury.

It is more likely to see 8%–12% range of headcount in enabler functions, with the other 85%–90% headcount being engaged in business functions. Cost cutting has heavily focused not just on lesser proportion of staff in corporate functions, but has gone forward with reducing the overall budget spent on such functions. This, in turn, has been facilitated by the outsourcing of a wide swathe of support functions, all the way from facility management and catering to IT application and infrastructure management. Offshoring, in turn, has helped to reduce such costs further.

Often in MNC organizations, increase in headcount in enabler functions is discouraged. Instead, third party outsourcing or assignment-based consulting is encouraged. This approach helps in spending just enough on deliverables instead of having a full-time employee to manage and be managed.

Much like the management span of control, the tooth-to-tail ratio in an organization needs to be identified both at the headcount level as well as the payroll level. An optimum organization needs to be decided on the basis of business requirements, without providing a buffer.

Often in HR, one finds a ratio based on headcount. We will have one HR person for every X number of employees. X can vary from 100 to 500. This figure is a quick rule of the thumb number without predictive validity. As an organization grows, one can follow two approaches:

- Set a coverage ratio of 1:200 and then keep hiring HR representatives to keep pace with growth.
- Set a target to improve the HR ratios even as the organization grows. Go from 1:200 to 1:400.

HR ratio based on headcount also assumes that an HR person is needed to perform several administrative functions and keep up engagement. On the other hand, as an organization grows automation improves helping every employee deliver more.

Increasing the number of HR partners has a lesser impact on engagement than improving the quality of people management. The role of HR is to ensure that managers do a great job of people management. Then, HR partners migrate to a coaching and consulting role from a pure relationship role. The HR headcount diminishes but business outcomes get better.

Just following a standard ratio does not help us re-imagine the function!

Becoming More Competitive Using Organization Structure

ORGANIZATION SHAPING THROUGH PYRAMID RATIOS

Ideally, every organization wants to be a like a pyramid. When we are talking numbers, two dimensions suffice and it is really a triangle, but the references have been to a pyramid.

The logic is simple. It may be difficult to arrive at an exact proportion of each level of employment. There are no basic ratios like 1:3:9:36 and so on. However, companies believe that the headcount at every higher level should be less than that at the lower level.

Let us take the organization, whose example was shared earlier. If we are to draw it into a pyramid, with length of the lines equivalent to percentage headcount, it would look something like this.

Role	**Role ratio**	**Role as a percentage of lower role**	**Role as a percentage of lowest role**
Engineer	48%	NA	
Sr. Engineer	27%	1: 1.8	1:1.8
Lead	13%	1:2.1	1:3.7
Project Manager	6%	1:2.2	1:8
Manager	3%	1:2	1:16
Senior Manager	2%	1:1.5	1:24
Director	1%	1:2	1:48

In this table, the percentages indicate the percent headcount in each role.

$$\text{Role as a percentage of lower role} = \frac{\text{Percentage headcount in a role (Senior Engineer)}}{\text{Percentage headcount in the target role (Lead)}} = \frac{27}{13} = 2.1$$

There are 2.1 senior engineers for every lead. This validates the fact that the organization has a tapering pyramid.

$$\text{Role as a percentage of lowest role} = \frac{\text{Percentage headcount in entry level (engineer)}}{\text{Percentage headcount in the target role (Project Manager)}} = \frac{48}{6} = 8$$

For every project manager, there are eight engineers. This is a healthy organization trend. If it were 2, then the company has far too many project managers.

One would see that in this simplified example, the ratios nearly double at each level. It can be equated to a progression of 2,4,8,16,32, and 64.

Each organization would have very different ratios based on their stage of growth and internal mobility. It is not unusual for manufacturing organizations to apply workforce ratios, primarily to their white-collar staff.

Every company, after a point of time, sets up internal universities to recruit fresh graduates from colleges to maintain their pyramid ratios and as far as possible have talent grown from within. There was a stage in the Indian IT industry when more than 60% of the workforce was composed of entry-level engineers. This led to a structure that looked like a triangle with its bottom stretched. This is not an ideal structure either, as it puts too much workload on managers to develop engineers.

In a healthy organization, it is natural that the role ratios between a level and the one above it are usually more than 1. It shows that in the organization, not everyone is promoted automatically. Consider the following scenarios.

1. Role ratio is less than 1. Suppose there are more senior engineers than engineers. Why does this happen? It could be because engineers are actually trainees and so their chances for doing billed work is less. It could also be that the company has not hired at the entry level in the recent past, as much as it used to. This could show a maturation process, wherein the company has adequate headcount and is in the process of improving the workforce productivity. Large manufacturing organizations do not suffer from attrition and so have stable employees at all levels. Campus hiring is just to create a pipeline for future talent.
2. Role ratio is more than 3. This is the usual case at the level of the CEO and his/her staff. There could be 10 SVPs but

only one CEO. That is the last stop in a career. While that is understandable, what about an organization that has a 4:1 ratio of lead to manager? This just means that the organization is suddenly tapering off and the leads are going to take a long time to become managers. Such a steep ratio would produce challenges of job rotation and career development.

ORGANIZATION SHAPING THROUGH PREDICTIVE ANALYSIS

How does an organization stay on top of its pyramid ratios? One obvious example is by growing talent internally and restricting hiring strictly to entry levels. This way, there are always people coming in through the ranks.

Second is to measure the role replacement ratios. Assume that a company has an attrition of 10%. Then, it needs to replace that extent of its headcount. Where there are internal successors identified, people are moved into these roles.

External hiring is the second big source for replacement hiring. It would make sense to divide replacement hiring into the following categories:

- Replacement hired at a higher level,
- Replacement hired at the same level,
- Replacement hired at a lower level.

By default, when there is a vacancy, the job requisitions are opened at the same level as the departing incumbent. It is often ignored that the positioning was also due to the experience and contribution of the incumbent. We need to review each position and make sure that at least a quarter of positions annually are actually replaced at a level less than the person leaving the job.

It would be fairly useful to review the % positions backfilled at the same level and set a goal of at least 25% backfill at a lower level.

Often, the usual representation of organization pyramids goes something like this.

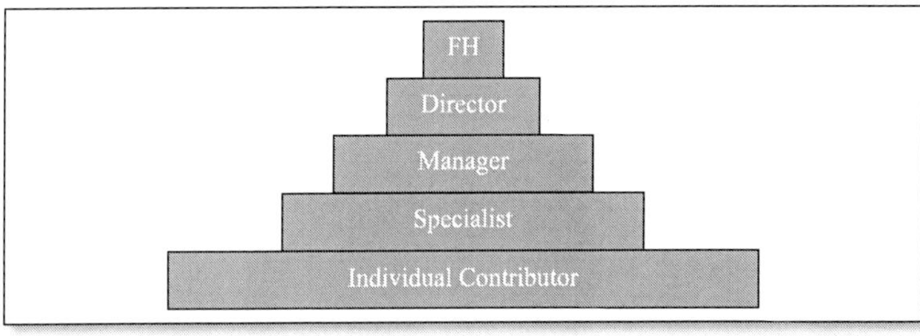

This kind of a structure is the ideal. Each level has lesser people than the level below that. However, this may nor may not be an accurate representation of an organization.

Consider a multinational organization setting up operations in a country. It will not have the liberty of hiring a lot of trainees from campus at entry levels. If it is looking to grow fast, the company would hire a lot of laterals at the higher band of specialist level as well as at a team-lead level.

The company then could have a pyramid like this.

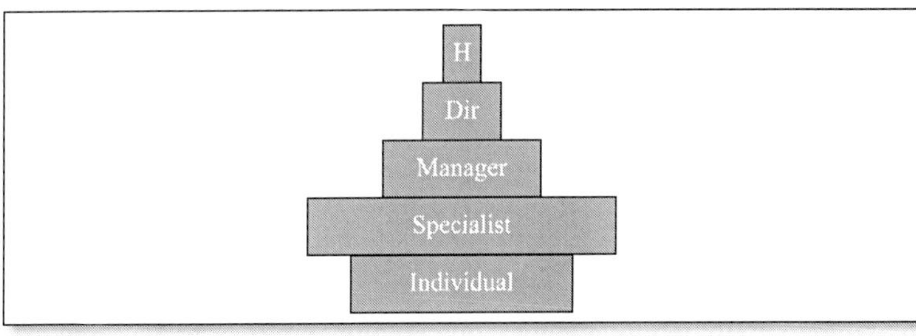

Let us examine this structure. Assume that the organization has industry standard attrition rates. Over a period of time, employees will expect growth. At the lower levels, they might expect to move in 3 years, while the time period would be longer and even based on vacancies only at senior levels.

The company then has to switch from a "default lateral hire" to "default grow from within" strategy. This migration could take 3–4 years, failing which perceived growth prospects of employees would diminish. This would also switch the focus of hiring from the specialist level to that of an individual contributor.

Year 1			
Level	**Numbers**	**Internal growth**	**External hire**
IC	30	30	
Lead	50	10	40
Manager	20	5	15
Year 2			
IC	60	60	
Lead	70	40	30
Manager	30	15	15
Year 3			
IC	100	100	
Lead	80	60	20
Manager	40	32	8

As we see in this illustration, the company has grown from a headcount of 100 to 220 over a 3-year period. However, it has consciously changed the pyramid shape from one that was bulged in the middle. Such a strategy also provides for a conscious and optimal mix of internal promotions versus lateral hiring. Of course, it is not an easy sell in the short term, as hiring managers always seek ready replacements and do not give the impression of having to allow talent to bloom. However, almost no great company was built on a strategy of hiring ready talent from outside all the time.

Organization Shaping and Employee Growth

Employees would like their organization to provide consistent career growth. Assume that an organization is in a growth industry and is growing as well as its competitors. Then, even if the company has the ideal pyramid, it still needs to have a good distribution of employees within the level.

For a long time, companies in India have been grappling with the challenge of employee expectation of growth. It is felt that employees would like an upward move, every 2–3 years. While this has acquired the contours of a truism, how far is this possible? Are all bands structured in a way that 80% employees can be promoted within 3–4 years?

Employers are more liberal with career moves at the lower rungs. With normal performance, an employee can hope to attain 3–4 promotions in their first 10 years. However, it is the rare person who gets more than two or, at best, three promotions in the next 10. As vacancy-based growth starts at senior levels, backlogs get transferred into the hierarchy. Expected tenure in band becomes important.

Level	**Expected tenure in level**
Engineer	3
Lead	4
Manager	5
Director	7

Given this reality, HR should share not just the career path but also the time expected for each progression for average performance and company growth rate. Then, for satisfying employee aspirations, one also needs to review the population distribution within each level.

This is an ideal situation. There are 20 managers eligible for promotion, of which at least 15 get promoted, creating 15 vacancies. Then we have 30 aspirants from leads, of whom 15 can be promoted. They can be backfilled by promoting from the 25 eligible engineers. This way employee growth can be cascaded down the path.

Level	Tenure in level	Numbers
Engineer	0–2	50
	2–3	25
Lead	0–2	50
	2–3	20
	3–4	10
Manager	0–3	30
	3–4	10
	4+	10

On the other hand, consider the situation where most of the employees are in the lead level and the situation looks like this.

Level	Tenure in level	Numbers
Engineer	0–2	40
	2–3	25
Lead	0–2	20
	2–3	30
	3–4	10
Manager	0–3	15
	3–4	30
	4+	20

This organization is relatively top heavy. Of the 50 manager aspirants, only 15 are promoted. For the 15 vacancies, there are 40 aspirants at the lead level and then there are 25 aspirants for 15 positions in the lead level.

Given that this shape has been created based on ad-hoc hiring, the company will tend to lose more employees at the lower two levels, as they have gained competencies of a higher level in their role and they could easily move to the next level in other companies.

Organization shaping then drives employee growth. When we do not analytically review the staffing plans holistically, attrition becomes an issue in the future.

For an organization to be more accurately represented, one needs to show the headcount as well as the tenure in band in years. This would also set the expectations correctly for employees and they do not go away thinking that they can consistently expect to be promoted every 2–3 years.

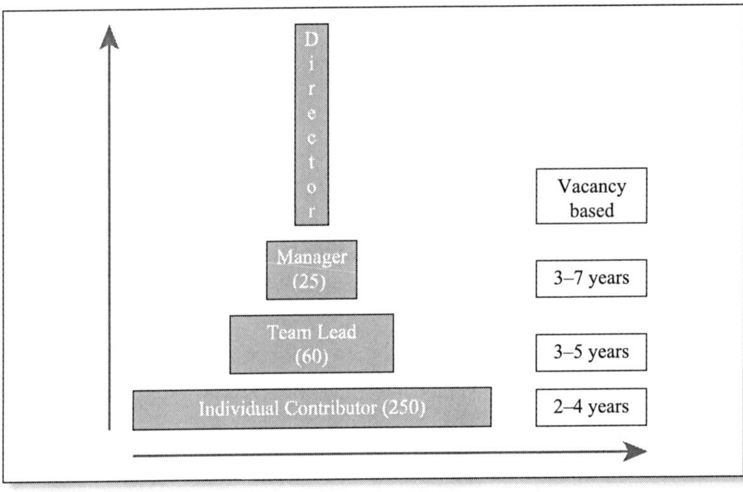

This representation also helps the employees to realize that there is no automatic growth and different employees grow differently on the basis of performance and assessed potential.

Look at Headcount in Offices

A company one of us had worked with had grown using acquisitions. Each acquisition brought with it R&D centers which were distributed across multiple locations. Over a period of time, the company had offices operating out of 50 locations. The company was incurring management expenses as well as co-ordination expenses trying to manage all these locations. Then, it took a decision to consolidate the headcount into 11 centers with growth hubs identified in each continent.

Often, companies end up in a sprawl of locations, each of which gets created for reasons at different points in time. As always, 80/20 rule applies to this too. It would also help to review the headcount at each location, identify the long tail and rationalize their number on an annual basis.

Measuring the Softer Aspects of Organization Structure

Organization structures look neat on the computer display. However, in reality, they are filled by people who interact with each other. Perception of the organization structure plays an important role in enabling the success of the structure.

It is possible to measure some of these as a one-off exercise and identify focus areas. For example, in a company with lots of matrix reporting relationships, one can identify the number of employees with matrix relationships and employees who are matrixed to more than two managers. Both are indicators of organizational complexity and need to be observed. However, identifying such information takes time.

Employee surveys are most commonly used to capture all perception feedbacks in companies.

A thoughtful organization design using analytics:

- Allows companies to be cost competitive,
- Increases employee motivation and reduces attrition by providing career growth,
- Helps develop future-proof staffing plans.

Organization Demographics and Succession Planning

Often countries are analyzed on their population distribution. Europe and Japan, for instance, have ageing populations, while India and China still have relatively younger population. India has the world's youngest population which will remain so for the next 10–15 years. Analysts refer to this as the demographic dividend.

For a long time, Indian IT companies had an average age in the mid to high 20s, representing their organization pyramid. Younger the workforce, more the need to invest in retention as employees are just getting started in their careers. Workforce becomes more stable, once they get into the 30s.

This is what is attractively packaged as the "Gen X," "Gen Y," millennials, etc. Adequate literature covers that. Let us check how national populations are represented.

This is the graph for India. This graph not only shows the age-wise distribution but also differences across gender. India has the

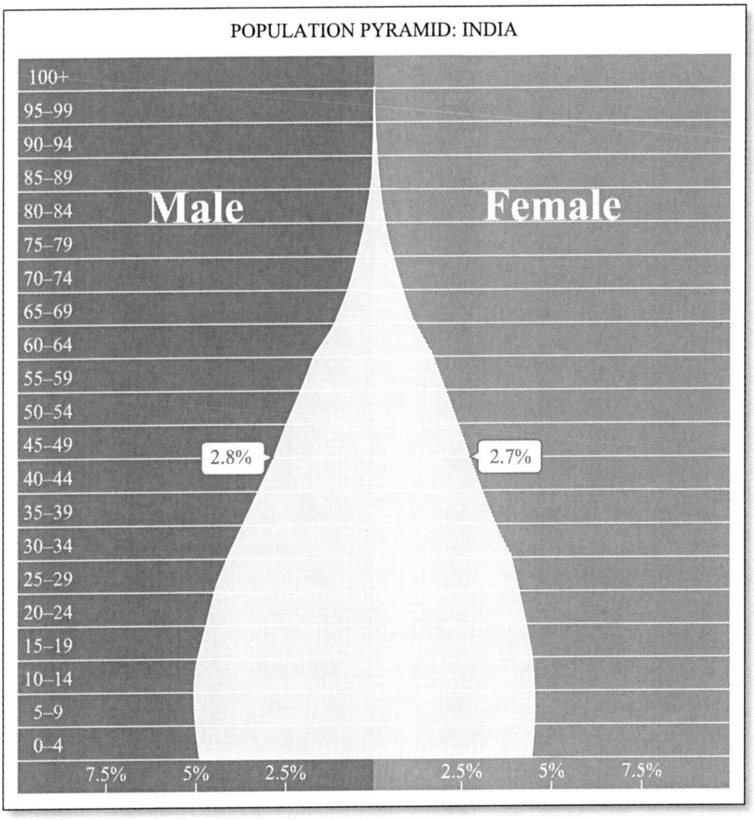

perfect pyramid with percentage population reducing with age. There would be enough youngsters to keep the economy running, though it will be a big challenge to make sure all of them are gainfully employed.

Let us look at Japan now.

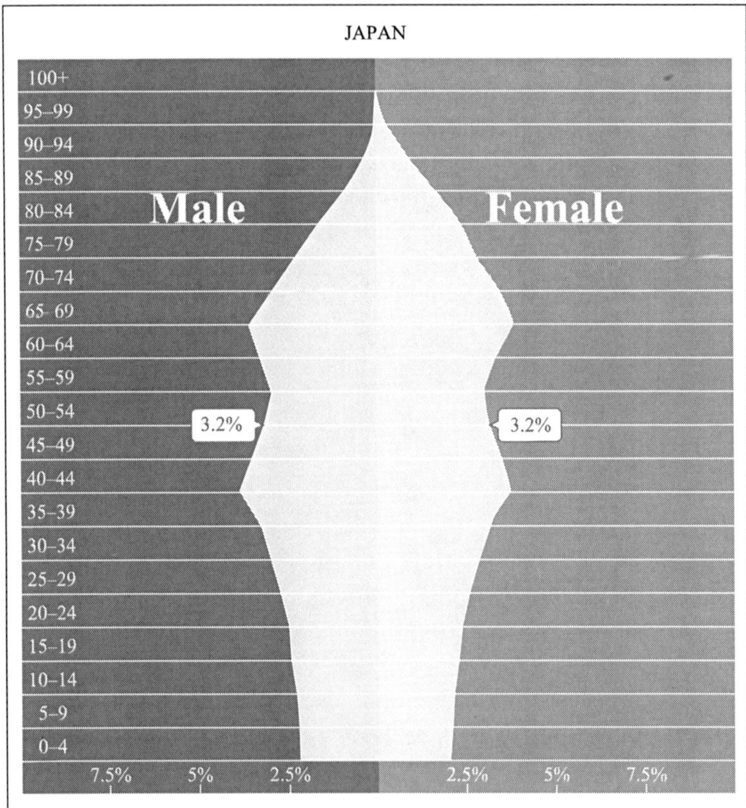

Source: populationpyramid.net (accessed on July 28, 2016).

Japan has a different distribution of population. 40–44 and 65–69 are the age groups with most people. There could be more people past the retirement age than the working population. This puts a greater demand on social welfare. Just looking at the demographics tells us that the nature of people problems in Japan and India are very different.

We have also come across some manufacturing organizations where the average age is in the high 40s. These organizations also have very low rates of attrition. What this means is that for several senior roles, both the incumbent as well as likely successors are of the same age and are likely to retire around the same time.

If we can visualize a similar representation in Indian companies, the IT firms will be similar to those in India. The challenge is one of engagement and employment. On the other hand, the visualization for manufacturing companies will be similar to that of Japan—older cohorts of retirement age. Succession planning in this case needs to be derived also from the age distribution. Do we have enough younger folks in the talent pipeline? Will we face a shortage of people in 5–10 years' time? How are we prepared for it?

Even in studies of gender diversity, we face the same issue. Gender diversity is increasing with more women coming into the workforce. At the same time, the representation of women decreases with seniority. A representation similar to the ones shared highlights these deficiencies in the manner that action can be systematically executed.

5

Acquiring High-quality Talent

Talent acquisition (TA) as recruitment is being increasingly referred to as one of the biggest processes in talent management. When the economy or a sector is growing very fast, TA becomes a differentiator to business. Even during a relatively steady growth, TA is key to bringing in people of the best quality at the right cost. TA as a process has a lot of transactional elements that make it more amenable to adapt an analytical approach. This also hinders progress sometimes as the more meaningful analytics dealing with quality need more coaxing and take a back seat. Here, we will look at both aspects of TA.

Business Levers of Talent Acquisition

TA, more than any other process, reveals the talent strategy of the company. A company could:

- Use a strategy of growing from within. Such a company usually hires the most at entry levels and primarily from college campuses. The company relies on a steady stream of employees progressing through levels and occupying leadership roles. Such a company rarely hires any lateral talent from outside. It minimizes the cost of executive search and the risk of a cultural fit, primary investment goes into the development of talent.

- Use a strategy of need-based hiring. Companies in nascent industries/fast-growth start-ups may not have the liberty of growing all their headcount from within. They go for need-based hiring and fill up positions across the board, including senior management. Such companies balance their investment into TA and talent development.

TA is also the only area in which companies compete with each other in the HR domain. On business and engineering college campuses, companies compete for talent. A better performance there, should translate into a better performance at the business front too.

In services companies, TA is also one of the biggest drivers of cost. If a company is making a 20% increase in its headcount, then the associated costs could be the equivalent of 3% payroll cost. Finding an optimum mix of experience and sourcing becomes important.

Often, in IT consulting organizations, one hears that:

- "Business is not the problem! Getting people is."
- "We can win this deal, if only we have five people with this skillset."
- "We are not able to convert our offers in the US and business is suffering."
- "We will start this line of business as soon as we hire someone who can drive it."

Needless to say, getting the right person on time is very important to keep businesses going.

Traditional Measures of Talent Acquisition

End to end talent acquisition process is depicted as follows. Often, TA is measured on two axes: speed and effort.

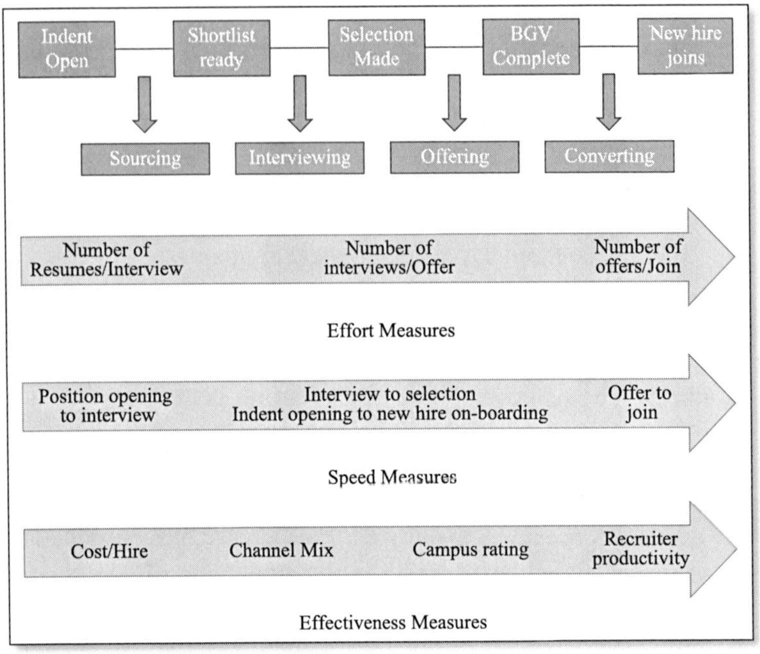

SPEED

It would be ideal for the recruiting manager to fill in the position as soon as it is thrown open. Imagine a vacancy opening up today and getting filled tomorrow! That at least is the ideal as far as cycle times are concerned.

In practice, hiring for each position goes through multiple steps. First is the process of sourcing. For the given position, resumes of eligible candidates need to be shortlisted. Then comes selection. Shortlisted candidates undergo the selection process of interviews, tests, and other assessment tools. This process takes time and can often be the most time consuming of all the steps. Next comes the process of making an offer to the selected candidate, verifying her credentials in parallel (including background verification), and having the person join.

There are two ways by which we measure this. For the hiring manager, the clock starts ticking from the time a position becomes vacant. It is his responsibility to get the work going. So, for him the cycle time is the duration from the time a slot is opened to the time it is filled. On the other hand, the TA team holds itself accountable from the time the position is open to the time an offer is made. After that, the joining time is influenced by the period of notice that a new hire should give her current employer. Based on need, the notice period can be bought out, but that is driven by the outcome and not by an indication of the process efficacy.

EFFORT

Even till a decade back, some companies in technology used to proudly mention the fact that they are receiving hundreds of thousands of resumes. Even the ratios were tracked and there were enviable numbers like only one in hundred applicants getting selected.

Typically, recruiting teams used to work on the following logic:

- How many offers we need to make for every join?
- How many interviews we need to do, for every offer?
- How many resumes we need to screen for every interview?

An inverted pyramid was formed, based on the following metrics:

- Offer conversion rate (% join rate. If we make 100 offers, how many join?)
- Interview conversion rate (If we do 100 interviews, how many are selected?)
- No-show rate (How many turn up for interviews, if we call 100 people?)
- Resume conversion rate (If 100 resumes are shared, how many are called for interview?)

Based on these numbers, the recruiting efforts were planned. Even today, these measures lie at the center of recruiting planning, with companies using analytics to ensure there is better conversion at each level. Let us just see what a difference of 10% in each step does.

Process	Company 1	Numbers	Company 2	Numbers
Offer conversion	80%	125	70%	142
Interview conversion	70%	179	60%	238
No-show rate	20%	223	30%	340
Resume conversion	60%	375	50%	680

In both cases, we end up with 100 new joins. However, company 1 is able to achieve this with lesser effort. This in turn means a greater process throughput. In the ideal world, to select 100 people, one should be able to just screen 150 profiles. Analytics is already playing a role in the same, as we will see later.

Effectiveness Measures

Acquiring talent is not governed only by cycle times. There are other dimensions as well. Cost is usually tracked by cost per hire. How many rupees are spent for every new join? Identifying the cost/hire is a great exercise, as it includes direct as well as indirect costs. Usually,

$$\frac{\text{Cost}}{\text{hire}} = \frac{\text{Cost}\left(\text{sourcing activity} + \text{technology} + \text{infrastructure} + \text{employee salaries}\right)}{\text{Number of new joins}}$$

Cost of hiring drives several operational decisions in hiring:

- Balancing out between hiring channels: Job portals are cost effective, but not sticky. On the other hand, referral programs are more expensive but sticky in terms of higher conversions. Cost per hire and conversion ratios help in deciding what positions should be promoted for employee referrals.

- Size of the TA team: Demand for recruitment varies with business. Unlike other HR functions, it is difficult to keep the team size constant. When demand is high, one needs more people but when demand is less, one needs a smaller team. TA teams typically have a more variable personnel cost, often employing people on time bound contracts and also by outsourcing the transactional activities.

Acquiring talent needs multiple channels: recruitment advertisements, job portals, employee referrals, search firms as well as social networks. How does one arrive at the right usage? Decision making is based on the following indicative factors.

Assume that we need to hire 25 engineers next month. From the table, it becomes clear that using job-boards and walk-ins should be our primary approach; however, since the conversion rates are low, this needs to be supplemented by employee referrals. On the other hand, if we need to hire three regional managers in sales, a walk-in interview will not help. Given it is a smaller pool, we also need to ensure all offers are converted. Then, we rely on referrals and use search firms.

Channel	**Set-up cost**	**Recurring cost**	**Turn-around time**	**Scalability**	**Conversion**
Referral	Nil	Medium	Medium	Moderate	High
Job board	High	Nil	Fast	High	Moderate
Walk-in	Low	Nil	Fast	Moderate	Moderate
Search firm	Medium	Nil	Medium	Low	High

These parameters are indicative. TA functions intuitively use such a decision-making matrix when arriving at their mix; especially in very large companies, employee referral schemes are highly effective as they leverage the power of the network.

Given that TA tends to use hybrid models of recruitment, it is imperative that every full-time employee is able to deliver the goals. As much as money, individual productivity is also important. TA teams track it in two ways.

First is number of new joins/number of full-time recruiters. Second is number of offers/number of full-time recruiters. Some TA teams use the latter as they feel it is a better representation of the efforts of the TA team; the former helps with measuring the output.

Large organizations also segregate entry level and campus hiring from lateral and mid-career hiring. Recruiter productivity is a better indicator of performance for hiring laterals. On campuses, it is the brand as well as the nature of employment that influences the success rate. Companies use indicators like "Number of key campuses on which the company was on day 0/day 1" to measure the effectiveness of the campus hiring team.

Ability to hire within the range is another challenge that most TA teams are grappling with, especially when it comes to lateral hiring. Typically, a company has a salary range for every level. Say for a team lead, it could be between ₹10 lakhs and ₹13 lakhs. Ideally, this range should be spread equally across the performance levels and tenure in the band. Suppose that a band has an experience span of 4 years.

Then, the best performer with 3+ years of experience should be getting 13 lakhs, while a person with highest rating but 1 year experience may get 11.5 lakhs. There are underlying complexities, but the more experienced and better performing a person is, the higher is his positioning on the band.

A company would ideally like all new hires to come within this salary range with similar rules. There may be a need to hire a few people even outside this range.

Let us illustrate this as follows.

We are sharing two simple distributions. Newhire 2 has more people in the lower third and lesser people in the upper third. On the other hand, the situation is reversed in Newhire 1. It is to the skill of the TA sourcing team and the brand of the company if the company is able to maintain the same graph for new joins as for

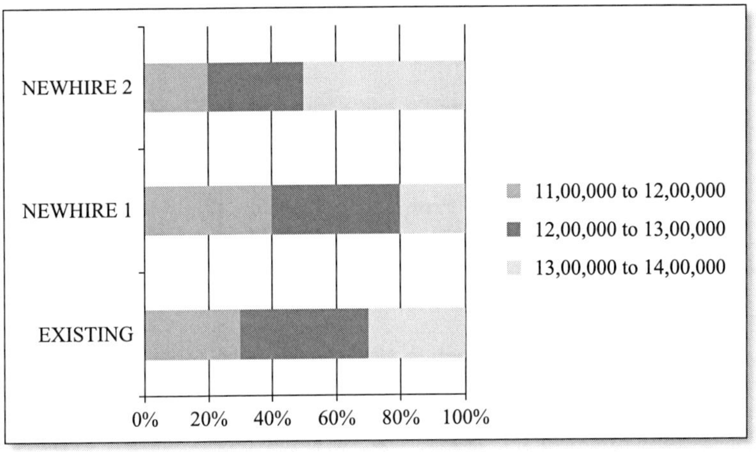

existing employees. Go lower and you risk a lower conversion, go higher and you risk employee unrest!

Emerging Measures of Talent Acquisition

We had earlier spoken about cycle time and cost of hiring. Under normal conditions, one would try to balance out the two.

Let us consider that we have 25 positions to be filled in regional sales. The company is losing market share fast. It is imperative that the new sales folks will need at least 2 months to become productive. Unless they join in a month, the company will struggle to meet its revenue goals for the year. It may need TA to use consultants more and do sourcing across the country. The company may even need to buy out notice periods. The cost of hiring will increase in the short term.

In this situation, will TA be focused on the cost of hiring or on the value of adding new hires in the quickest possible time and gaining sales?

Increasingly, experts are beginning to point out that while cost/hire is a useful measure, it should not be the primary measure. Cost should also be seen together with criticality of the position and the value added by that position.

Opportunity Cost of Cycle Time

When backfilling a role, there is another important dimension that is not sufficiently articulated. It is often assumed that a person leaving a job, under normal circumstances will be performing at near full ability. However, once the person decides to leave, his workload is distributed and the efficacy comes down by half or more before the day of separation. On the other, a new hire, however well qualified he may be, starts at zero. It takes time for a person to understand the organization, operating model, etc. It might take 3–6 months before the replacement starts operating at near optimal levels.

This drives the business case for retention. Let us consider a simplified hypothetical example. An employee is paid ₹50,000 a month and at the least delivers a value equivalent to the same amount. April goes on fine. But by the end of April he decides to move on. Organization triggers hiring actions but at the same time reassigns work. If the employee has 2 months' notice period, then he may be delivering at half his effectiveness in the first month and nearly at zero in the second month. Assume the replacement joins on 1st June. Using the same model, it would take 2 months for him to be at an optimal delivery level.

Apparently, things are fine and the position has been occupied continuously. On the other hand, the company had incurred a cost of ₹300,000 in this period, while the returns have only been ₹150,000.

Month	Cost	Value
April	50,000	50,000
May	50,000	25,000
June	50,000	0
July	50,000	0
August	50,000	25,000
September	50,000	50,000

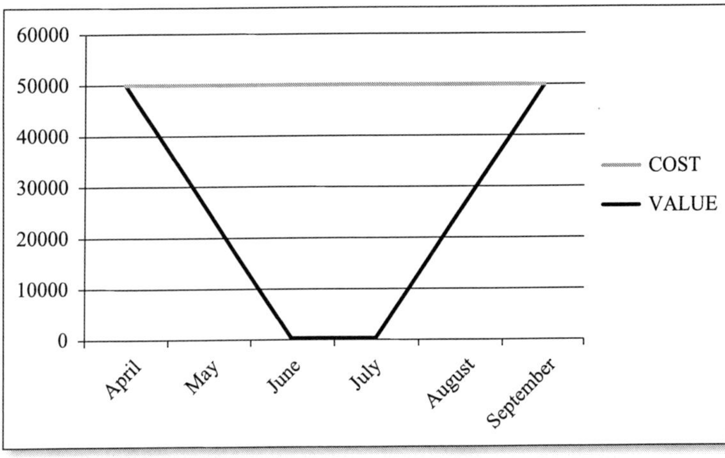

Does this mean that it is okay to let the job vacant, without incurring a cost? Not really; there is opportunity cost of business not fulfilled or customers not handled as well as they should. This is felt by the hiring manager and is transferred onto the TA team. The following graph illustrates the same.

Validity of Hiring Specifications

What happens when a company is flooded with resumes and needs to select 1 out of 50 or one out of 100? There needs to be a standard set for shortlisting and processing these applications. Given the large numbers, any standard that is set needs to be simple and appear fair. Such information should also be available for all candidates.

What is so easily available? Only college education as performance in college is universally applicable. So, companies start by drawing the guidelines on the basis of the following:

- Academic qualification (diploma/graduate/4-years graduate/ post-graduate/PhD, etc.),
- Type of graduation attended (arts/sciences/technology/ management),

- Quality of institute (premier/well-known/emerging/not known),
- Performance in education (first class/70%/consistent first class, etc.).

This makes sense in a country like India, where often a professional education qualification is seen as the preferred choice for good students. Most good students go in for an engineering graduation. The better students clear tests to get into premier institutes such as the IITs and NITs. Even within these institutions, there is a pecking order in terms of specialization. For a computer engineering aspirant, the choices would be computer science, IT, electronics and communication, electrical and electronics, and so on.

A company hiring for a certain number of engineers then follows an algorithm that looks like this:

- Engineering graduate or no?
    - If engineering graduate, premier college or no?
        - If premier college, first class or no?
            - If first class, consistent all through or no?

Based on such rules, candidates are shortlisted. The criteria are objective and can be shared transparently. However, this also creates a scarcity-based talent model. Students who tick all the boxes are in heavy demand from multiple companies. At the base, students who tick off just one or two boxes end up competing with a lot of others and can even end college without being employed.

It is not unusual to hear from companies that there is a shortage of good talent. In a country of 1.2 billion people, this is surprising. So, what is going wrong?

While the criteria are objective and measurable, they do not accurately measure what is needed to perform well on the job. Does an IIT qualification automatically mean that the best programers come out of there, to the exception of every other pedigree? Do the best engineers always come from the best schools?

Researchers have been analyzing the correlation between on-the-job performance and academic qualification. More than one study has found that there is little correlation between the academic background of a person and their on-the-job performance. In the words of the Google head of People Operations "noted that Google had determined that 'G.P.A.'s are worthless as a criterion for hiring, and test scores are worthless.... We found that they don't predict anything." He also noted that the "proportion of people without any college education at Google has increased over time"—now as high as 14% on some teams.

That is not to say a college education is not needed or a high GPA is bad. It is just that other things being equal, academic performance or even performance on a hiring test does not indicate future performance.

Future performance is predicted by competencies a prospective employee possesses. Google talks about humility, ownership, learnability, and emergent leadership. These can be assessed only through structured assessment of competencies.

It is often amusing that most companies in India are faced with a talent shortage and there is high competition for good programming talent, for example. How can a country of 1.2 billion have a talent shortage?

That happens because most companies are focused on the tip of the iceberg—people working in successful companies with a pedigreed degree. On the other hand, if the problem is redefined and they start looking at alternative talent pools and select on the basis of competencies and train, the challenges will be mitigated.

That in turn needs use of analytics to identify what competencies matter and how to develop them.

Importance of Quality of Hire

TA teams world over hold targets for meeting numbers, service levels and costs. However, not often does the quality of hiring gets reviewed or assessed. How does one create a TA function that delivers quality workforce?

Some companies have tried to put a quality of hiring measure. Let us go through different measures first.

As discussed earlier, one can start by looking at the pedigree of the candidates:

- What percentage of new hires has a professional qualification?
- What percentage of new hires is from named competitors?

In the absence of everything else, these measures act as a surrogate for quality. As discussed, competency-based hiring is a better predictor of on-the-job performance. However, what is the first step to competency-based hiring? Enough selection tools should be created for hiring for competencies and interviewers trained in that:

1. What percentage of roles has competency-based selection tools?
2. What percentage of critical roles includes validated assessment tools?
3. What percentage of interviewers has been trained in competency-based selection?

These measures ensure that the checkpoints are aligned with competencies needed for quality hiring.

Once the new candidates are on board, it is expected that they reach an optimum level of performance within 3–6 months. In companies, this is given as the probation period, after which the employee is confirmed in service. In case the inputs are of inconsistent quality, there would be variations in the confirmation rate of new employees. This can again be tracked as:

4. Percentage of new hires whose confirmation is delayed.
5. Percentage new hires that are let go within the 1st year on performance grounds.

After a year, the new employee has integrated with the company and is being assessed for performance. An analysis of performance review information, in turn, helps us create a quality measure:

6. What percentage of new hires having less than 6 months experience gets an "above average" rating.

7. What percentage of new hires having less than 6 months experience gets an "average" rating.
8. What the performance rating distribution is of new hires versus the distribution for existing employees.
9. New hire retention levels.

From the above-mentioned list, it seems like the best way of measuring quality of hires is to use a combination of measures. It could be a challenge to create a composite measure unless we assign relative weightages to the components of the quality measures.

QUALITY OF HIRING IS MORE IMPORTANT THAN PLAIN COST OF HIRING

Let us take two companies and assume they are hiring for similar positions. One of them spends just ₹25,000 per hire, while the other spends ₹35,000 as it wants to get the fit right.

Company	Cost of hiring	Year 1 replacement cost	Year 2 replacement cost	Total cost
Company 1	25,00,000	8,75,000	9,25,000	43,00,000
Company 2	35,00,000	5,25,000	2,40,000	42,65,000

Let us look at the cost for 100 new hires.

Company 1 incurs a cost of ₹25 lakhs for 100 hires while company 2 incurs a cost of ₹35 lakhs. The finance and HR organizations are happy in company 1 having saved ₹15 lakhs.

Let us look at the second year. Company 1 has focused on cost but not the profile of workforce that would help in retention. To some extent, the first year costs for company 2 were higher as they also invested in recruiting instruments based on analytics. Of the 100 people who joined, company 2 has an attrition of 15% while company 1 has an attrition of 35%. In the second year, company 1 has an attrition of 25% while that for the same group of people in company 2 has come down to 5%.

Assume that the costs remain same and the companies refill all vacancies. Let us also assume that attrition affects backfills in the same ratio. (Of 35 people hired as replacements, 35% quit in the second year).

Let us look at the costs now. At the end of year 1, company 1 has saved 40% when compared to company 2. But after 2 years, the running costs of company 1 are more and even though the cost of one-time hiring was higher for company 2, the overall costs are actually less.

This is not to say that a higher quality hiring process should be more expensive all the time. However, it is important that hiring costs are blended with other workforce quality measures to arrive at qualitatively better decisions.

Talent Acquisition for Predictable Joining and Performance

Let us go back to our original example of a company needing to select 100 new hires. Let us take the more productive company, but expand to include the hidden costs of recruitment. For simplicity's sake, let us just focus on the time managers spend:

Process	Company 1	Numbers	Additional effort	Time spent by managers
Offer conversion	80%	125		
Interview conversion	70%	179	54 (179–125)	108 hours
No-show rate	20%	223	152 (375–223)	25 hours
Resume conversion	60%	375		

Let us review the numbers. The managers screened 152 resumes more than required, resulting in 25 hours of additional work (assuming 10 minutes per resume screening to shortlist). They also interviewed 54 more candidates, so as to provide a buffer for the final joining numbers. At 1 hour per interview for two managers, this is another 108 hour additional effort.

In this entire process of using a hiring pyramid, 133 hours of extra management time has been spent. In other words, for each join, the hiring manager spends at least an hour on wasted activity. 16 person days of management time, is at least ₹100,000. In other words, the hidden cost of hiring efficiencies adds ₹100 per offer in hiring costs!

This is just a very conservative estimate. A manager has many priorities and spending such time takes attention away from other priorities. This time is immaterial when one is hiring for senior positions or roles with a unique skillset. On the other hand, TA incurs such extra efforts even for fairly generic roles. Analytics helps us question these long-held assumptions. Can a company use analytics to identify the exact fit people, who would be willing to join, much like sabermetrics for TA?

It then becomes important to create an ideal state. If I need to have 100 joins, can we interview just 120 people? Can we get that 120 from just 200 resumes? Instead of a taken-for-granted pyramid, can we do with a tapering rectangle?

Analytics companies are helping solve this exact problem. Technologies used are:

- Context-based search. Resumes are written freestyle. Earlier search technologies used keyword search to identify skills. But that is not so useful any more. The new algorithms read the profile of joins and identify what is the characteristic of new joins in terms of
    - Nature of company,
    - Experience level,
    - Location,
    - Technology,
    - Compensation.

Then they identify the parameters that distinguish the joins. For example, they can plot a zone of join based on company, location, and joining salary; then they can target that particular profile to get more conversions with the same effort.

- Companies are also using competencies to move to hire for assured performance. We might make big investments and hire people of the same quality. The new talent pool with luck would be as competent as the existing pool. Ideally, it should be better. Companies analyze the competency profiles of existing employees and then try to hire candidates with similar profiles from the talent pool.

This increases the design time for HR and training time for managers—but ideally, if the results are not only a more productive process but also a higher level of performance, why not?

S. No.	Company 1	Company 2
1.	65	85
2.	70	90
3.	75	95
4.	90	95
5.	105	102
6.	120	99
7.	140	103
8.	90	95
9.	65	91

S. No.	Company 1	Company 2
10.	80	95
11.	105	85
12.	75	90
13.	80	95
14.	110	100
15.	130	95
16.	90	90
17.	120	101
18.	75	95

Measuring and Improving Process Capability

Manufacturing processes need to conform to high standards of reliability. Usually there are two measures to evaluate the performance of a process. One is process control. Process control is the "voice of the process" that is derived from how consistent the process has been performing over a period of time and indicates the consistency of output. Process capability, on the other hand, is a measure of goodness of the process comparing the "voice of the process" with the "voice of the customer".

Applying to TA, process control gives a view of the number of joins/offers the process delivers on a consistent basis. Process capability will give an indication of how well it is able to meet the customer needs.

Let us take two different scenarios. For the sake of brevity, let us take performance over 18 months of a recruitment function. Let us consider that the monthly demand is 100 joins in both cases. The actual performance of the two functions is as below.

Company	SD	Process control	Process capability
Company 1	22.41	0.3	0.2
Company 2	6.36	1.3	1.0

For simplicity's sake let us assume that the business has a tolerance of 20, even though it is a wide range! The customer has a target of 100 per month and is okay as long as the joins are in the 80–120 range.

The formulae for process control index (Cp) and process capability index (CPk) are as follows:

$$\text{Cp} = \frac{(\text{USL} - \text{LSL})}{(6 \times \text{SD})}$$

For the purposes of this exercise, the upper specification level (USL) is 120 and the lower specification level (LSL) is 80.

$$\text{CPK is least of } (\text{USL} - \text{mean})/(3 \times \text{SD}) \text{ or } (\text{mean} - \text{LSL})/(3 \times \text{SD})$$

Standard deviation (SD) for company 1 is 22.41 while that for company 2 is 6.36.

The values of Cp and CPk are as follows:

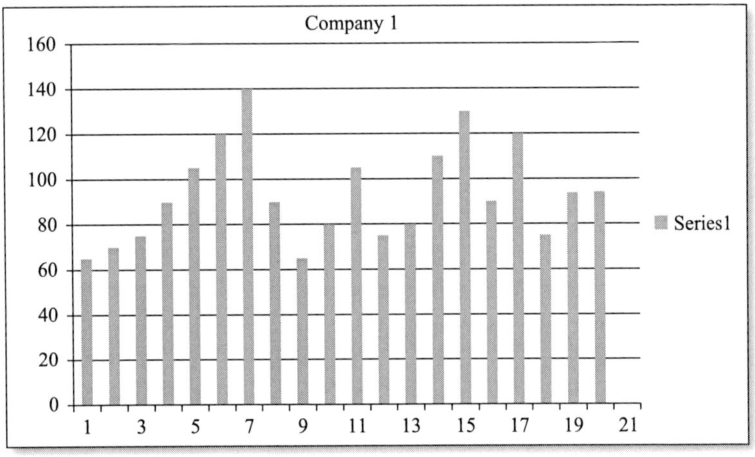

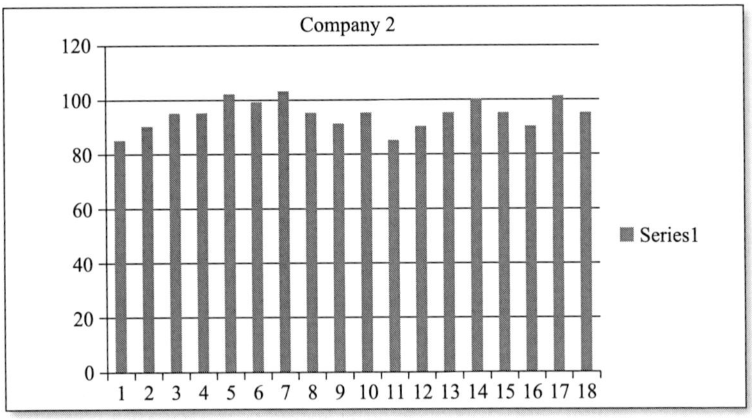

What are the takeaways from this?

1. On an average, company 1 gets 93 joins a month, while company 2 gets 96. Not a big difference.

2. However, the process control index Cp for company 2 is 1.3. This indicates that the process is good and the amount of reviews can be reduced. On the other hand, the Cp for company 1 is 0.3, indicating an unpredictable process.
3. Let us look at CPk now. The process in company 1 is more within the desired range, but is there any skew? The CPk for company 1 is 0.2. This indicates that the process is not meeting customer expectations. Not only is the process not meeting expectations, but also for any given month, it can be higher or lower than the expectations. Company 2 has a CPk of 1. While this is not ideal, in comparison with Company 1, they deliver more within the range and the numbers also reveal that they consistently deliver a little below the goal of 100.

   For a goal of 100, Company 1 may deliver between 70 and 130, while Company 2 would deliver around 95. This is a more predictable process, in need of fine-tuning. A visual representation of the same is given below and it is obvious that the process is far more reliable in company 2.

One could argue that measuring TA processes with the rigor of six sigma adds more challenge. However, usage of concepts like ranges, limits as well as SD provides a lot of clarity, especially when the nature of demand is uniform.

Articulating using process language also helps the business to take into consideration the variabilities so that their business planning can be more grounded.

6

Results-oriented Talent Development

Since the publication *War for Talent* by McKinsey in 1997 (Michaels, 1997), finding the right talent has been an ever growing challenge for the companies. And the process of finding the right talent is not cheap. There have been various studies to estimate how much a new hire cost to the company from the joining date to the date of being productive, and the rule of thumb being that based on the level of hire, cost can range from 1.5x to 3x of the salary for a fully productive employee. Imagine the total cost for hiring 1,000, 5,000, or 10,000 employees per annum. Now here is the challenge. A company may be able to find the talent and bring them on board by spending huge amounts of money but any leakage of the talent will hit company manifold in costs. Hence, after hiring, the next big challenge for any company is to retain the talent as the replacement cost per employee will be even much higher than the hiring cost!

Talent development works as a double-edged sword: first, by developing employee expertise or skills to help the company deploy trained employee on higher positions and second by retaining the employee for longer periods as employees start appreciating benefits of longevity than short tenures. Following are some of the reasons why companies invest in talent development:

- Skill development,
- Retention,

- Ensure availability of roust talent pipeline,
- Enhance employee engagement,
- Increase job performance,
- Foster continuous change,
- Employer branding.

There are various ways of talent development in any organization and these are often categorized as formal and informal methods. Classroom-based development is formal, which is complemented by other methods called informal methods. Broad list of informal methods includes:

- E training or virtual learning,
- Mentoring,
- Coaching,
- On-the-job training/learning,
- Informal or social learning,
- Self-directed learning,
- Job rotations,
- Project assignments,
- Attending conferences and seminars,
- Tuition reimbursement.

All of these talent development methods involve cost—both in terms of direct cost spent on these activities and indirect cost based on employee time spent on these activities. Globally, training spend per employee (2014) ranges from USD 1,200 to USD 2,000 and average training hours per employee range from 36 to 42 depending upon the size of the company and industry type. In India, the average employee spend in year 2014 was USD 375 and the average number of training hours ranged from 40 to 49 hours per employee. Across the globe, companies in the year 2015 spent USD 355.6 billion on employee training (Training Industry Inc., 2016) and in India it is estimated by various sources to be around USD 26 billion.

Above cost figures show that there is a significant spend on training by companies. As a rule of thumb, cost of training in any organization ranges between 2% and 3.5% of the payroll cost.

In companies where the payroll cost is 60% of the total revenue like services companies, training spend becomes a significant cost, forcing the C-level to ask questions on what is the return on investment (RoI) on the training budget. And if the data shown to the C-level for demonstrating RoI of training spend are not convincing, then the training budget is the first casualty when any company or economy is not performing well.

Measuring RoI of talent development initiatives has always been a challenge, but it is seen as a priority by many organizations. A study by Palmer (2010) found that only 8% of the companies actually evaluate return on talent development initiatives. So how can a company measure value of investment in a talent development initiative? The earliest known and popular model has been given by Donald Kirkpatrick's (1959a, 1959b, 1960a, 1960b) four-level learning evaluations model published in a series of four articles in the *Journal of American Society of Training Directors*. The four levels of the model are:

- Level 1: Reaction—captures reaction of participants immediately after the intervention/program, is over, mainly in the form of smiley sheets regarding participants' views on logistics of program, facilitator, content, etc.
- Level 2: Learning—captures participants' response on knowledge or skill increase after attending the program.
- Level 3: Behavior—this level measures the application of learning by the participant while on the job after attending the program.
- Level 4: Results—here focus is to capture change in the performance levels of an employee after attending the program.

These four levels still fall short actually connecting investment with business level outcomes such as profitability and revenue growth. Jack Philips (1996) added the fifth level as RoI.

- Level 5: RoI—to measure benefits over the cost invested for a program or initiative.

Later on, two more levels were added—Level 0 as the base level and Level 6 as the optimization level by Pease, Bradford, and Walker in 2014, making the total number of levels 7. Briefly, these levels mean:

- Level 0: Base level—this level captures basic data like utilization rate of each program/initiative meaning how many participants attended the program against the available seats.
- Level 6: Optimization level—this level attempts to show the actual impact of talent development investments on business outcomes such as revenues growth, profitability, productivity, retention, etc., by connecting the dots, and also goes a step further in highlighting where talent development initiatives are working or not, thus giving choice to company for optimizing investments for higher returns.

So all the seven levels can be shown in a model linking business impact and analytics value-add of each level as shown in Figure 6.1.

Let us illustrate the above-mentioned seven levels with the help of an example so that talent development practitioners can apply the same at their workplace. ABC Company hires 300 engineers with 3–4 years' experience in 2014. After 2 months of joining, 150 engineers are put through a two weeks' training program. ABC Company can use the seven levels of talent development measurement as follows:

1. Level 0: This level captures basic data; in this case, 150 persons were nominated and 140 participated successfully for two weeks.
2. Level 1: This level simply requires administering feedback forms to those who attend and collect the feedback related to facilitator, logistics, etc., and analyzing feedback form data and then using visualization techniques such as histogram, graphs, pie charts, etc., to present the feedback data to stakeholders.

Figure 6.1 Data-based Talent Development Measurement Value Chain

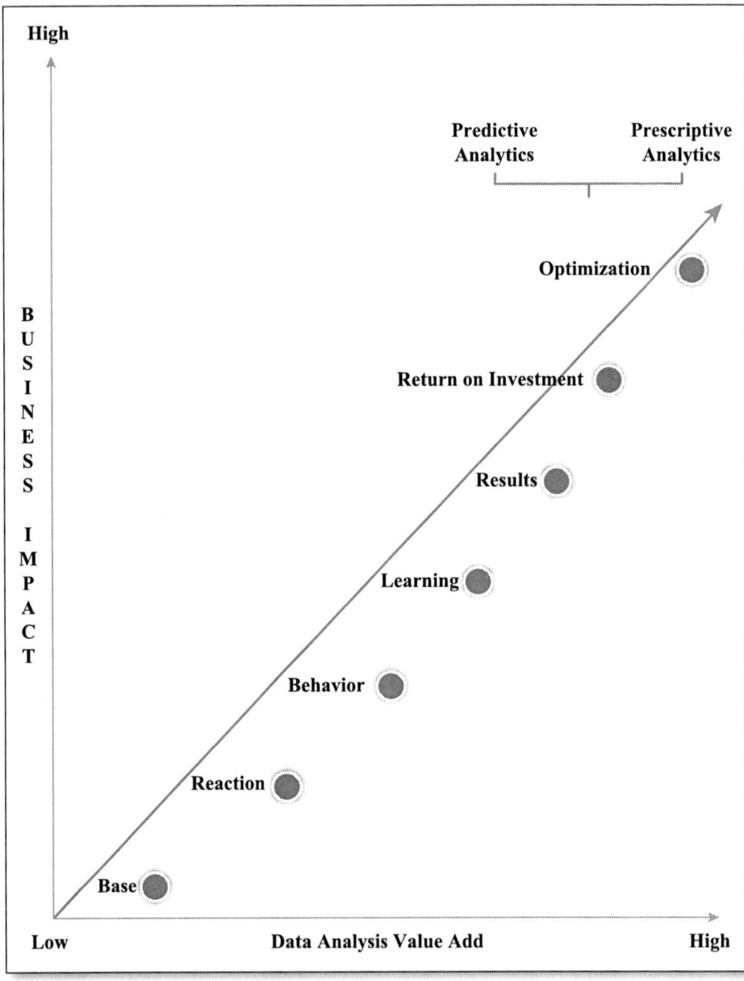

Source: Authors.

3. Level 2: This level is related to learning gain by the participant. This can be measured typically by conducting a quiz-type test within one month to measure knowledge retention by the participant.
4. Level 3: This level requires measuring changes in participant behavior and for this a structured form needs to be used to

capture the behavior changes displayed by the participant who has undergone training. The form has to be filled by the manager of the participant with the form having columns like the list of behavior changes intended, pre-training behavior displayed, and post-training behavior displayed, using the Likert scale to measure responses.

5. Level 4: This level concerns the results level and requires capturing either monthly or quarterly on KPI indicators mapped to the competencies/skills intended to be improved by the program attended by the participant. If the program focused on handling difficult customers or presentation skills, etc., then improvements in these as reported by direct manager can be used as a fair measure to capture the benefit of behavior change (level 3) leading to right outcomes, that is, improved customer handling of the quality of presentation.
6. Level 5: This level requires measuring RoI of the program. The best method to measure this is by using the A/B group testing or split testing technique. In this technique, the group which underwent training is called the controlled group (A) and the group which did not receive training is called the non-controlled group (B). For example, if the objective of the training was to improve dealer satisfaction or increase product sales by the sales team and if data show increase in dealer satisfaction levels or product sales figures for Group A as compared to be Group B, then it is fair to conclude that training has contributed to business outcomes (dealer satisfaction/increased sales) like revenue increase. Ideally, if resources permit, any organization should use A/B testing for levels 3 and 4 also.
7. Level 6: This level deals with the optimization and predictive effectiveness of the training to the participants. This level helps in measuring the ultimate utility level of a training program to the participant and organization. Let us use an example of ABC Company explained earlier. Out of 300 engineers, 140 attended the program. Let us say that 1 year after attending the program, 80 out of 140 got promoted to the next level. How the Bayesian theorem can be used to find out the predictive effectiveness of training for those

Table 6.1 Applying Bayesian Theorem to Training Impact

Training attended	Promoted	Not promoted	Total
Yes	80 (57.14%)	60 (42.86%)	140 (100%)
No	55 (34.37%)	105 (65.63%)	160 (100%)
Total	135 (45%)	165 (55%)	300 (100%)

Note: Row percentages in parentheses.

who attended the training program? Here is how this is done with help of the Bayesian theorem by putting data in a matrix form (Table 6.1).

$$\text{Predictive Effectiveness of Training} = \frac{\text{Odds of being promoted after training}}{\text{Odds of being promoted without Training}} \times 100$$

where

$$\text{Probability of being promoted after Training (p)} = \frac{\text{Odds of being promoted after training}}{\text{Probability of not being promoted after attending Training } (1-\text{p})} \times 100$$

$$= \frac{57.14}{42.86} = 1.33 \text{ or } 133\%$$

$$\text{Probability of being promoted without Training (p)} = \frac{\text{Odds of being promoted without training}}{\text{Probability of not being promoted without Training } (1-\text{p})} \times 100$$

$$= \frac{34.37}{65.63} = 0.5437 \text{ or } 52.37\%$$

$$\text{Predictive Effectiveness of training} = \frac{133}{52.37} = 2.54 \text{ or } 254\%$$

Interpretation: Predictive effectiveness of training calculation shows that chances of being promoted are 254% higher for those who attended training than those who did not attend training, everything else being equal.

Hence, a benefit of attending training improves chances for the individual to get promoted and for the organization it indicates that the use of training leads to better outcomes in future.

Measuring Return on Investments on Talent Development Initiatives

As technology is advancing fast and organizations are witnessing digital transformation, it is becoming easier and cheaper to collect and store vast amounts of data related to talent development initiatives and connect it with various business levels and other outcomes relevant for the organization. As the talent development initiatives can impact vast parameters of people management, typically organizations across the globe use the following metrics to gauge the impact of talent development initiatives:

- Employee engagement,
- Employee retention,
- Business-like productivity, reduction of costs,
- Customer satisfaction,
- Reduction in failure rates,
- Talent pipeline depth,
- Leadership performance,
- Innovation,
- Teamwork.

Measuring all of these parameters is not easy as some of the development initiatives pose measurement challenges. For example, measuring informal or social learning or self-directed learning is not amenable to easy measurement. At the same time, if development has become strategic and shows business outcome impact, then it has to move from tactical skill type focus to connecting development initiatives to business performance. For the sake of making measurement easy and meaningful, classifying outcomes into different levels as follows may help:

1. Organizational level,
2. Individual level,
3. Program/Intervention level.

Another approach for classifying metrics and measures is to align them to the needs of business leaders so that investment connects to outcomes and business performance is demonstrated. Using this as a guiding principle, we can categorize outcome-based metrics under three broad categories as shown in Figure 6.2:

1. Organizational capacity-related: This category captures metrics related to building and growing talent depth in the organization.

Figure 6.2 Typology for Talent Development Measurement Levels

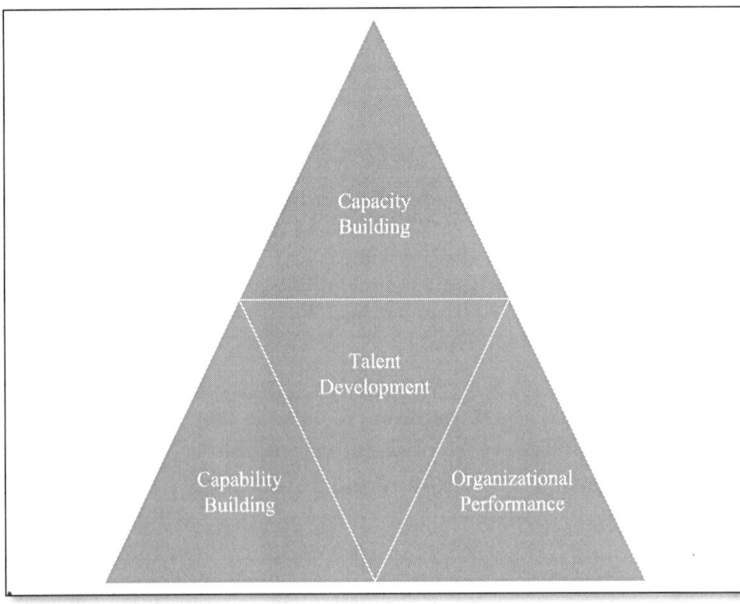

Source: Authors.

2. Organizational capability-related: This category covers metrics capturing skill or competency development.
3. Organizational performance-related: This category captures metrics related to business growth.

Identification of measures or metrics[1] that will be relevant for each level and those which can be connected to business outcomes will further provide clarity on what to measure and how to measure. Any measure must satisfy some criterion to be qualified as a metric fit for measurement. Here is a list of those characteristics:

1. It should be fairly usable by all the types of organizations though each organization may need specific measures for its context.
2. It should be easy to understand and deploy.
3. Data should be easily available or identifiable with some effort.
4. It should make use of current data as well as should be flexible enough to incorporate new data.
5. It should provide insights into both leading and lagging indicators.
6. It should have link or should be connected to performance as otherwise it does not make business sense.
7. Metric should be credible with stakeholders.

Right Metrics and Measures for Strategic Alignment

What will be key metrics and measures for talent development initiatives which will combine all the characteristics of good metrics and measures listed above? Practicality demands that the

[1] Metrics and measures are used interchangeably in the business context though there are subtle differences. Metric is a derivative of measure. For example, the number of training hours offered in year and the number of training hours utilized in each program are measures. Metric for this will be the utilization rate which is derived by dividing the total number of training hours by the actual training hours used/attended.

number of such metrics and measures be minimum, otherwise a long list will become overwhelming for any talent development practitioner to track and meaningless for stakeholders from the sense-making point of view. Before covering examples of metrics under each category, it will be useful to provide a linkage between all categories and business outcomes with the help of a model or framework as shown in Figure 6.3.

A map linking various talent development interventions where typically any company makes investments and their linkage to business results are shown in Figure 6.4. In this figure, connection between talent development programs, indicators, metrics, and business results including financial performance is presented in a simple manner. However, in each company such flow connecting various elements will vary depending upon the type of talent development programs in use and business outcome to be measured. It will also vary due to a company's priority at that particular point of time to measure the impact of investment in a particular program in use. Another cause of variation will be the type of data available and the ease of measuring such data. Based on the context and feasibility, each company can broadly draw a talent investment–business outcome linkage map as shown in Figure 6.4.

According to Lavoie (2014), business leaders across the globe are increasingly looking for data to make talent development investment decisions. However, a CEO survey done by PwC in 2014 shows that 80% CEOs want data for talent development investments but only a small percentage is able to receive it (Saratoga, 2015). Another study by Vickers (2010) i4cp found that high-performing companies more often measure talent investments and some top measures used are as follows:

- Financial performance,
- Talent pipeline,
- Cost reduction,
- Employee engagement,
- Leadership success.

Figure 6.3 Metrics for Measuring Impact of Talent Development Investments

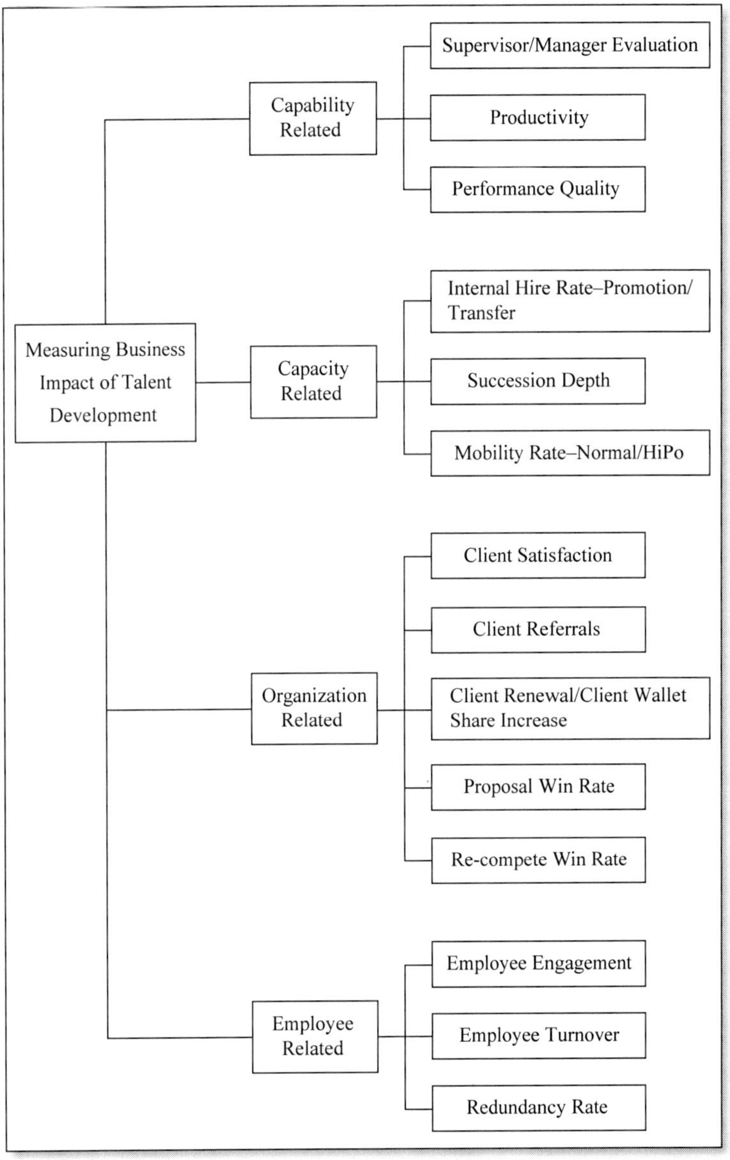

Source: Authors.

Figure 6.4 Talent Investments–Metrics–Business Outcomes

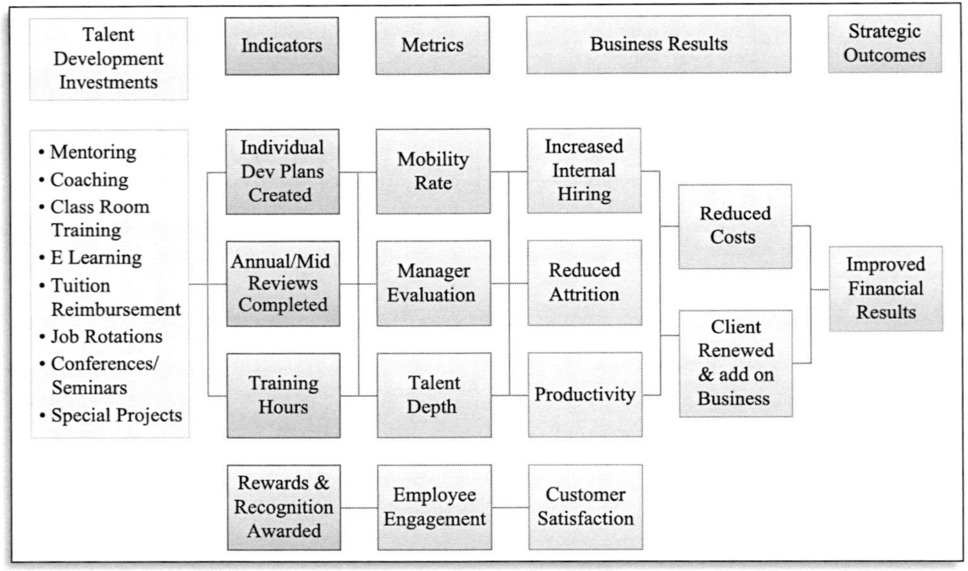

Source: Authors.

Here are some industry examples of talent development investment measurements:

1. Sun Microsystems used predictive analytics to measure the impact of a mentoring program on financial performance. Sun did a two-phase study of comparing a control group with an experimental group for a mentoring program. Results of the analysis showed that $6.7 million were saved through improved retention, while the total cost of the mentoring program was $1.1 million (Sun Microsystems, 2014).
2. ConAgra Foods created a Foundations of Leadership (FoL) Program to align leadership across the company. The RoI of the program was studied by third party—Bellevue University's Human Capital Lab using a control group approach. The study analyzed the performance of 600 trained and 1,600 untrained supervisors and found that the program improved the productivity and reduced employee turnover. The study further found that those who went through the training improved their chances of promotion by 2x (ConAgra Foods, 2010).
3. GoogleEDU, the employee training division of Google, makes use of data in aligning training to business strategy. For example, it uses data to offer more programs to certain employees than others and this is based on data collected from manager evaluation of the employee performance and training transfer, suggestions by team members, career stage of the employee, and even location. Google also uses data to create training redundancy by eliminating training programs which are no longer working, and offer more of those programs which are delivering better employee performance (GoogleEDU, 2012).

7

Talent Engagement and Retention

Talent engagement is an idea whose time has come. In fact, some argue there is far too much focus on just engaging the employees at the cost of enabling them to align their performance to that of the company. Just how much engagement is required?

Engagement has one of the tent poles of HR analytics. Most technology companies rely on human capital. Bill Gates was supposed to have once remarked, "The market capitalization of Microsoft is zero at the end of the day. It does not come back up unless all of them return to work the next day." Obviously there was some maturity in tracking attrition, analyzing it, and identifying patterns in the same even before analytics became a happening area. Tools and platforms have been created that help in integrating existing information and create a degree of predictability.

Business Levers of Employee Engagement

Initially, companies counted only one measure to track employee satisfaction. It was felt that satisfaction would lead to motivation which would lead to performance. Turnover rate was taken as the measure for satisfaction. If the employee turnover rate is less, then they are more satisfied.

Workers in factories hardly quit. However, there are also cases of workplace disruptions including strikes that shut down plants. Does it mean turnover alone is not enough to measure satisfaction?

So HR started adapting tools from market research. Like customers, employees were also surveyed to find out how satisfied they are with the company. Normative 4–10 point scales were used to capture the employee's perceptions on policies, processes, and their impact on employee engagement.

Taking the marketing paradigm forward, companies did not stop with gauging satisfaction. They found that satisfaction alone was not enough to predict turnover levels. You could have a high satisfaction and a high turnover.

Then additional dimensions were added. Employees were questioned on the following:

- Intent to stay (loyalty).
- Intent to recommend the company to others (advocacy).

The measures for engagement started increasing. But what about the business value?

One of the classic *Harvard Business Review* case-studies in the 1990s related to the employee–customer–profit chain in the American retail giant Sears. In the early 1990s, Sears had a new CEO and were looking at large-scale organization transformation (Rucci, Kirn, & Quinn, 1998). After a highly involved process, the company expressed that it wants to be a "Compelling place to work, shop and invest." A team was entrusted with identifying the total performance indicators for the same. After iterations, they came out with a model connecting employee motivation to business outcomes. The model was formed after rigorous statistical analysis on a 70-question employee survey.

They identified "attitude about the job" and "attitude about the company" as predictors of employee behavior. In turn, they found that answers to six questions impacted "about the job". These covered,

- liking the work,
- pride in the company,
- impact of quantum of work on attitude about the job, and so on.

Similarly, response to four questions, such as

- confidence in the future of the company,
- understanding business strategy, and so on had an impact on the attitude about the company.

That was the crucial first step in identifying the drivers of engagement. The challenging piece remained on connecting the engagement levels to business performance. Sears were able to establish that a 5% improvement in employee attitude will drive a 1.3% improvement in customer satisfaction resulting in a 0.5% improvement in revenue growth. They were actually able to predict the store performance just on the basis of engagement survey outcomes. Subsequently, the model was revised to factor in both business and employee measures.

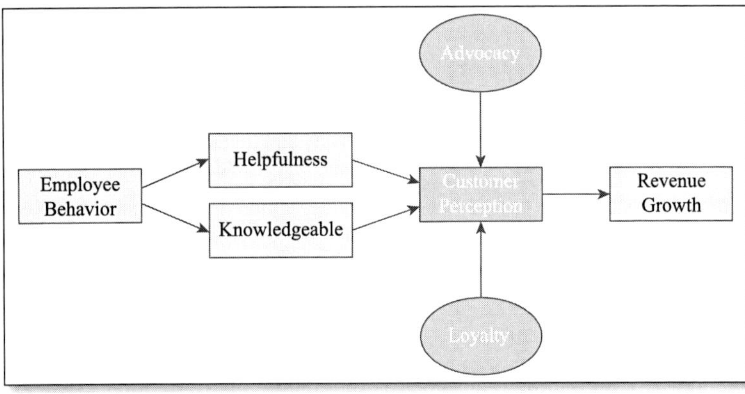

The study that became a *Harvard Business Review* article was the first to clearly identify a linkage between employee motivation and corporate performance. The company estimated that it could have added $200 million in additional revenues because of a 4% increase in employee attitude.

Then *War for Talent* happened. Silicon Valley always had a shortage of talented programers and in the dotcom era companies outdid one another to offer benefits and perks to ensure longevity. Even best employers started losing people. Employee turnover became not just a long-term challenge, but one on which one needed instant improvement. This created its own set of questions. What is the shortest (least-cost) path from being 2, 3 on employee survey to 4 (on a scale of 5). Then RoI was needed for different programs and their impact.

To an extent, the 2008 economic downturn took the sheen off employee engagement. Large-scale layoffs became the new norm.

Sears happened in 1990s, before the "analytics" era was upon us. But we have another equally powerful illustration from another retail company, Lowe's. Lowe's had very clear linkages established at the store level between sales promotions and improvement in sales, linkage between revenues and shrinkage, etc. However, while the executives felt there is a link between employee engagement and business success, the models were not there.

The company set out to develop such a model using business measures and the outcomes from their employee surveys. Often we are curious to know about the following linkages:

- Can I increase revenues by increasing person days training?
- Can I increase retention by improving manager engagement?
- What are the three programs having the biggest impact on employee engagement?

Lowe's used a statistical modeling technique called SEM to validate their hypothesis. Analysis showed that employee engagement had a positive impact on customer satisfaction which, in turn, had an impact on shrinkage numbers. They also discovered a two-way linkage between manager engagement and employee engagement (Coco, Jamison, & Black, 2011). This, in turn, helped them refine a model that can help estimate the impact of engagement on business. They found that higher engagement resulted in an average 4% higher volume per sale. Factoring in cost savings, they conservatively estimated a difference of a million dollar sales per annum between the most engaged stores and the ones with least engagement.

These are studies that clearly show a positive correlation between employee engagement and company performance. Companies that rely on human capital like Google go all the way to ensure the right

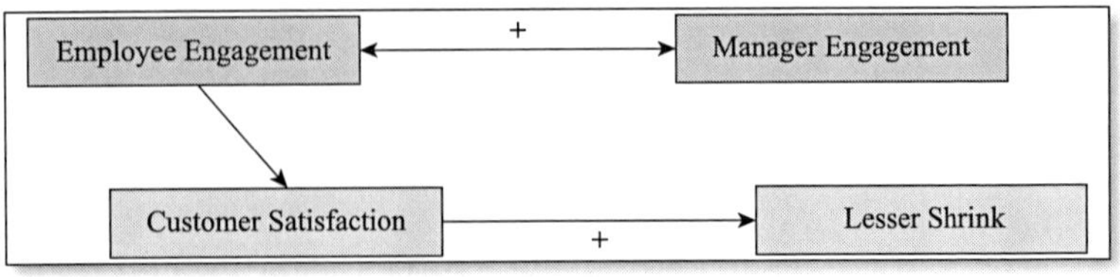

talent is attracted and retained. However, cost constraints often come in the way of long-term engagement of most companies.

Traditional Measures of Engagement

First and the biggest is measuring employee turnover. One could argue that employee turnover is a part of workforce demographics. While that is true, it is also the first measure everyone uses to identify the strength of engagement.

SHRM defines employee turnover, as the "rate at which employees enter and leave a company in a given fiscal year."

Measuring Attrition

Unlike the headcount, attrition is always a percentage rate. It is measured in annual, quarterly, and monthly intervals, though sometimes companies in high turnover industries track manpower leakage almost on a daily basis.

A simple formula for deriving attrition is:

$$\text{Attrition rate} = \frac{\text{Number of employees who quit during an year}}{\text{Average headcount for that year}}$$

When multiplied by 100, this gives the attrition percentage.

It is easy to find the number of employees who quit during any given 12-month period. How do you arrive at the average headcount?

It depends on the degree of accuracy you are looking for. A basic formula would be:

$$\text{Average Headcount} = \frac{\text{Headcount on 1st April} + \text{Headcount on 31st March}}{2}$$

If you need greater resolution,

$$\text{Average Headcount} = \frac{(\text{Headcount month 1}) + (\text{Headcount month 2}) + \ldots + (\text{Headcount month 12})}{12}$$

Headcount of a month is usually calculated by averaging the headcount on the first day of the month and the last day of the month.

Month	HC	Exit
Apr.	1,200	15
May	1,250	18
Jun.	1,270	25
Jul.	1,450	45
Aug.	1,475	30
Sep.	1,550	20
Oct.	1,625	10
Nov.	1,660	10
Dec.	1,650	15
Jan.	1,700	18
Feb.	1,725	20
Mar.	1,725	15

What will be the attrition rate by the first method?

$$\text{Attrition} = \left(\frac{241}{1475}\right) = 16.3\%$$

Now, if we average out the headcount across the year, then the denominator becomes 1,525. The attrition rate then is:

$$\left(\frac{241}{1,525}\right) = 15.8\%$$

We are able to see a 0.5% difference in attrition on the basis of how the averages are arrived at. While there is no right or wrong, any average that considers more sampling is likely to be more accurate.

LTM or YTD?

There are no arcane terms. As far as attrition is concerned, there are two different ways of arriving at an annualized number.

In most companies in India, the fiscal year (FY) runs from April to March. On April 1st of the next year, you will be able to identify the attrition rate for the previous year.

However, business is more dynamic to wait for a year to find out the attrition rate. Often, updates are required on a quarterly or monthly basis. Then what do you do?

LTM

LTM stands for last 12 months. In some places, TTM is also used (trailing 12 months). This works on a rolling rate principle. Suppose we want to know the attrition rate in August. We have only seen 5 months in the fiscal. So, we use the attrition formula for the preceding 12 months.

$$\text{LTM attrition for August 2014} = \frac{\text{Number of quits}}{\text{average headcount from September 13 to August 14}}$$

This is similar to how businesses calculate their revenue run rate. While the company may have done \$500 million last fiscal, on the basis of their last 12 months' revenue, they say our run rate is 575 million dollar.

Advantage of going with the LTM basis for attrition calculation is that you are always basing it on information available. There are no assumptions being made here.

However, suppose a company wants to set attrition goals for its managers. The going rate is 18% and the company wants to bring it down to 15%. So, it sets that all managers should keep attrition at 14%. Appraisals have arrived. How to calibrate the performance of managers?

One way could be to just consider the LTM attrition as of appraisal time. This would include performance over the past 6 months. However, what if you want to only give importance to performance in this fiscal?

Here year to date (YTD) comes into play.

YTD

One calculates the going attrition rate and extrapolates it for the rest of the year.

Let us start with a simple example. Assume that the attrition rate for a company at the end of April is 2%. Then using the YTD method, we assume that the attrition for the rest of the year also would be 2% per month. Total attrition on a YTD basis becomes 24%. (Not good for our managers!)

Let us take forward for a quarter.

Month	Initial headcount	Final headcount	Attrition
April	800	820	12
May	820	845	10
June	846	866	9

What is the attrition for this quarter?

We see that the average headcount for April, May, and June is 810, 833, and 856, respectively. Average headcount for the quarter then is 833. Company lost 31 employees.

$$\text{Attrition rate for the quarter is } \left(\frac{31}{833}\right) = 3.7\%$$

On a YTD basis, we extrapolate it for four quarters by multiplying by 4. The YTD attrition rate is 14.8%.

This estimation happens to be a more conservative way of forecasting attrition. In effect, the company is growing by 22 employees a month, while it is losing at the rate of 10.33 a month. Extrapolating for the year, attrition could be

$$\text{Annualized attrition} = \left(\frac{12 \times 10.33}{932}\right) = 13.3\%$$

While rate extrapolation is a very quick way of forecasting, we can project headcount growth and attrition and arrive at a more accurate estimate as shown above.

YTD calculation is estimation. However, it is completely based on current environment and does away with any impact from the past or business actions from the previous year.

A usual mistake done by people is to take the rate for a period and state that as the attrition rate. Just taking the rate for a period as that for the year will set us up for shocks in the future. It is always better to estimate the annual rate and then share it accordingly.

Both YTD and LTM have their backers and their uses. It makes sense to be aware of both and use appropriately. YTD is a better measure of short-term spikes, while LTM levels out such spikes and presents a more realistic picture.

Employee Retention

Some companies are trying to move away from tracking attrition and are focusing on their ability to retain employees. The primary measure of retention is average tenure.

AVERAGE TENURE

Attrition finally is about employees leaving. What about those who stay? This is where the length of tenure becomes important. Objective of engagement is to get employees to stay with the organization.

Let us take two companies. Assume that one has an average tenure of 7 years, while the other has a tenure of 2 years. A company with a longer tenure has more stability and a better knit culture. There could be three reasons why a company has a shorter average tenure:

- The company is growing very fast and adding new people rapidly.
- The company is new!
- There is a high amount of churn.

The last is what should be of concern. It would be useful to benchmark across the industry and then see whether one's own company is able to retain people for a longer time.

It is also possible that tenures are longer in industries where the demand for talent is low and value propositions are similar. In general, government has longer tenures but that does not automatically indicate highest levels of engagement. In a company with longer tenures, change management could be difficult.

LEAD INDICATORS OF ENGAGEMENT

While attrition is universally used as the measure for engagement, it suffers from the following:

- It is at the fag end of the engagement process. It is too late to do anything when an employee quits.
- An increase in company-level attrition happens sometime after the engagement has dropped. It would be easier to do it by measuring engagement on a real-time basis.

This is where surveys come in handy. Most organizations conduct an employee survey at a periodic interval of 12–18 months. The surveys usually focus on assessing the overall satisfaction level and, with time, added elements of loyalty and advocacy.

The survey numbers were very helpful and independent of which industry you are in—a satisfaction rate of 80% is always more handy than 60%. When the scores drop from a survey to the next, the leadership can also use it as a lead indicator of higher turnover.

A monolithic survey may make a lot of sense at an organization level. However, in modern times when Moore's law drives a lot of things, 18 months really becomes a very long period of time. Shorter, snappier polls are gaining currency. Even mood meters, that track employee's mood on a weekly basis, are seen as relevant.

By nature, surveys are confidential and one does not know about who gave what feedback. This limits the predictability of engagement. We may say that 30% of people in engineering are unhappy, but we may still have to guess about who constitute the 30%.

Hence, there is need to create a cause and effect analysis for lower engagement and for attrition.

MODELING FOR SURVEYS

It is beyond the scope of this book to write on how employee surveys are designed and implemented. However, the following points need to be kept in mind when using a survey for measuring engagement.

1. Critical sample size: Often companies either have a small sample or try to cover all employees. HR pushes employees and managers to participate and shoot for 100% participation. While a higher number looks good, it is not necessary for a valid survey. It is more important to have the following:
   1. A stratified random sample that ensures adequate representation from all employee demographics. Let us consider the following.

Level	**Actual number**	**Survey number**
1	20%	10%
2	30%	80%
3	50%	10%

This survey participation, for example, has a very different profile than what the company has. So, any inference made on the basis of this data may not fit in with what the company thinks.

2. Statistically valid sample size: Companies try to have all employees participate in the survey. That is good from an employee involvement principle. However, accurate assessment can be made with a much smaller sample size. Using confidence interval, confidence level, and stratification it is possible to arrive at reasonably accurate modeling of very large populations using sample sizes in the hundreds.
3. Input and output: Often dipstick surveys are used to gain inputs on perception. This works as long as we do not have one final outcome in our mind.

   Let us take an example of a restaurant. It is easy as long as they ask for your feedback on a five-point scale on the ambience, food quality, speed of service, etc. But the moment they ask you about the overall satisfaction, the dynamics change. What do you make out of the following?

   - Satisfaction with Ambience : 4.5
   - Satisfaction with food quality : 3.8
   - Satisfaction with speed of service : 4
   - Overall satisfaction : 3.7

A manager sitting with this data will be confused. Sometimes, people just think taking an average of all scores should result in the overall score. In such a case, the average score here is 4.1. But the overall score is less than the average. So what has happened?

Possibly, in framing the dimensions, a crucial element that customers value has been left out. One can look at factors like ambience, food quality, speed, etc., as inputs that result in the overall satisfaction as an output. What if value for money is a factor that is important but has been left out? And the restaurant is perceived to be overpriced? Does that impact the overall score?

Often, in employee surveys as well, one is faced with this question. When formulating, have we identified all drivers of engagement? Are there dimensions that are overrepresented and underrepresented?

This is where drawing up of a framework for engagement becomes important. At a very high level, a company can create a framework similar to the model shown below.

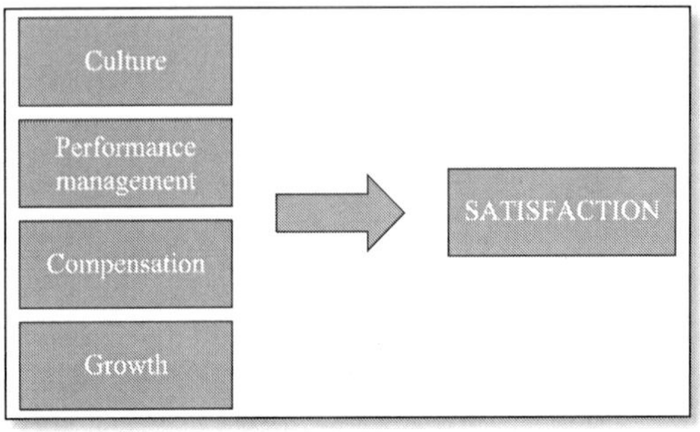

Lately, the models do not just stop with measuring satisfaction but also result in conscious actions. Does a satisfied employee:

- Express intent to stay for a longer time? (loyalty)
- Recommend the company to others? (advocacy)

Such modeling, of course, requires familiarity with statistical tools and techniques. Statistics also takes us to the realms of predictability.

It would be tempting to look at satisfaction, advocacy, and loyalty as three axes that constitute a cube and analyze the patterns. It can definitely be done, but with a caveat. The three measures are to some extent interlinked and are not mutually exclusive.

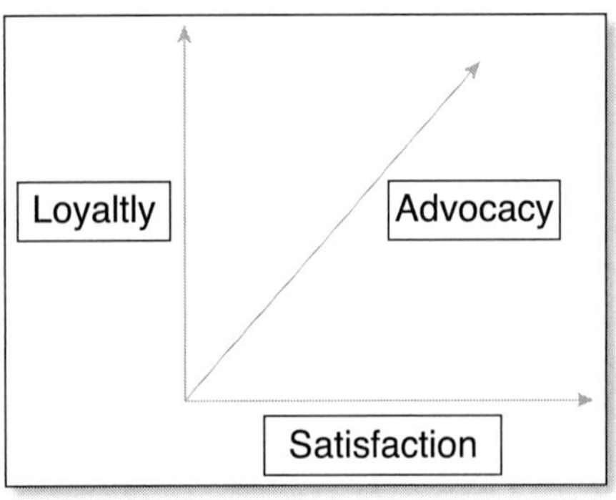

LEAD INDICATORS AND PREDICTING EMPLOYEE ENGAGEMENT

In manufacturing, two parameters of the shop floor are looked at with great concern. One is tardiness/late coming and second is absenteeism. Both, of course, have an impact on the productivity. However, what connects them to engagement?

There is a theory based on withdrawal. It is said that people tend to withdraw from spaces when they do not like being in that space (Adler & Golan, 1981). Let us take it forward to the work environment. In the flextime environment, one is never sure of the starting time of the office. It would be a challenge to say an employee is not engaged because he/she is not coming "on time" to office. However, the following are observed to be lead indicators of diminishing engagement:

- Change in work timings: An employee starts coming later and later to work. 9:30 becomes 10, 10 becomes 10:30 without any increase in the hours at work.
- Increasing use of "work from home" options without any personal need for the same.
- Unpredictability of attendance: The person may be taking leave more frequently and often without any notice.

All the three indicate that the person is becoming more withdrawn from the workplace and does not want to engage with the organization or colleagues. An *Academy of Management Journal* paper from 2006 "How important are job attitudes? Meta-analytic comparisons of integrative behavioral outcomes and time sequences" by Harrison, Newman, and Roth (2006) details out the correlation between these factors as well as an outcome like employee turnover.

On the other hand, we also tend to look at employees who are supportive of their co-workers, talk well about the company, and volunteer for discretionary work as those who are more engaged. Organization citizenship behavior, as originally conceptualized by D.W. Organ (1988), has the following key components:

- Altruism,
- Conscientiousness,

- Sportsmanship,
- Courtesy,
- Civic virtue.

There are studies that also correlate organization citizenship behavior with higher engagement as well as more positive business outcomes.

So there is potential to leverage what is being anecdotally used to track engagement to actually be used as a mainstream measure.

EMPLOYEE REFERRALS AS A LEAD INDICATOR

As stated, employee surveys measure the "advocacy" factor as well. While the advocacy scores measure intent to recommend the company, does it happen in practice? Often large companies say that more than 30% of their new hires come from employee referrals.

Health of your employee referral program is a good indicator of the level of engagement. Do you get a flow of recommendations even when there are no positions? Or on the other hand, are you hard selling your referral program and still not successful? Most importantly, is the offer conversion rate higher when it is made through referrals?

Each of this is a good lead indicator of the level of employee engagement.

THE ENGAGEMENT CURVE

Like economics, engagement also follows a pattern that has been observed across companies. One typically sees a J-shaped curve on engagement scores if we plot tenure on one axis and engagement score on the other. Employees with 1–12 years of experience show very high engagement levels and then it starts dropping for next group of 10 to 20–22 years of experience, and finally rises again for employees with 22–30 years of experience. Why so?

- Studies have shown that this happens because euphoria of first employee after college and subsequent 2–3 job changes in the next 10–12 years' period keep the engagement levels high.
- As the employee progresses on chronological age, his/her cognitive faculties start developing very quickly and become quite discerning about everything, including job and personal achievements, and a sort of cynical outlook develops due to more knowledge processing and exposure.
- After this stage, in late 40s and early 50s onwards, an employees' outlook towards life and work changes as the employee becomes more receptive and appreciative of whatever happens around him/her, presumably due to more maturity dawning and because cynicism gets replaced by security and likeness for everything due to short working years ahead. This liking outlook shows in increased engagement levels and hence that "handle" of the curve represents the start or renewal of falling engagement levels once again!

USAGE OF ANALYTICS TO FINE-TUNE ACTION ITEMS FOR RETENTION

Let us consider the technique of exit interviews. Companies always had an exit interview format and it is still part of the relieving formalities of an employee. Companies also analyze exit interviews. However, exit interviews have ceded space in analytics due to the following reasons:

1. Timing: An employee tends to be more transparent with his emotions when he is still considering leaving the company. By the time his last day comes, he is not interested in a reversal of situations which could make him stay. Also, he does not want to hurt anyone on the way out. So he reveals only a portion of what really caused his exit. More often than not, they say that their attrition is caused by "personal reasons" effectively blocking off the company's efforts to identify the real reasons.

2. Aggregation: The challenge for any reporting on engagement/turnover is the heading given to causes. Summarizing results in headers such as:
   - Job-related,
   - Personal reasons,
   - Performance reasons.

   Taking action at that level is often difficult.

The problems of aggregation dog employee survey outcomes too. It is not unusual to have tables like the following as priorities for action planning.

Level	Junior	Middle	Senior
Priority	Career growth Compensation Training	Work-life balance Job rotation Benefits	Collaboration Communications

There are only a few things that can be done to take action on a sustained basis. Also, this does not differentiate in terms of employee expectations at different businesses, locations, etc. Here is where supplementary analysis comes in handy to do the fine tuning. Let us consider the following situation:

BU	A	B	C	D	E	F
Attrition	14%	9%	10%	20%	12%	16%

Let us suppose that the company attrition rate is 12%. So, the business units (BUs) A, D, and F are higher than the company.

A lot of literature exists connecting the impact of manager with employee engagement. So can we clearly say that the managers of BUs A, D, and F should be relieved of their managerial roles and fresh blood be brought above them? Or there are other factors we need to look for?

Let us consider a few factors in the spirit of our deep and wide analysis (assume this is a technology company):

- Manager maturity (as indicated by the number of years in the role),
- Demand for skillset,
- Team average tenure with company,
- Employee survey scores.

To simplify it, let us segregate the data.

Factor	A	B	C
Manager maturity			
Skillset demand			
Team tenure			
ESAT score			

Notes: Manager Maturity ranges from high to low. Black for high, white for average and gray for low.

Demand for skillset: Black for less demand, white for moderate demand and gray for high demand.

Team Tenure: Black for high tenure, white for moderate and gray for low.

ESAT Score : Black for high, white for average and gray for low.

These details make it more complex and do not point fingers on managers at all!

Business Unit A

BU A has a manager who has been playing that role for a while. The demand for team's skillset is moderate. The team has been with the company for some time and even the employee satisfaction scores are reasonable. There would be a need to examine the manager's personal style and make corrective actions.

Business Unit B

The demand for skillset is moderate and the ESAT scores are reasonable. However, the team itself has not worked in the company for a good length of time. They may be still settling in. Also, the manager has just moved into people management. A right approach would be to coach and develop the manager so that he/she becomes better.

Business Unit C

While the manager has reasonable experience, he has also delivered high employee engagement scores in the survey. The attrition should not be high, looking at it conventionally.

But let us consider the external environment. The demand for the skillset of the team is very high. This, in turn, leads to far higher attrition than the company is enduring otherwise. High turnover, in turn, creates a churn resulting in low tenure of employees. A right approach would then be to re-examine policies to make sure the unique demands of the BUs are met.

Factor	**A**	**B**	**C**
Manager maturity			
Skillset demand			
Team tenure			
ESAT score			
Action	Check style	Coach manager	Change policies

Note: Manager Maturity ranges from high to low. Black for high, white for average and gray for low.

Three units, three different challenges—only by using analytics will HR be able to take decisive action. Using templates for solutions will result only in frustration.

BUILDING UP FOR RETENTION PREDICTABILITY

It is fascinating that two people from the same background join a company and one leaves within the year, while the other goes on to become CEO after 25 years! A company cannot be so different for two people?

A lot of literature exists on what helps higher employee engagement, leading to retention. Gallup's Q12 based on their research has become iconic in this field, even though with time some elements like "Have a best friend at work" or "I received recognition in the last 10 days" have become open to criticism. (Crush, 2009)

Let us visualize an empirical model to envisage what all go into building an algorithm for predicting retention.

Let us assume that two people join with exactly the same background. What would be the factors impacting the initial engagement?

- Have I received the right fit in terms of level and compensation?
- Are people nice to interact with?

Within a month, the impressions will start getting formed on the following:

- Is my manager good to work with?
- Does the company have a legitimate strategy?
- Do colleagues talk well of the company?
- Are my job expectations clear?

After 6 months, the following impressions start getting formed:

- Is the culture democratic? Can I express myself without fear?
- Is my manager enabling me to be successful? Is he/she approachable?
- Am I feeling stretched?
- From a pay and benefit perspective, is the company delivering what it had promised, especially bonus and variable payment?
- How easy or difficult it is, to get things done here.
- Is my team composed of competent staff?

After 1 year, the following takes precedence:

- Have I started achieving what I was hired for?
- Am I getting visibility to senior management?
- Am I getting selected for task forces?
- If in a remote center, do I have the freedom to visit HQ when needed?
- How much discretion do I have to spend my budgets?
- How much discretion do I have in hiring my team?
- Is there any investment being made into my development?
- Did I get a fair performance review?
- Did I get a fair pay increase?
- Is this an exciting area to work?

After 2 years, a person might start having these questions:

- What is my visibility into the next higher position?
- How strong are my networks within the company? Do I like working here?
- Does it ring a bell, when I say I work here? Is there social recognition?
- Am I able to get time for family when required?
- Does senior management rely on me to deliver results?
- What are my long-term wealth generation prospects?
- Am I being recognized adequately for my efforts?

This is one shot at identifying the factors that are important for a person in managerial levels/mid-career. The factors could be very different for someone in the early stage of their career. These could vary slightly for someone at senior level of leadership. (It might just come down to working relationship with CEO☺)

For the sake of simplification, let us summarize as in the following table:

This is just one part of the modeling. There are other questions of a more personal nature like:

- Proximity to native,
- Quality of life in place of work,

Level	Important factors	Good to have factors
Junior	Training Cutting edge work Pay Benefits	Work culture Supervisor quality
Middle	Career growth Responsibility Work culture Management quality Pay	Work-life balance Benefits Cutting edge work Higher education
Senior	Success on the job Peer respect Leadership vision Influence ability Wealth generation	Perks

- Job and locational preference of spouse,
- Nature of financial commitments.

All these of course fall into the mythical bucket of "personal reasons" as stated in exit interviews!

HR organizations model retention with the sincere belief that it is all under their control. It is not. External market reasons play as much a role in retaining an employee, especially at junior levels, as intrinsic reasons.

We have organization factors, individual factors, and market factors. For simplicity's sake, let us give a weightage for each factor, so that these add up to 100. Let us also assess an employee's current level of engagement using a 1–3 scale, where 1 is low.

Factor	Learning	Work quality	Pay and benefits	Manager	Team	Personal
Weight	15%	25%	20%	15%	10%	15%
EE 1	2	3	3	2	3	2
EE 2	3	2	1	1	2	3

Let us multiply to arrive at strength of retention:

$$EE\ 1 = (0.15 \times 2) + (0.25 \times 3) + (0.2 \times 2) + (0.15 \times 2) + (0.1 \times 3) + (0.15 \times 2) = 2.55$$

$$EE\ 2 = 1.95.$$

The range for scores is between 1 and 3. One might classify as the following segments:

- 1.7: High risk,
- 1.7 to 2.4: Moderate risk,
- 2.41 to 3: Low risk.

Based on intrinsic reasons, EE 1 is low risk and EE 2 is moderate risk.

This has to be aligned to the market condition. We might again use a 1–3 index, with 1 as high demand and 3 as low demand. In which case, we take the score again and multiply. Assume that EE 1 is in a low demand area while EE 2 is in a high demand area.

Then, 9 becomes the desired score (3 on engagement and 3 on demand). Treating intrinsic and extrinsic factors equally, we arrive at final scores. EE 1 = 2.55 × 1 = 2.55, whereas EE 2 is 1.95 × 1 = 1.95.

Even when the intrinsic motivation is high, the risk of EE 1 leaving is higher, as the demand is much higher in her area. On the other hand, EE 2 is at a lower level of engagement but not a flight risk, as in his work area, demand is less.

At an enterprise level, such fine-tuned modeling is difficult. However, data science and big data come in handy here and help us model on far more parameters that are important. For example:

- Tata Hotels recruits primarily from tier 2 cities in India as they find their attitude to be better.
- TVS group looks at children of its employees from group companies favorably for entry-level hiring.

On the one hand, we use data scientists to create the algorithms that create a right fit equation for predicting turnover. On the other hand, we also need to capture the data that is crucial. We do have information from workforce data. We can create the external demand factor based on actual data. Employee's own perception and needs, have to be arrived at on the basis of the following:

- Surveys that track individual preferences,
- Strength of connections, participation, etc.

Predictive Modeling for Attrition Analysis

As technology and analytic tools have advanced, organizations are employing sophisticated statistical models to mine attrition data and understand at the granular level what trends and patters emerge with what probability of success. Many companies have employee data like performance ratings, promotion history, training programs attended, engagement data, salary data, tenure on various positions/roles, age, leave, etc., and added to this, data from social media can be used effectively to find which employee will quit. Also data like traits of employees who have been successful performers in the company can be used to profile employees who will not fit with these traits and, hence, pose the risk of quitting company. Here are some of the popular predictive models used for attrition analysis:

1. Descriptive statistical techniques: HR function has lot of historical data and an easy way to use this data for predictive analytics is by using descriptive statistics approach. Descriptive statistics methods like forecasting with past data (stationary series), moving averages and exponential smoothing can be used at the very simpler level to predict attrition for the next month or quarter at aggregate level. Even seasonality in attrition—which is a common phenomenon in some organizations—can be factored by exponential smoothing forecasting method to predict attrition in the next month or quarter due to seasonality factors.
2. Regression analysis: To further improve predictive validity, a commonly used statistical tool for predictive analytics is regression analysis. Regression modeling frequently used includes:

a) Ordinary least square (OLS) regression: This is used to study the relationship between independent and dependent variable using equation y = mx + b. For example, regression of attrition and engagement will give result like – A (Attrition) = –2E (Engagement) + 2,000, which means that for every 2 points increase in the engagement score, attrition will go down by 2 points – 2,000 – 2 = 1,998. Also the graph plot is a linear line indicating variables fit on the line and nothing more. However, this model does not tell whether change in engagement levels will lead to the employee quitting or staying. For this another type of regression modeling will work.

b) Logistic regression: This method tells very clearly whether employee will quit or not—like 0 or 1 modeling—assuming 0 for stay and 1 for quit. Here the graph plot will be like "S" curve which highlights when attrition will go up or fall.

3. Artificial neural networks: These are predictive models based on brain analogy and work on the basis of experience or training as in the case of brain. Neural networks are ideal for working with complicated and imprecise data to identify patterns and trends.
4. Classification methods: These include decision trees and memory-based reasoning/case-based reasoning. These are like algorithms which are suitable for identifying patterns in non-numerical data.
5. Clustering: It is another model to predict groups which are similar or closer to each other based on some traits or attributes. This tool can be useful in identifying clusters of employees who display high or low relationship between job attitudes and turnover. Clustering will show patterns like dense areas (high correlation) and spare areas (low correlation) based on attributes.
6. Survival analysis: This technique is borrowed from medical sciences where it is used to predict survival of a disease-affected patient based on medicine used for the treatment.

Survival analysis is an analysis of time to predict when an event will happen and the time elapsed before the event happens. In employee attrition, it helps in pointing out when the event (attrition) will happen with what probability and how long will it take for the event to occur with what probability. For example, analysis may show that there is 80% probability that 10 employees will quit after 8 years or 50% probability that 6 employees will quit after 5 years, and so on. Survival analysis includes analyzing the following and taking action:

a) When an employee will quit, at different time period in months or years
b) What is the probability of quitting taking place for that time period?
c) Take action before the predicted event happens.

8

Measuring and Managing Competencies

Competencies are the connecting blocks of mature HR practices. People capability maturity model designed by the Software Engineering Institute provides for five levels of maturity in HR practices. Practices such as recruitment, training, and compensation occur at Level 2.

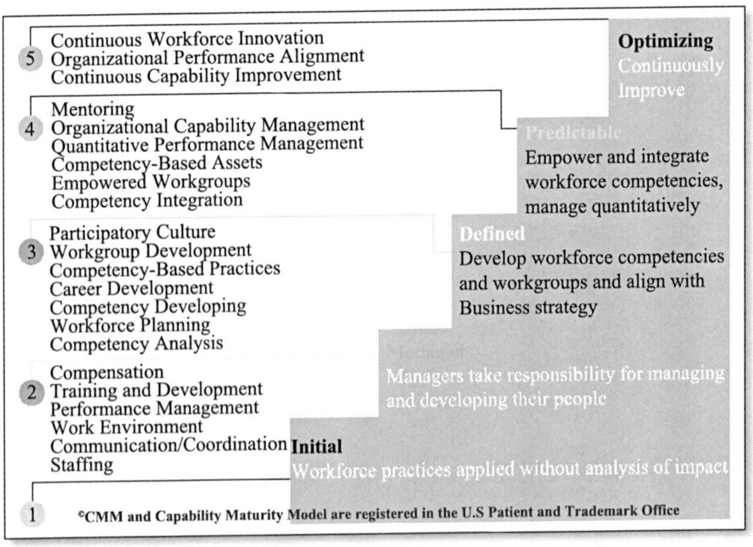

As the schematic shows, business and HR are linked using competencies as defined in Level 3. The business expectations are converted into competencies needed from the workforce. Then the competencies are embedded into workforce planning, career development as well as into recruitment, training, promotions, etc. At a higher level of maturity, the processes are made predictable by baselining process performance and then predicting based on the trends.

Emerging practices in HR rely on competency-based assessments to not only arrive at the best individual decisions but also:

- Decide on the focus areas for L&D,
- Hire effectively based on competencies that drive retention and performance.

Competency Baselining

Most companies have identified a set of competencies that are mapped onto the roles. A table could look like this.

ROLE: Testing Lead

Competency	Level
Communications	2
Collaboration	2
Analytical ability	1
Testing	3

Next step is an assessment of all role-holders. This could be done using a self and manager feedback, 360° survey, or a proper formal assessment. In general, at the end of the assessment, an employee gets a score. Expanding the above, the assessment could look like:

Competency	Level	Score
Communications	2	3/5
Collaboration	2	4/5
Analytical ability	1	3/5
Testing	3	3/5

The company can then consolidate the score from all such assessments and arrive at a baseline score for competencies as follows.

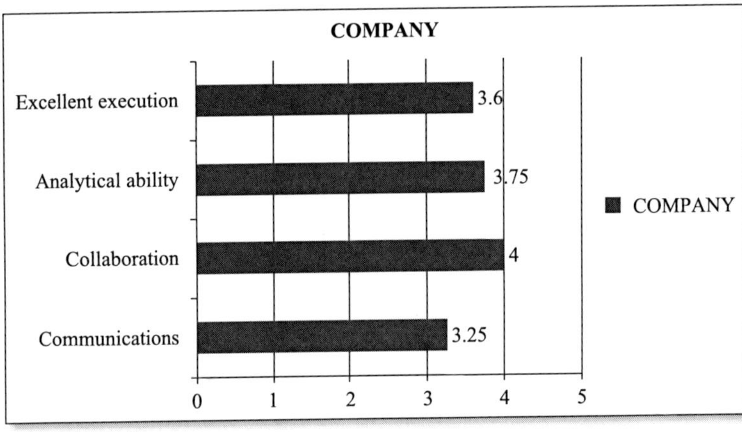

This can then be used to share with the individual employee where he/she stands with respect to the mean score of all role-holders.

Such a comparison will still need to be positioned appropriately, as the averages can be in fractions and the employee can only score in discreet numbers. As it is done elsewhere, percentile scores can also be used to share the findings. This is as far as the individual is concerned.

The organization can then perform a regression of the competency data with performance data. How is the competency profile of the top 10% performers different from that of the others?

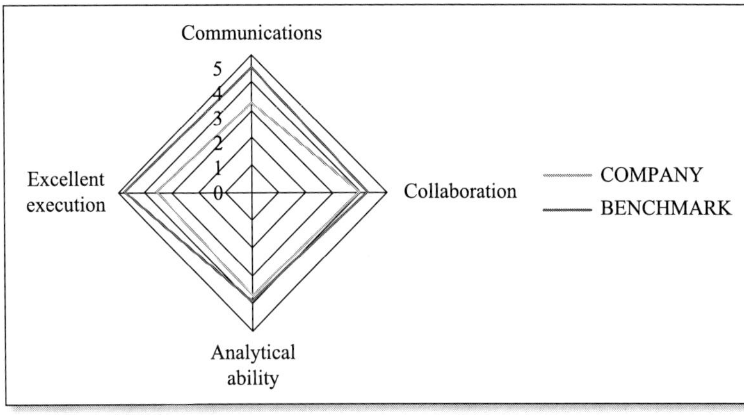

Are the differences across all competencies or only one or two competencies account for the performance variation?

Research shows that a different level of proficiency in just three competencies out of a larger basket can influence performance by more than 75%. Analytics helps us to find what these competencies are. Using the simplified table above, assume we get the following data.

Competency	**Average**	**Top 10%**
Communications	3.25	4.3
Collaboration	4	4.1
Analytical ability	3.75	3.9
Testing	3.6	4.3

This data clearly shows that on collaboration and on analytical ability, the scores do not differ much. Top performers are assessed at a higher level on communications and testing. It is possible that proficiency in these has a greater impact on performance.

The company needs to validate this after considering other variables such as nature of work and quality of supervision, etc. Let us assume that even after that, testing and communications emerge as differentiators.

Usage of Competency Baselines

The first usage of such baselines happens in training. The company can focus its training efforts on improving the communication skills of all role-holders. It can also provide opportunities for all test leads to get better in their functional skills by providing development opportunities.

Secondly, the employees can not only drive their individual development plans but also assess them against the requirements of the higher role. While it has not become a mainstream practice, a lot of companies do perform potential appraisal. Let us say that the employee is looking for his/her next promotion to that of a manager. Let us do a competency comparison.

Competency	Lead level	Manager level	Score	Threshold score for the next level
Communications	2	3	3/5	4
Collaboration	2	2	4/5	2
Analytical ability	1	2	3/5	4
Testing	3	3	3/5	3

The employee needs to improve proficiency in communications and analytical ability to be considered for a promotion. The last column says about the threshold level assessment on the lead level that can be extrapolated to the entry level proficiency for a manager. Accordingly, we get a gap of 1/5 on both competencies. This essentially means that the employee needs to display the behaviors expected from these competencies more frequently to be considered for a move up.

This is a simple way of doing it. For critical roles such as of a manager and director companies often do a stand-alone competency assessment to decide on promotions.

Thirdly, competencies can be tracked at a team level as well, by aggregating the competency assessment scores. Creating simplistic data, we get the following.

Competency	Team 1 lead	Team 1 manager	Team 2 lead	Team 2 manager
Communications	3.8	4	3.4	3.9
Collaboration	4.1	4	3.7	4
Analytical ability	3.2	3.4	3	3.7
Testing	3.6	3.8	3.6	4

This information can be correlated with project/team performance. Let us assume that the team is tracked on:

- Percentage of on-time delivery,
- Number of escalations,
- Attrition percentage,
- Defect rate.

Figure 8.1 is an illustration of the same. The graph maps a measure called "cost of quality" used in measuring quality of programming. The measure has been mapped on one axis. On the other axis, we have two indicators:

- Tech index: This is based on the cumulative competency scores such as programming, analysis, and testing.
- Competency index: This is a composite of competency scores across technology and behavior.

The chart shows cost of quality scores across different projects against their tech and behavioral competency indices. The progression clearly shows that higher the competency scores, lesser the cost of maintaining high quality.

It is possible to compare the competency scores with the business measures using correlation and regression to arrive at the following:

- Whether competencies are impacting team performance.
- What is the impact?
- What needs to be done to enhance the competency level of the team?

Figure 8.1 Correlation: COQ to Competency Baseline

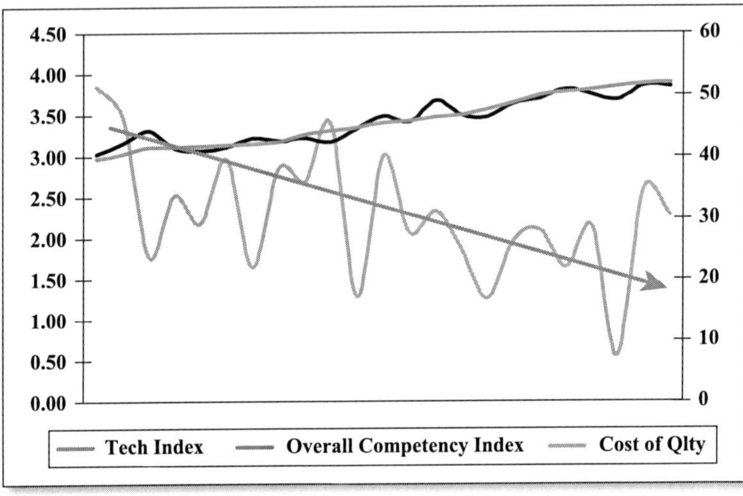

Source: Created by Samit Deb.

We are using competencies to assess and develop employees. However that is just with existing employees. What about new joins? Should we not also assess them against desired competencies?

Mature companies use competency-based hiring instruments. Assume that communication skills is the biggest predictor of on-the-job performance. Then, it becomes important to spend some valuable time in the selection process assessing whether the candidate displays proficiency levels commensurate with top performers of the organization. This helps in ensuring that the right profile candidates are selected and they start performing earlier.

Leadership Development

Competencies form the base of all leadership development activities. Assessment centers are performed using leadership competencies and development plans arrived at.

How do leaders of one company compare against best in class leaders? This information is an added input when a company is trying to be competitive with the market leader. Assessment companies have the global trends on the average scores as well as on the scores for top performing companies. A radar chart then helps baseline the existing competency levels against industry-leading competencies and then use that to fine-tune development plans.

A radar chart, as follows, helps in this benchmarking.

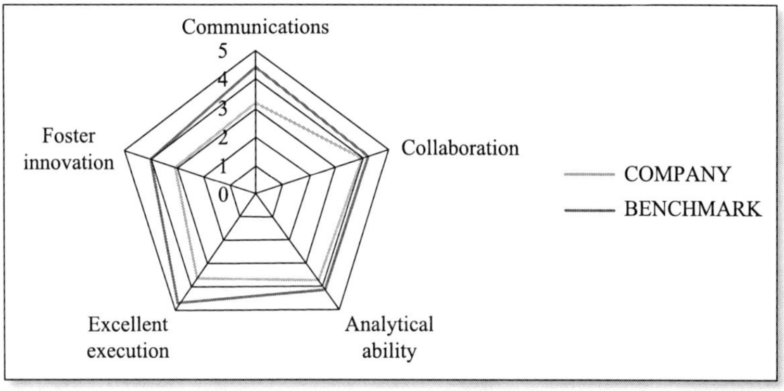

Using Competencies in Talent Acquisition

As stated earlier, a company can move to a higher level of HR process maturity by integrating competencies to all HR policies. While it is one thing to assess and map competencies to performance, it would greatly benefit to use the competency information for hiring new talent into the organization.

Often companies have 12–15 competencies identified for each role. Even if we prioritize a few for each role, it would still mean 5–6. Assessment centers are a validated method for objectively assessing potential employees. However, it is still an implementation challenge to use assessment centers for all roles, especially those that are done in high volume.

Typically, for entry-level roles, interviews are used for selection and these do not exceed more than an hour or so. In which case, how does one prioritize what competencies to focus on?

This is where correlations help. Employees are assessed against different competencies. As shown in the example above,

Competency	Average score for all role holders (1–5)	Average score for high performers
Communications	3.7	4.5
Team working	4.1	4.2
Innovativeness	3.1	3.8
Analytical ability	4	4.2
Client orientation	3.5	3.7

the competency profiles for high performers are called out. The crucial 2–3 competencies that differentiate high performers from the rest are isolated. The limited time in interviews can be focused on assessing these competencies to arrive at better quality of hires.

As the table above shows, the biggest differences between average performers and high performers stem from the competencies of innovative thinking and communications. When one is interviewing, it would aid to focus on these two competencies.

9

Optimizing Compensation and Benefits for High Performance

Compensation and employee welfare costs are deemed important enough for it to deserve a line for itself in the annual P&L report of companies. These tend to be one of the top five costs for any organization. Let us consider the following companies.

Company	**Segment**	**Headcount**	**Employee cost/ Revenues**
Infosys	IT services	165,000	57.50%
TCS	IT services	300,000	55.50%
Marico	FMCG	1,938	6%
Tata Motors	Manufacturing	65,500	9.2%

One finds that there is a wide difference in employee costs across the three segments represented here. Employee costs account for more than half the costs in IT services. On the other hand, in Tata Motors it is only 9% and in Marico, it is even less. In a manufacturing company like Tata Motors, oftenthe cost of raw materials is the highest amount costs; in services companies, billing hours of people is the primary raw material. In fast-moving consumer goods (FMCG), cost of materials and cost of sales and marketing outstrip employee costs.

Let us now detail out the table a little more.

Company	Segment	Headcount	Employee cost/ Revenues	Employee cost/Net profit	Employee cost/FTE
Infosys	IT services	165,000	57.50%	2.7	1,800,000
TCS	IT services	300,000	55.50%	1.8	1,514,000
Marico	FMCG	1,938	6%	1.7	1,469,040
Tata Motors	Manufacturing	65,500	9.2	1.5	3,200,000

Source: Derived and simplified from annual reports 2014–2015.

In all four companies, the employee costs outstrip the net profits. Even when the cost is as low as it is in Marico, it is still higher than the profits. So, any path to higher profitability necessarily incorporates an optimization of all employee expenses.

The last column is interesting because it is on the higher side, for an average Indian employee. All this indicates is that Infosys, TCS, and Tata Motors incur a significant payroll and benefit cost overseas, that when averaged and aggregated looks quite high. Marico possibly pays more given its lesser headcount. In manufacturing and FMCG, there is also contract labor and how they are expensed is something that is outside the scope of this book.

Business Levers of Compensation and Benefits

Often in areas such as training and employee engagement, we start off from an activity measure, derive the cost, and then try to assess the business impact. On the other hand, compensation is an area, where the costs and business impact are very well articulated.

As mentioned above, the cost of compensation and its impact on the overall profitability is the first business lever. Not long back, General Motors, the venerable American auto manufacturer, went into bankruptcy because of an employee benefit; in the olden days, they had guaranteed lifetime healthcare benefit for all. Over a period of 50 years, the cost of administering this benefit alone brought the company to its knees.

Compensation is an area that is also governed by government regulations, which set the minimum wages. Compensation strategy becomes a fine art of balancing between the regulations, market pay as well as employee performance.

Incentive compensation is used as the default tool to align the sales goals with sales compensation. A lighter shade is the investment on rewards and recognition programs. Stock options and long-term incentive programs are used to align the long-term growth of the company to employee motivation.

So, while employee expenses are an important line item in financial statements, there is an equally big expectation to achieve business goals using the motivation of incentive schemes and reward programs. In effect, if HR has to stand its ground from the CFO just looking at the people investment as expenses, an analytical approach is de rigueur.

Organization Structure and Cost of Management

Management is important. At the same time, it is expensive. And as the levels increase, the compensation rises exponentially. Let us look at this example.

Role	**Number of people**
Engineer	48
Senior engineer	27
Tech. lead	13
Project manager	6
Manager	3
Sr. manager	2
Director	1
Total	100

Span of control will be the first measure used to identify whether this is an effective structure or ineffective. Let us assume that levels above project manager are managerial roles. Here, we have 6 + 3 + 2 + 1 headcount in such roles; 11 managers for 100 employees give us a manager span of control of 9. It is a reasonably good number.

Now, let us include the average compensation costs for these roles as well.

Role	Number of people	Average salary pa	Total compensation
Engineer	48	400,000	19,200,000
Senior engineer	27	700,000	18,900,000
Tech. lead	13	900,000	11,700,000
Project manager	6	1,200,000	7,200,000
Manager	3	1,800,000	5,400,000
Sr. manager	2	2,200,000	4,400,000
Director	1	3,000,000	3,000,000
Total	100	698,000	69,800,000

Let us relook at the ratio now. The average salary of an employee is 698,000. The average compensation of an individual contributor is 565,909. On the other hand, the average salary of a managerial employee is 16, 66,667. In other words, every manager costs nearly three times an individual contributor and, hence, direct management costs would account for 33% of the payroll. With due respects, managers administer value; they don't create. In an IT services company, all value comes from individual contributors like software developers, architects, and sales people.

This is just for 100 people. Any mid-size organization employs people in thousands. To that extent, the cost of management increases proportionately. And we are not even talking about the leadership layer.

Level	Average Salary pa	Percentage of total payroll
Individual contributor	565,909	71%
Management	1,666,667	29%

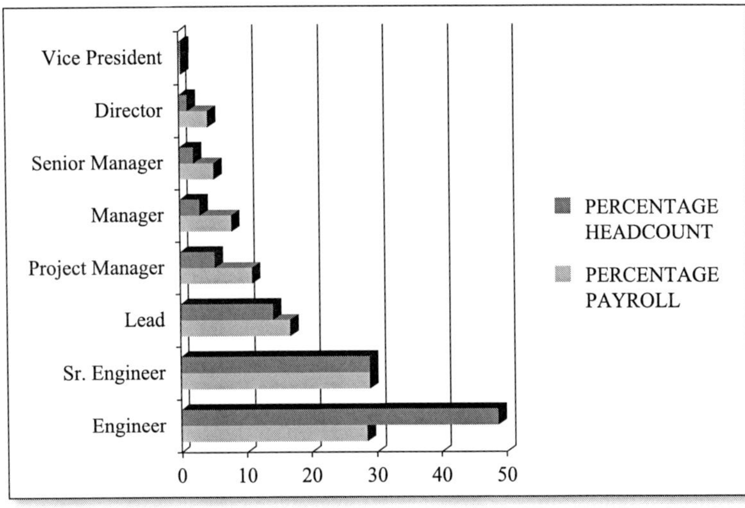

This graph clearly shows the difference. Engineers maybe 48% of the headcount, but they cost only 27% of the payroll. On the other hand, the director and senior manager level is just 3% of the headcount, but 12% of the payroll.

Let us complicate things a little more. Let us improve the headcount by 10 times. There are not only going to be more senior managers and directors, but even people at the level of vice president. For argument's sake, let us say a company needs 1 vice president, 3 senior directors for every 1,000 employees, while the structure for every 100 employees is replicated as above; 1 director for every 100 employees. You need to pay vice presidents really well!

Role	Headcount	Average salary pa	Total compensation
Engineer	480	400,000	192,000,000
Senior engineer	270	700,000	189,000,000
Tech. lead	130	900,000	117,000,000
Project manager	59	1,200,000	72,000,000
Manager	29	1,800,000	52,200,000
Sr. manager	19	2,200,000	41,800,000
Director	9	3,000,000	27,000,000
Sr. Director	3	4,200,000	12,600,000
Vice president	1	6,000,000	6,000,000
Total	1,000	709,000	709,600,000

Level	Average salary pa	Percentage of total payroll
Individual contributor	565,909	70%
Management	1,666,000	28%
Organization leadership	4,650,000	2%

The drop in the proportion of individual contributor payroll has been taken up by the leadership layer. For the cost of a vice president, we can employ 15 engineers and they generate revenue!

This is simplistic. Vice presidents not only hold the fort but also strategize for the company. They not only are busy in meetings with each other but also with customers, which help the company get more business that keeps engineers occupied—fair point. However, the takeaway from this example is that:

- Span of control is an important measure.
- Dividing the payroll costs by management levels provides greater insight.

- Performance measures need to be tighter before increasing the salaries of leaders.

Google famously once tried to do away with all managers and tried to create a truly collegial workplace. However, they dropped the experiment once the engineers started coming to the founders for things like travel reimbursement. Managers were reinstated. There are several experiments in organization structuring and design. Maybe one day companies like Morningstar (a tomato processing company), who have been successful without a single manager, could become the norm. For now and the near future, management remains integral to organizations.

Traditional Measures of Compensation

In general, two measures take preponderance in public discourse. First is the compensation quartile positioning of the company, when compared to a peer group. Second is the annual average percentage increase in the base pay. What is also tracked by employees is the percentage payout of incentive/variable payout. The latter two are more popular than arguably any other measure in HR.

Mature organizations also track the following:

- Cost of defined benefit plans like hospitalization insurance. This is usually the most expensive benefit and undergoes an elaborate annual renewal process.
- Coverage of reward and recognition programs. How many unique employees were covered at least under one of the programs?
- Compensation on a cost-to-company (CTC) basis. Employees do not really consider the investment into benefits like provident fund (PF) as something that is contributed by the company. In reality, at least 15% of the cash compensation is contributed through benefits. Unless this is tracked at the organization and employee level, there is no proper appreciation of this investment.

Organizations try to maintain or reduce the total cost of compensation year on year. It is expected that any investment into salary reviews or introduction of other benefits should lead to a corresponding decline in employee attrition. Attrition of employees based on their compensation quartile as well as percentage increase in salary is tracked.

In addition to this, the traditional measure of comparatio is also adapted by companies. Comparatio is used to assess the positioning of the employee's compensation with respect to the market pay for that position. Market benchmarking allows us to establish the minimum, median, and maximum for each position. Comparatio then is a simple calculation as follows:

$$\frac{\text{Compensation of the employee}}{\text{Market mid-point for the position}}$$

A comparatio of 1 means that the employee is being paid the market rate for the position.

It is possible to arrive at the group comparatio for different roles and assess the market positioning of the role.

How Far Does Annual Compensation Increase Help?

No questions asked. Organizations do a benchmarking of their competitors every year and based on business needs decide on the comparatio to be used. Then, the percent adjustment needed to achieve market positioning is arrived at. Employees are then positioned across the median, based on their individual performance appraisal ratings.

This usually is the annual merit increase process. However, it so happens that in several organizations, the attrition peaks usually after the salary increases. Some of it has to do with the employee having a certain expectation and leaving when it is not met. However, it is not unusual to find employee grievances around fairness and internal equity. Neither is it unusual to see consistently good performers not necessarily topping the pay charts.

Very often one comes across employee angst around "I joined on the same day as XYZ, my performance ratings have been superior to him and yet, how is he making more money than me?"

Such oversight happens, because companies lack an analytical framework to visualize what the compensation distribution should be and what it is. An annual process helps us make increments but the starting point of it should be internal inefficiencies in salary distribution.

Differences exist between the compensation of otherwise equivalent employees due to the following reasons:

- Different salary at the time of joining.
- Variations due to salary increases in different years. One person might have been rated "Outstanding" but received little or no raise as that was a bad year for the economy. On the other hand, his peer could have been rated "Outstanding" in the following year, when the economy rebounded and the company gave out good substantial raises.
- The employees were under different managers. Each had a different peer group for comparison, leading to one manager giving an increase on the higher side of the range.

Such factors add up over a period of time and result in variations that are large enough to make the employee feel less engaged.

How does one address this using compensation analytics? The solution lies in moving away from looking at employee compensation as a one off to reviewing it holistically on the basis of the following:

- Role spans and an employee's positioning on it based on tenure and performance.
- Employee's compensation progression based on performance in the span.

Let us say that a company has a role with a role span of 3 years. Employees in this role will attain full proficiency in 3 years, when maintaining "meet expectations" standards. If the employee has been consistently exceeding expectations, he/she would attain full proficiency in 2 years. Let the company have four performance ratings: exceptional (E), exceeds expectations (EE), meets expectations (ME), and does not meet expectations (DNME).

For us to review this against employee compensation, we need to map the cumulative performance of the employee in the role against the current compensation. We are looking at performance in band as well as compensation as a continuum and not stand-alone events.

To start with a simple assumption, let us just examine the scenario for employees who have been consistently rated E, EE, ME, and DNME. Then the actual plot would be something like:

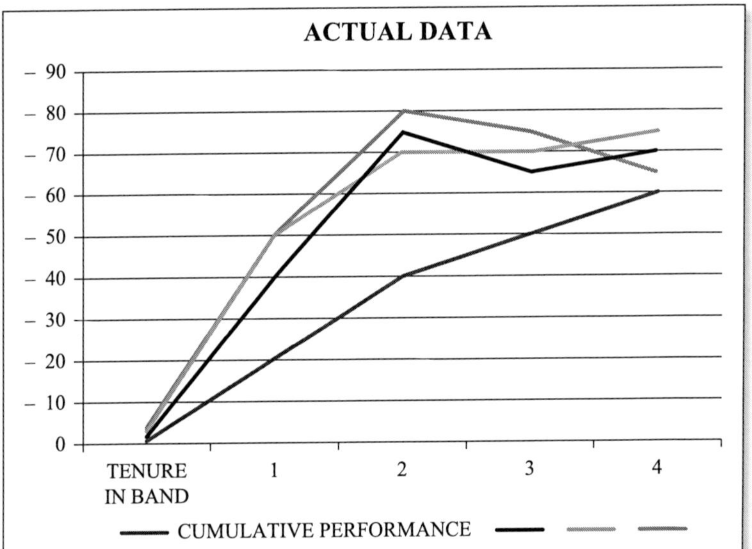

This shows that the person who is performing consistently lower than expectations, (if he/she is lucky enough to retain the job) is definitely at the lower end of the pay scale. For all the other three, there is a clustering at the top. After 2 years, the consistency of performance does not seem to be a big differentiator. This is slightly exaggerated, but in the long run there does exist a clustering of compensation.

How should this graph look like? An average performer should be at the mid-point of the role when their tenure equals the mid-point of the salary range for that role. The exceptional performer should be at the top end, in Q4 by the 3rd year.

The graph then should resemble this:

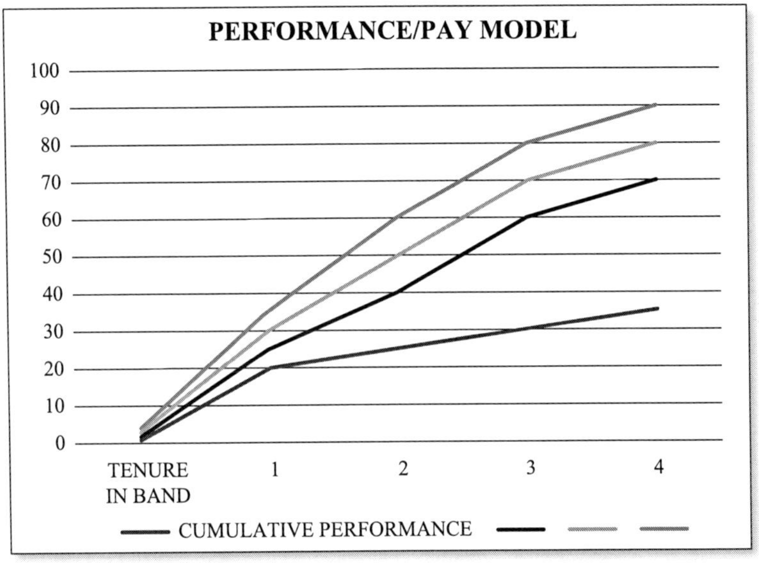

As is visible, the model also makes sure that the employee compensation is not solely determined by performance on the job. There could be two people rated as EE; one with 2 years' experience and another with 6 years' experience. It makes little sense to give both of them same increases, even though the performance rating has been the same.

This is where the role span comes into play. Compensation increases linearly till the 3-year mark. After that, a person continuing on the same role could be delivering diminishing returns year after year. As such, the pay increases should be muted with time.

Is it possible to create a template that helps in this? Such a template should be able to include cumulative performance levels as well as tenure in the role. An illustrative table follows.

	CUMULATIVE PERFORMANCE IDEAL			
TENURE IN BAND	1	2	3	4
1	20	25	30	35
2	25	40	50	60
3	30	60	70	80
4	35	70	80	90

The cumulative performance level is taken as the marker. Here, we are looking only at four combinations that serve as guidelines. An employee could be ME, E, and EE in 3 years while another could be EE, EE, and ME. These scores fall within the overall range and can be calibrated. There are four annualized performance ratings, resulting in 24 combinations.

Such a framework based on existing compensation information is useful in validating the compensation strategy. This exercise should be conducted when the compensation planning is initiated. Using this matrix, the compensation manager can identify outliers as they exist across the company.

At present, most companies do not consider the cumulative performance evolution. Then outliers are handled as exceptions and actions are taken based on managerial discretion. A systematic top-down approach using tenure in role and cumulative performance rating allows outliers to be highlighted early and actions to be taken in a timely fashion.

Often, one is at a loss to understand why employees leave, even after getting a good raise. Only after an investigation is HR able to identify systemic issues that have created a perception of unfairness. Articulating fairness as a compensation goal and using tools to ensure fairness in action reduces post-salary increase blues!

We Are a High Performance Organization. Are You Sure?

While purists may scoff at the format as well as the "auctions" used to hire players, the Indian Premier League cricket tournament promotes merit. It rewards the pace bowler, big hitting batsman, and the nifty all-rounder based on their performance. Teams bid for players and the annual pay packets can be in millions of dollars. A team would have two opening batsmen; one costing 10 crores per annum and the other, 50 lakhs; A 20X variation. Players do not mind it much as they feel that with consistent performances they will be able to command premiums as well. The IPL does not classify players into opening batsman, opening bowler, and spinner and then arrive at a median salary.

Organizations are somewhat different from sports or entertainment. It is said that the best programer can be 30 times more productive than the average programer. However, an organization finds it difficult to create a talent market due to the following reasons:

- The deliverables are interlinked and it is not easy to completely isolate one person's contribution.
- The employees have a 30-year career, when compared to a star athlete, who has a 10–15-year career.
- The expectation is for a few stars but many solid performers. The compensation base is set on an average employee delivering average performance.

However, companies rigorously rank their employees on a performance curve with the intent of allocating salary increases on the basis of performance reviews. This is showcased as one of the primary vehicles of meritocracy.

Even allowing for all variables, just how much more should be the incentive for the top performer? Is there a top performer band?

At the end of normalization, most employees are in the middle of the curve. After benchmarking, the average salary increase is arrived at, so that the median is fixed first. If there is a 10% gap between market salary and internal median, then it is decided that there would be a 10% adjustment. What about the top performer? Does he/she get 5% more, 10% more?

In practice, managers and organizations are very comfortable with central tendencies. Once the average increase is arrived at, a premium of 5% or so is added to the salary increase for the top performer. A compensation matrix looks like this:

Performance rating	**E**	**EE**	**ME**	**DNME**
Percentage workforce	10	40	45	5
Salary increase	16	12	8	0

The increases are in steps of 4%. An employee, who has outperformed everyone, ends up getting just 8% more than the average performer. In informal discussions, employees say that the effort required to achieve the top rating is just not worth the returns. Drawing a comparison chart, one gets the attached picture:

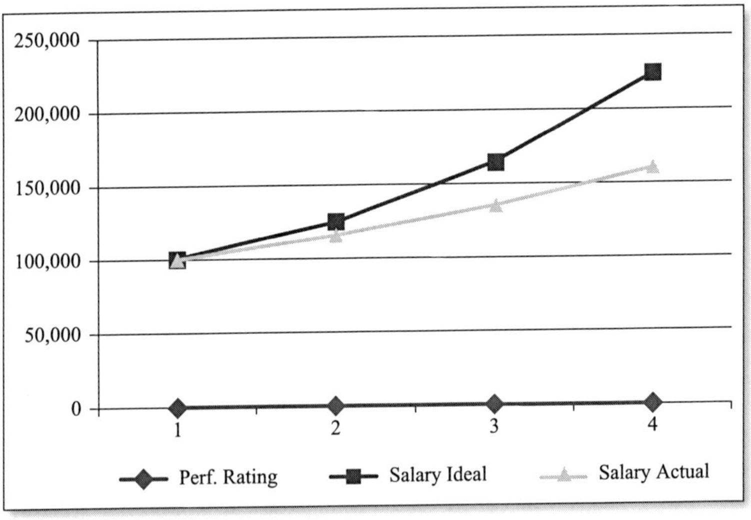

Please note that the ideal distribution here aims to create increasing levels of differentiation between each performance level. This can be achieved by focusing not only on the median number but also on the difference between each performance level.

Performance rating	E	EE	ME	DNME
Percentage workforce	10	40	45	5
Salary increase percentage	16	12	8	0
Desired salary increase percentage	22	14	8	0

Starting point for all this will be the simple scatter plot of employee compensation against performance.

Valuing Benefits Using the CTC Statement

Consider two friends discussing their salary.

Friend 1: How much do you make?
Friend 2: I make 12 lakhs.

Friend 1: How much is fixed and how much is variable?
Friend 2:15% variable. It is usually paid. So, 10.2 fixed and 1.8 variable. What about you?

Friend 1: I make 10 lakhs, but it is fixed. No variable pay though.
Friend 2: Anything tax friendly?

Friend 1: No. All based on payroll.

While the conversations are usually on salary, take home, taxation benefit, and so on, benefits are never mentioned in the discussion. While doing compensation analysis, it strikes you when nearly 12% to 20% of employee payroll costs in India are in the form of benefits.

Let us consider the benefit cost of an employee who gets a salary of ₹10 lakhs. Let us assume that the person has a basic pay of 40% of the total CTC. A simple explanation of this would state:

Basic:	400,000
Allowances:	600,000
Total:	10,00,000

Let us look at the benefits:

PF (@ 12% of basic):	48,000
Gratuity (15/26 of 1 month's basic):	15,000
Telephone reimbursement (@2000 pm):	24,000
Tuition reimbursement:	75,000

This is an illustrative list. If you consider the amounts mentioned alone, we get up to 16% of the cash salary.

Companies include defined benefits like PF to arrive at the cost-to-company number. In reality, the CTC, when an employee utilizes all benefits, is 8%–10% more than the CTC numbers.

For employees to shift their mindset from a cash compensation base to a cash+benefits base, we need to clearly articulate a total compensation statement that does not start with basic pay, but with CTC.

Component	**Amount**	**Percentage**
CTC	1,175,000	100
Base pay	850,000	72
Variable pay	150,000	13
Benefits	175,000	15

It is sometimes very difficult to value benefits like employee stock options and the like. However, it is recommended that as far as possible, value the generic benefits and show them and use them in discussions with employees. Using an analytical approach, HR should establish the landed cost of each benefit instead of treating benefits as a line item.

Portfolio Management of Benefits

While the basic salary may be 40% of the basic pay, it is a one line item. On the other hand, benefits, even when they account for 15% of the CTC, are comprised of 7–8 line items. This fragmentation ensures that no single benefit is too costly, but at the same time makes it difficult for companies to assess their relative importance.

To measure the impact of benefits, we need to consolidate the following:

- Benefit,
- Target population,
- Number of beneficiaries,
- Percent workforce beneficiaries,
- Cost of benefit.

Benefit	Target	Target population	Beneficiary number	Percent	Cost	Cost/ Beneficiary	Cost/ Employee
Library	All employees	1,000	250	25%	2,50,000	1,000	250
Extended maternity leave	Women employees	300	50	5%	25,00,000	50,000	2,500
Food coupons	All employees	1,000	1,000	100%	2,50,00,000	25,000	25,000
Car lease	Managers	200	120	12%	86,40,000	72,000	864
Tuition reimburse-ment	Individual contributors	800	100	10%	50,00,000	50,000	5,000
Gymnasium	All employees	1,000	100	10%	15,00,000	15,000	1,500

Such an analysis helps us to take stock of how different programs are doing. Food coupons are popular, as they cover all employees. At the same time, benefits like library or gym, which are open to all employees, are not used by as many employees as they should.

Having such information helps us to identify targets for rationalization. Total cost of benefits listed here is 4.3 crores per annum. If we are to reduce this by 10% next year, what do we do? In such a scenario, we look at the following options:

1. Dropping a benefit altogether,
2. Offering it on a cost sharing basis. It can be 50:50, 75:25, etc.,
3. Reducing the eligible population. For example, move the company-leased car benefit to directors and above,
4. Effecting an across-the-board cut.

However, before effecting these cuts, one also has to compare the benefits with their impact:

- Has the benefit utilization been increasing year on year? Is the popularity of the benefit increasing?
- Is there any correlation between benefit utilization and retention? Does a long-term benefit, like car leasing, help in retention?
- Within the target population, some utilize the benefits and some do not. Does the intent to use a benefit indicate intent to stay for a longer tenure?

Armed with such data, we will be able to create a portfolio of benefits as following:

Benefit	**Coverage**	**Utilization**	**Cost/ Employee**	**Utilization trends**	**Impact on retention**
Benefit A	All	High	Low	Flat	Nil
Benefit B	Individual contributors	Low	Medium	Improving	Positive
Benefit C	Managers	Medium	High	Declining	Neutral

A portfolio of benefits, formed on the basis of utilization and impact metrics, gives a view grounded in facts on evolving the benefits strategy.

Tailoring Variable Pay to Performance Based on Data

As mentioned earlier, Sysco Corp., a $40 billion wholesale food distributor based in Houston, found that its compensation system for drivers—paying them by hours worked—did not provide as much value to the organization as it could. According to company, the model was not providing better customer satisfaction or profitability. Instead, Sysco changed to a reward structure it calls activity-based compensation. Drivers earn a base pay that is supplemented with incentives for more deliveries, fewer mistakes, and good safety records.

To be on the safe side, Sysco did not roll out the program nationwide. It tested it in certain pilot markets first, and then tracked the results of the operating company. Four metrics were targeted: satisfaction level, retention, efficiency (delivering more cases in less time), and delivery expense. Under the new compensation structure, Sysco found that drivers were not only more efficient, they were also more satisfied. The company's retention rates for drivers improved by 8% and expenses, as a percentage of sales, went down. After quantifiable results showed the benefit of the change, Sysco rolled out the program nationwide (CFO, 2006).

10

Making the Transformation Possible

The human resource management (HRM) function has undergone many transformations since its inception as a personnel and welfare department in the late 19th century. Every transformation had added a new outlook or objective for the HRM function and each time HR practitioners have been successful in adapting to as well as adopting new transformational shifts. However, after the first decade of the 21st century, HRM is again at the threshold of another transformative stage, which is being labelled as people analytics, talent analytics, HR analytics, etc.

The beginning of this transformation started with the use of data in selection of baseball players who delivered stellar performance resulting in multimillion returns for the team owners. This entire baseball story got published as a book titled *Moneyball* in 2003 which subsequently caught eye of corporate world as it gave a key message on talent management that need of the hour is to *find the talent who is being paid below average but has big potential.* Thus began the journey of data use in identifying talent and making data-based talent decisions in the corporate world initiating the latest transformative agenda for the HRM function.

However, this transformational demand on HR practitioners is vastly different from earlier transformational changes as it poses fundamental mind-set shift for HR practitioners. Unlike previous transformations—this one is "subtractive" in nature than more on the "additive" side, requiring HR professionals to create space for a lot of unlearning. The challenge is further accentuated by the nature of the work style of HR practitioners so far, which has been more making talent or people management decisions based on qualitative criteria and positioning HR professionals as touchy-feely types, whereas HR analytics demands making talent or people management decisions largely on the basis of data and being more objective in decision making. Given the momentum that HR analytics has gained in the last 4–5 years, there is hardly any choice for HR professionals other than embracing this new transformational shift and operationalizing it as a key discipline of the mainstream HRM function.

The implementation of HR analytics requires HR professionals to be fully aware of key "must haves" for successful execution. Using a mix of McKinsey 7s Model, here is a list of key dimensions (Figure 10.1) for operationalization of HR analytics and each will be discussed in detail subsequently:

1. Skills
2. Systems (process and technology)
3. Structure
4. Support (leadership and culture)
5. Staff
6. Strategy (HR strategy)
7. Data presentation and communication

All of these dimensions are critical for the implementation of HR analytics by any HRM function. Some salient features of the model in Figure 10.1, before discussing each dimension in detail, are:

- Support dimension, which includes culture and leadership and hence this dimension permeates across all other dimensions and thus underlines its importance by being on the top of this model.

Figure 10.1 Graphical Representation of HR Analytics Implementation Schema

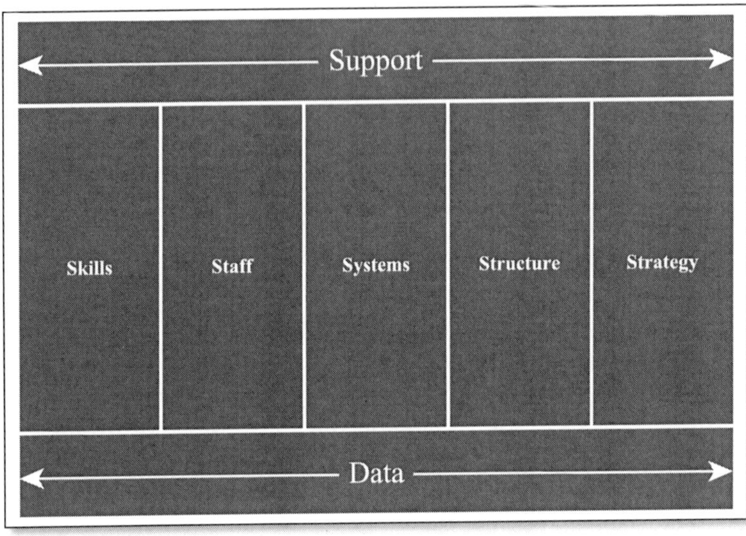

Source: Adapted from Watermen, Peters, and Phillips (1980).

- Data, like support, is another key dimension which is sacrosanct for other dimensions and, hence, has crucial role in implementation plan.

Now let us discuss in detail all the dimensions of Analytics Implementation Schema as shown in Figure 10.1.

1. Skills: Implementation of HR analytics requires HR professionals to possess these skills:
   a) Business acumen: complete understanding of business of the company/BU, how company/BU makes money, and key value drivers of the business from the HR perspective such as impact of employee wages, benefits, productivity, and employee development investments, and how these in turn impact business outcomes like revenue and operating margins.
   b) Statistical skills: basic knowledge of statistics to be able to use and understand the meaning of various statistical

tools like measures of central tendency, dispersion, distributions, correlations, regressions, probability, etc.

c) Research methodology skills: familiarity with the research methodology field, like familiarity with sample selection techniques, tool or instrument creation, scientific approach to problem identification, and model/framework selection.
d) Financial skills: basic understanding of key investment evaluation methods such as cost–benefit ratio, RoI, net present value (NPV), and internal rate of return (IRR).
e) Data presentation skills: these are required to make sense of data along with statistical techniques, and include graphs, plots, charts, and curves.
f) Data analysis: basic skills required include ability to create a basic model, frame hypotheses, and test and validate the same using data analysis tools and techniques.
g) Data interpretation skills: this skill is different from data analysis skill as interpretation requires the ability to read patterns or interpret analysis results to draw insights and actions.
h) HR domain skills: deep and wide understanding of various HR disciplines such as workforce planning, recruitment, performance management, development, rewards, etc., and their interrelationships.

Patrick Coolen and Auke IJsselstein have created an "HR competencies/skills wheel" required for successful implementation of HR analytics (Figure10.2). This wheel also gives a glimpse of the type of interface required with various other functions and the kind of people needed to staff the HR analytics team, and is covered next.

2. Staff: This dimension deals with "people" part of the implementation model. An HR analytics team needs various type of skills apart from those listed above and these other skills include IT skills such as storing and retrieving data, software use, advance statistical skills like algorithm and

Figure 10.2 HR Capability/Competencies/Skills Wheel

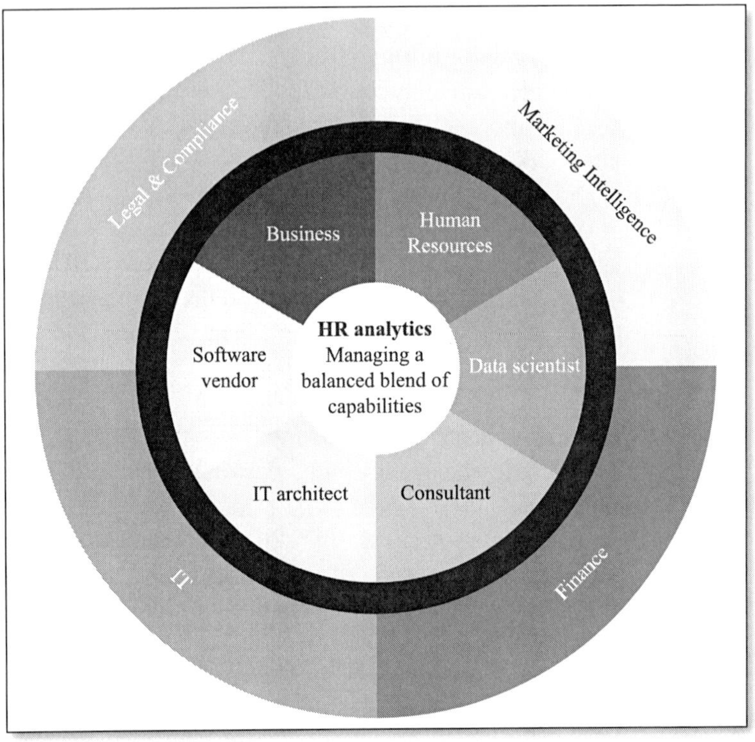

Source: Reproduced with permission from Coolen and IJsselstein (2015).

model building, costing skills, business operations and marketing skills, psychology and sociology skills to link data with human and group dynamics, etc. So given the varied nature of skills required by an effective HR analytics team, here is suggested composition of team—organization can borrow resources internally from other functions or hire from outside depending on need:

a) HR analytics team leader: someone from a non-technical background, though from HR domain, is ideal and has excellent influencing and communication skills with analytics expertise. Main role is to sell HR analytics to business leaders and get their buy in. Additionally helps in adding HR perspectives and context to interpretation of data analysis results. Care needs to be taken while selecting a person for this role as a wrong person without appropriate gravitas and skills can kill the HR analytics initiative.

b) Data analyst/statistician: someone who knows how to do statistical analysis. He/she can be from HR or from other functions like marketing or finance.
c) Data scientist: role of this person is to do big data crunching, create models/algorithms, and interpret data results.
d) Data specialist: who maintains and ensures data is available in the right format, and oversees the data governance process.
e) Other team roles/members required may include persons with legal knowledge, finance, business operations, etc. who can be drawn internally from other functions based on requirements.

3. Structure: This dimension deals with issues like whether HR analytics should be part of the HR function or not, and the type of structure required. As far as the first is concerned, it is ideal to host HR analytics within the HR function as it is the HR head who is accountable to the CEO for HR decision making and budget, etc., and it also helps in giving HR language flavor to the analysis and results interpretation. Regarding the type of the structure, an organization can choose from the following formats based on its need, size, and scale:

   a) Centralized: here HR analytics group is at the corporate level and rolls out the HR analytics framework and data analysis results organization wide.
   b) Decentralized: in this form each division or business unit has its own HR analytics team for implementing HR analytics.
   c) Center of excellence (CoE): in this form there is an expert team at the corporate/central level coupled with an embedded HR analytics member for each function or BU who is supported by the CoE team. CoE is more

of an enabling setup for the implementation of HR analytics across the organization. The CoE approach also recognizes the fact that HR analytics needs a different kind of skills and abilities than other CoEs, such as learning and development, compensation, etc.

d) Functional: here, each function of HR, such as, learning and development, workforce planning, or compensation and benefits, etc., has its own analytics team or a person to do analytics.

4. Systems: This dimension deals with the systems or processes and technology assets required to produce and store data for analysis—reports and dashboard types, generation periodicity, tools or software assets or technology requirements, data standards, protocols, templates, etc.—to ensure consistent application of HR analytics across the organization.
5. Strategy: Essentially, this piece covers HR strategy encompassing HR analytics strategy and roadmap. Unless HR analytics is made an integral part of the overall HR strategy for the organization, utility of HR analytics diminishes. Strategy dimension also includes clarity on HR analytics strategy covering analytics roadmap, objectives, metric selection, and their link to business outcomes in a phased manner.
6. Support: This is one of the key dimensions whose importance cuts across all other dimensions as shown in the model. It has two sub dimensions, namely leadership and culture, and each is elaborated below:

a) Leadership: means the C-level team of the organization such as CEO, COO, CHRO, CFO, CTO, etc., and they being on board for sponsoring implementation of HR analytics by providing budgetary and other resources required for its implementation. C-level support also ensures that data which resides in other functions such as finance, operation, marketing, etc., are made available to the HR analytics team for analysis. Also more important is that the CHRO includes HR analytics as a piece of his/her overall HR philosophy for the organization to position HR analytics.

b) Culture: another key sub-dimension of support piece. Culture of an organization has various nuances impacting implementation of HR analytics. Basically organizations either have a culture on a spectrum where one end is the culture that believes in use of data for various types of decision making including HR decision making, and on the other end is culture which does not believe in the use of data in decision making. Reason for lack of cultural support for data primarily comes from high transparency and accountability caused due to data-based decision making. Also use of data in driving key HR decisions such as recruitment, promotion, rewards, development, etc., has the potential of upsetting the political fabric of the organization. So one needs to be sensitive to the prevailing culture of the organization and how does that culture support or oppose the use of data in HR decision making before deciding to implement HR analytics.

7. Data: Last key dimension of the model is data, and its importance for HR analytics is akin to blood running through a human body. For this reason, data has to be treated as an "asset" to be monetized through analytics. There are certain key aspects related to data in the whole plan of HR analytics implementation and these are covered below:
   a) Nature of data: Typically, HR data is either unstructured (text form) or structured (numerical), and good amount of HR data is unstructured such as social media data, resumes, survey comments, appraisal feedback, exit surveys, training feedback, etc., requiring heavy coding to make it machine usable. Other key challenges related to data need to be taken care of and include:
      i. Missing data: most of the time there is large amount of data missing or not available affecting meaningful analysis.
      ii. Data reliability/integrity: primarily arises due to lack of standardization of definitions, process inconsistency, and methodology used for storing

data. This can also impact quality of analysis and, hence, needs to be sorted out before implementing HR analytics.

iii. Data governance: deals with policy, processes, responsibility, accountability, accessibility, legal aspects, etc., for data storage, use, and communication to appropriate stakeholders for decision making. It is ideal to have a data governance group to take care of these governance-related challenges.

b) Presentation: Another element related to data is presentation of analysis results and here are some key points to take care of this part:

i. Know the audience: tailor presentation of analysis results according to the audience. For example, the type of presentation for CEO will be different from that for CFO, and similarly for other business leaders also. Within HR, the type of presentation will vary whether it is for CHRO or HR leadership or unit HR managers or various CoEs of the HR function. Also it is better to know analytics familiarity of audience to make it easier to understand.

ii. Avoid cluttering: too many analyses at a single place can lead to confusion or inability to grasp the message.

iii. Focus on key points: identify the purpose of presentation and restrict to that like whether it is for employee engagement analysis or exit survey findings, etc. Too many things at the same time can lead to loss of focus.

iv. Insights and actions: more time spent on key insights from analysis and actions for future generate more interest and buy-in than discussing results or analysis outputs.

c) Communication: It is another side of the coin while one side is presentation covered above. It is being dealt separately as communication of data to non-quantitative audience like HR makes it more important. There are two elements of communication requiring attention:

i. Storification: weaving a story around the data results and insights makes attention, understanding, and retention of analysis findings easier. Story also helps in contextualizing the analysis findings and, thus, gives organizational flavor, increasing the receptivity. Also data analysis narrated in the form of story works very well with audience both at intellectual and emotional levels. Storifying analysis results and insights is a skill which develops overtime, and HR practitioners can learn it.

ii. Visualization: along with story, use of visuals adds power to results and insights communication. In fact, story and visuals make the results and insights self-explanatory for audience to a large extent. But the fact is that visualization is a poorly used and exploited technique in HR data presentation and communication. There are various methods of visualization depending upon the purpose of visualization such as sharing of data, sharing of information, concept, or strategy. Depending upon the purpose, visualization technique will vary. Some of the ways to visualize data analysis and results using different colors are:
   a) Bars,
   b) Charts—pie, line, radar, layer charts
   c) Diagrams—Venn diagram, cycle
   d) Boxplots
   e) Graphs/plots of various types such as scatter graph, curve graph, etc.
   f) Tables
   g) Matrices
   h) Continuum
   i) Cause–effect Chains
   j) Maps—to highlight data findings for different locations/geographies/units/functions, etc. Also heat map
   k) Network—with nodes
   l) 3D diagram

Executing Transformation—Rubber Hits the Road

After ensuring that various dimensions for operationalization are in place, the next step is to start the execution. Given the vastness of data and what analytics can do to data, it often becomes challenging to decide where to begin. Many a times HR professional equipped with analytics tools start on fishing expedition to find out something interesting from data. Analysis will always throw up something interesting which may be of less business value or no value at all. HR professionals often grapple with questions when rolling out an HR analytics program; some questions are as follows:

- Where to start?
- Which metric is important to measure and analyze?
- Should focus be on attrition or employee engagement or compensation?
- What type of data is needed?

Here is a step-wise suggested approach to kick-start HR analytics:

1. Begin with question: The "question" to be asked is "what is the business challenge which has the HRM relevance?" Every organization at any point of time faces business challenges related to people management like attrition, employee engagement, productivity, poor customer satisfaction, etc. This question—"what are the key business challenges where HR can impact?" should be asked to business leaders like CEO and COO. Selection of a business challenge based question to start HR Analytics will get buy in and support of business leadership for doing HR Analytics. Support and buy-in of leadership is lukewarm if analysis is done of a question which is more close to the HR function like performance appraisal rating trends, etc. The next step is to select the top most challenge and take it forward. Some sample questions can be:

a) Why is turnover high in some BUs?
b) What are the drivers of sales team productivity?
c) What is the impact of training on productivity?
d) Why is C-SAT low in some BUs?
e) What will be our talent gaps for the next year based on attrition?

2. Create a model and hypothesis: After selecting one of the key business challenges, the next step is to frame a hypothesis and a model capturing that hypothesis. For example, hypothesis can be that low employee engagement impacts customer satisfaction, meaning that if an employee engagement is lower, then it impacts a business outcome, like customer satisfaction. A simple pictorial causal model between two variables—employee engagement and customer satisfaction—can be created to give visual power to the hypothesis. The next step is to identify the top variables or drivers of employee engagement. For identifying these variables, one way is to use judgment or experience. Other valid method to avoid errors is to read published literature on this topic and based on organization context, a list of drivers of employee engagement can be selected. Once narrowed down, these variables can be added to the engagement variable in the causal model.
3. Select right measures/driver/variables and data: Once a list of variables or measures of employee engagement has been selected, then the next step is to identify which out of these can be subjected to analysis based on data availability within the organization. For example, studies may show that travel or food quality is related to engagement, then the question to be asked is whether data related to these measures (travel distance/food quality) are available within the organization to perform the analysis. If the answer is no, then these need to be dropped. Also is there any past baseline or benchmark data to compare trends and results overtime to draw robust conclusions. If there is no past records of using such measures or non-existing benchmarks, then it is belter to drop these, as analysis results will be difficult to defend.

4. Conducting analysis: once data has been collected, the next step is to perform statistical analysis such as correlation and regression using tools such as Excel, SPSS, R, SAS, etc. Statistical analysis will help to validate or reject the hypothesis and model. If it is rejected, then new variables have to be selected to perform the next iteration of analysis to check results based on statistical significance.
5. Interpretation of results: After statistical results have been obtained, these have to be interpreted to make sense of results. A simpler interpretation of results has to be written keeping in mind the audiences with whom interpretations will be shared.
6. Presentation of results/findings/insights and actions: The final step is to share the outcome of analysis with the stakeholders who have interest in getting this business challenge. All the presentation techniques/tips outlined earlier, such as using graphs/charts, creating a story around results using HR language, highlighting key analysis insights and action steps, have to be followed to make an impactful presentation. It will be good foresight to prepare a list of possible questions and keep answers ready to make the presentation more professional.

Building an HR analytics capability in any organization is a journey rather than an event. There are no right or best steps or best processes to do this; however, there can be a guiding framework based on the work done by other organizations successfully. Each organization can tweak the framework based on its resource availability and need of the hour. Over a period of time with continuous improvements, HR analytics capability evolves.

Let us explore a few myths before completing the book.

People Analytics: Hype Versus Truth

There is a lot of hype around people analytics and in any tide of hype, lot of “meaningless” boats get prominence while large "meaningful" ones remain in the backdrop. This analogy aptly captures the current picture in the world of people analytics. This hype versus truth spectrum ranges from advocacy (Bernard Marr)[1] for splitting HR into two functions of people analytics and people administration to *uberization* of HR in the future. In between there are lot of prophecies such as people analytics is a new fad marketed by consultants or people analytics is the way forward for making HR accountable like other business functions. Elsewhere, David Green,[2] in a recent post, wrote that it seems that HR has suddenly discovered a gold pot in people analytics and every CHRO is running after it! Here is our take on hype versus truth in people analytics:

1. **Hype (H):** Data has value and is like an asset which can be monetized for powerful insights, having impact on business outcomes. Hence, data has to be treated as "strategic" in nature.
Truth (T): There is no doubt that data analysis can provide powerful insights but truth is that organizations treat data as "transactional" making it unfit for any kind of analysis and creating a familiar situation of *garbage in garbage out.*

2. **H:** People analytics can help in identifying drivers of organizational performance, making it easy for HR folks to align HR initiatives and programs with those drivers to maximize the organizational performance.
T: The reality is that we know lot about individual-level drivers of performance such as pay, training, rewards, communication, etc., but how these individual drivers of performance are connected to organizational performance is not clear as all individual performance gets aggregated into a project and several projects add up into a function or unit or account and, thereafter, sight of

---

[1] https://www.linkedin.com/pulse/20131118060732-64875646-why-we-no-longer-need-hr-departments?goback=%2Enmp_*1_*1_*1_*1_*1_*1_*1_*1_*1_*1&trk=nmp_rec_act_article_detail

[2] https://www.linkedin.com/pulse/hr-analytics-new-gold-rush-david-green

contribution gets lost. So we do not know organizational-level individual performance drivers.

3. H: Big data in HR will help HR in becoming a truly "strategic function" in the coming years.
T: HR function's ability to use big data for HR will depend on extracting "value" (V) from "variety" (V) of HR big data. These 2 Vs (of 4 Vs of big data) are central to success of people analytics. Analyzing, interpreting, and making sense of data is not easy.

4. H: Buying a high-end technology solution marks the successful initiation of people analytics function in the organization.
T: Technology at best can be an enabler of people analytics. There is whole lot of ground work which needs to be done within HR function/team and organization to harvest the benefits of people analytics. One of the major reasons why people analytics does not take off in many organizations is simply buying a highly marketed technology solution and then assuming that the organization is ready for people analytics. And also technology is expensive and when it does not give promised results, disillusionment sets in.

5. H: Large datasets based on years of employee data are needed for high-quality insights.
T: No doubt that large data are needed, but tiny datasets and anecdotal evidence cannot be ignored and can be source of powerful insights. Water cooler or corridor chats or food court murmurs, all can be equally good data points for insights on effectiveness and impact of HR programs and policies.

6. H: Models and algorithms bring perfection and rigor to the practice of people analytics by bringing out patterns from large amounts of employee data which is impossible for an average person to visualize.
T: It is well known that even the best model and algorithm with the best data can be imperfect as there are human limitations to include everything while creating a perfect one for capturing everything of

a "whole man"[3] that matters and that may get missed out in these, and also, no perfect algorithm can give a perfect outcome.

7. H: People analytics will eliminate "human biases" as everything becomes number based and numbers speak for themselves.[4]
T: People analytics has its own biases because it measures what can be measured. However, people are people, and so far there is no exact science to exactly measure and predict what and why people do by uncovering all the biases and motives.

8. H: Job performance data can be converted into objective measures making measurement simple and capturing each employee's contribution to the job and organization easy.
T: Over-objectification or over-simplification of the measurement of performance creates the risk of missing the richness of what makes that job special—or complex—or what makes each person's contribution unique. For example, an HR manager spending time on a difficult employee or a client-facing manager who is soothing down an angry customer, all are complex tasks not amenable to easy measurement.

9. H: People analytics will help in eliminating errors in decisions related to people management matters such as hiring, promotion, potential, rewarding, and deployment.
T: It is true that errors will get reduced, but we run the risk of facing unintended consequence of committing *fundamental analytic error'*. In social psychology, we often commit *fundamental attribution error*, meaning we attribute causes to intrinsic factors (within individual) rather than to extrinsic factors (context or situation). Hence, people analytics runs the risk of unfairly making individuals who are not performing well a scapegoat based on data analysis, while ignoring the weaknesses and constraints of the system where individual is working. Truth is that system is always powerful than an individual and most of the time overpowers even the best talent in the world.

---

[3] http://www.panarchy.org/whyte/organizationman.html
[4] https://hbr.org/2013/04/the-hidden-biases-in-big-data

10. H: People with HR domain background are best-suited for HR analytics.
T: Deep HR domain knowledge surely adds value in making sense of data patterns from "people" perspective but a broad-based people analytics team comprising people with knowledge and background ranging from business, financial, statistics (data scientist), sociology, psychology, philosophy, IT, and data specialist makes a deadly combination of a dream team for people analytics.

11. H: HR function moving from charting, dash-boarding, reporting to predictive analytics signals the completion of installing people analytics in the HR function.
T: Doing the analytics piece is half part of the people analytics equation. True value and proof of pudding lies in converting people analytics insights into meaningful actions for business outcomes, which is often tough.

Appendices

HR analytics is relatively a new area in HR function and the adoption of HR analytics is picking up, albeit slowly. Majority of companies with global employee footprint are still struggling with creating a "global dashboard" of various HR metrics, while adoption of predictive and prescriptive analytics is still lagging. A study done by Meta Group and another by Bersin by Deloitte in the year 2013, and adapted by John Macy (2015), found that in a 10-year period (2003–13) the adoption of strategic HR analytics, such as prescriptive and predictive analytics, has increased from 4% to merely 14%, whereas the use of descriptive analytics and reporting has decreased from 96% to 86% during the same period (Table A.1). According to Macy, for any HR analytics to be of strategic value, it should be 50% predictive and prescriptive and rest reporting and descriptive. However, given the slow growth rate, it may take decades to reach that level for any organization.

Clearly, many organizations are struggling to adopt HR analytics and are at various stages of adoption of the HR analytics value chain discussed elsewhere in the book. Apart from other factors responsible for this slow adoption, one of the factors is related to "taking the first step with clarity on where and how to get started." To address this challenge, from "practitioners" perspective, three contributors who have led the implementation of HR analytics in their respective organizations have distilled their experiences in Appendices A, B, and C.

Though deployment of high-end analytics becomes a challenge due to lack of tools and techniques, skills, and right data, yet even a simple dataset which can be easily obtained can provide rich insights about what is going on in the organization and how it impacts key business parameters. Appendix D gives an illustration

Table A.1 Workforce Information Management and Analytics (Maturity Model—Comparison of Level 2013–2003)

2013	Bersin by Deloitte	Meta Group	2003
	Level 4		
4%	**Predictive Analytics**	**Predictive Modelling**	1%
	Development of Predictive Models, Scenario Planning, Risk Analysis and Mitigation, Integration with Strategic Planning	Time-sliced data, multi-scenario analysis to generate views of the future	
	Level 3		
10%	**Advanced Analytics**	**Correlated Analytics**	3%
	Statistical Modelling and Root-Cause Analysis to Solve Business Problems, Proactively Identify Issues and Recommend Actionable Solutions	Relates workplace information with enterprise data to determine the impact of workforce investment	
	Level 2		
30%	**Advanced Reporting**	**Contextual Embedded Analytics & Metrics Delivery**	21%
	Proactive, Operational Reporting for Benchmarking and Decision-Making, Multidimensional Analysis and Dashboards	Presenting relevant analytics at a decision point to provide just-in-time decision support. Graphical scorecards and dashboards that highlight exceptions for further drill down and analysis	
	Level 1		
56%	**Operational Reporting**	**Information Distribution**	75%
	Reactive Operational Reporting of Efficiency and Compliance Measures, Focus on Data Accuracy, Consistency, and Timeliness	Standardized information, simple format delivered as paper based reports or HTML page to Line of Business Managers	

of how using "employee identity number (EIN)" for data analysis for a set time frame can provide rich insights.

One of the key areas of employee investment is training and development and each year every organization spends millions of dollars/rupees on employee development. Often getting approval for this spend every year becomes a challenge for HR as leadership keeps asking for RoI of spend in terms of hard numbers. Any HR function without such hard data to showcase RoI of training and development has to accept cuts in spends. A large automobile group in India used data to track the benefits of training spends at shop floor and successfully showcased its RoI to leadership as explained in Appendix E.

The story is not complete without actual illustrations of talent management analytics being used successfully in corporates. Appendix F focuses on the power of analyzing text to arrive at outcomes. Appendix G shares an example on using contextual search to upscale a talent acquisition process. Appendix H articulates on arriving at an RoI for talent retention. Appendix I is all about leveraging specific statistics for establishing engagement drivers.

Appendix J is one of the leading edge illustrations on the emerging practice of predictive analytics. Appendix K signs off the lineup with visual illustrations of the future: organization network analysis.

The appendices, we hope, complement and support what has been articulated through the book.

References

Meta Group.(2013). acquired by Gartner in 2014.

Bersin, J., O'Leonard, K., & Wang-Audia, W. (2013). *High impact talent analytics: Building a world class analytics and measurement function*. Oakland, CA: Bersin by Deloitte. Retrieved July 18, 2016, from http://marketing.bersin.com/rs/bersin/images/hita100113sg.pdf

Macy, John. (2015, October). HR will never be strategic. Retrieved June 21, 2016, from https://www.linkedin.com/pulse/hr-never-strategic-john-macy

APPENDIX A

HOW TO GET STARTED IN HR ANALYTICS

Having spoken at many conferences in the US, Canada, and the UK, I've had the opportunity to speak to many HR professionals from a variety of industries. When I ask people if they have started the journey into HR analytics, many respond with a great desire to get started but serve up one of the following five challenges as a reason not to move forward:

1. Our data isn't good enough.
2. We have no leadership support.
3. We're busy working on other initiatives.
4. We have no budget.
5. We don't have the skillsets.

Let's take a brief look at each of these popular challenges.

Our Data Isn't Good Enough

I've met quite a few companies who feel that the quality of their data is insufficient to move forward with analytics. Most of these are embarking on the implementation of a new HRIS system in the hope of resolving their quality issues. These implementations are estimated to take 18–36 months.

The companies that impress me the most are the ones that are actively investigating their data quality to determine which data they can use to start HR analytics and are forming a priority list of what needs to be fixed in other data areas. This, I believe, is the fastest route to getting value from analytics when you question your data quality. After 25 years in analytics (in engineering, supply chain, and HR), I can tell you that all of your data does not have to be perfect to move forward. In fact, the reality is that your data will never be perfect. There will always be reasons why you have special "nuances" in your data to support business processes that don't quite match your technology processes.

We Have No Leadership Support

I've been there and I feel your pain, but this is never a reason to not move forward. When it comes to analytics in HR, often the leadership cannot envision what is possible. While 50% of new CHROs are being selected from outside of HR in 2015 (and 30% in 2014), the fact remains that most HR leaders in place today came from traditional HR (aka non-analytical) backgrounds. It will take specific examples of what can be accomplished with HR analytics to help these leaders see the value. In speaking with HR analytics leaders who have taken this approach, they report that it takes about a year of these examples and much communication before leaders start to envision other business applications for HR analytics.

In December 2014, I conducted an informal survey and asked HR analytics professionals around the globe what their biggest challenge was in moving forward. The overwhelming response was "leadership support." It was not the support of HR leaders though. It was gaining the support of leaders outside of HR. In some of these cases, HR must realize that analytics pertaining to the workforce may not be the biggest issue facing other leaders in the company.

We're Busy Working on Other Initiatives

...and you always will be. When I see that 85% of the companies say that HR analytics is very important but 86% of the companies report no HR analytics capabilities in HR, it tells me that many companies are buried so far under in their day-to-day tactical work that they have no time to consider anything strategic. In the current world of rising workforce costs and headcount reductions, it is difficult to find internal resources to support HR analytics. In these cases, it might be well worth having a third-party expert start your analytics initiative with a small pilot project that can be managed externally.

We Have No Budget

You don't always need one. In the previous conference presentations, I gave a specific example of how I, with a team of volunteers across the globe, managed to produce a great deal of analytical value for very little money. What's the secret? Don't focus on what you don't have; learn to leverage what you already have. No one said that the first attempt at an HR analytics had to look pretty! So, you don't need to pay a vendor $500,000 to get the value out of analytics.

We Don't Have the Skillsets

I have helped several companies develop and execute their HR analytics roadmaps, select technology, and communicate the value of analytics to their employees. The key to remember in this area is that it is more important to know which skillsets you need and when. I have seen some companies hire a statistician in the beginning of their journey only to realize that they will not need this talent for at least a year. This risks having an under-challenged employee that may not have the patience to wait for your journey to catch up to his/her skills. Several smaller companies assessed their needs and realized that they would not have enough of this type of work to justify a full-time employee. In these cases, they outsource their analytical projects.

SO, LET'S GET STARTED

I would never dare claim that getting started in HR analytics is easy. It is admittedly challenging in that it requires a great deal of thought, assessment, and the persistence to change traditional mindsets. It is truly an uphill battle, but if you thrive on challenge, it is greatly rewarding. Here are a few suggestions to get you started:

1. Start small and find an area of the company that is feeling some sort of pain related to the workforce. They will be thankful for any help you can provide and they will be your biggest supporter if you can show results.

2. Assess the current state of your HR analytics program. An Internet search on "HR analytics road maps" will yield several expert views on the progression of HR analytics capabilities. Compare your current capabilities to those sample maps and determine which new components you would like to add to your company's capabilities in the next year or two.
3. Focus on specific business questions. If you do not know the specific questions you are trying to answer or the specific problem you are trying to investigate, you risk wasting a lot of time and money on something the company doesn't value.
4. Don't buy HR analytics technology until you know how you plan to use it. These investments are very expensive so it is best to conduct several analytics projects without this technology to get an idea on what your company really needs. Only then should you search the market for technology that matches your needs.
5. Analyze your data in context. Numbers are great and many people are skilled at "slicing and dicing data." But, what does that data mean to the business area or the problem you are studying? This is where HR analytics experts need to partner with experts in the specific business area to be able to interpret what the data is really telling you. For example, what are the possible root cause reasons for the movement of metrics in the data? People working in that area every day are best suited to provide this insight.
6. Expect the unexpected. Your first few projects will take longer than you anticipate as they reveal multiple categories of challenges along the way that you did not anticipate. While painful, these will also be the projects from which you learn the most about how to do HR analytics within your own company.
7. Seek outside help at the beginning of your journey. Many people have been down this path before you who can offer advice on what went well in their HR analytics journey and what did not. Learn from the wisdom of others.

Tracey Smith is one of the "Top 50 Global Influencers in HR Analytics" and presents at conferences in the US, Canada, and the UK. She holds degrees in Mathematics, Engineering, and Business and has over 25 years of experience in the areas of Human Resources, Supply Chain, and Engineering. Tracey is the author of "HR Analytics: The What, Why and How" and "Strategic Workforce Planning: Guidance & Back-up Plans." She is also the owner and editor of "NI Magazine," an e-magazine dedicated to the HR analytics and workforce planning communities.

(*Source:* www.numericalinsights.com (accessed on 22 August, 2016).)

APPENDIX B

SEVEN DEADLY SINS OF HR ANALYTICS INITIATIVES

The right HR leader can play a vital role in enabling workforce analytics initiatives. Effective sponsorship will ensure that an analytics initiative has the support required to succeed, the resources—both people and technology—to be impactful, the support to create and communicate a clear, compelling vision, and the leeway to focus its attention on key business challenges or issues.

Conversely, the wrong HR leader can help to kill a talent analytics initiative before its first breath. With the best of intentions, a misguided leader will—intentionally or not—engage in behaviors that virtually guarantee the failure (or significantly impeded the traction) of future workforce analytics initiatives. In some cases, these errors are committed with the best of intentions. In other cases, good intentions are not the issue, but rather ignorance, naivety, or hubris (or a combination of the three) plays a role.

If you, as a HR leader, want to really support your organization's HR analytics efforts, there are specific things—"sins," if you will—you should seek to avoid. Granted, "sin" may be a strong word, but hey, it got your attention and may have influenced your desire to read this! However, these are dynamics that—if you can avoid them—help set up your workforce analytics initiatives for success.

So, in no particular order, here are seven dynamics that can surely make analytics initiatives more difficult (or set the stage for failure at inception):

1. "Burger King"—having it your way (and changing "your way" at a whim)
2. "Teacher's pet"—solving for your pet issue
3. "Penny wise and…"—refusing to invest strategically
4. "Headcount neutral"—requiring cuts in other areas to fund analytics

5. "Other duties as assigned"—making analytics a leader's part-time role
6. "Dummying down"—assigning analytics to report to a "less analytically inclined" leader
7. "Know it all"—believing you are the person to "sell" analytics

"Burger King"—Having It Your Way

This is one of the most common issues—a senior leader decides that analytics is going to support their "vision"—which (unfortunately) is often no more than a better way to see my "dashboard" or "scorecard" or to demonstrate that, "I am doing what I said I have been doing" (or, actually, "others are doing what I said I was doing"). It's not about measuring the most relevant people-focused business drivers, but rather providing a more technologically sophisticated "veneer" on their "pet" metric, report, scorecard, or dashboard.

Compounding this is the leader who cannot fix on a given objective or set of objectives, but instead change their "order" as one might change what they order from one trip to Burger King to another. They start out with no vision regarding what they want and then, in the absence of any clear vision, their interests shift from one metric to the next ad nauseam. Those who are lovers of the "Burger King" approach to analytics do not want insights necessarily; as much as anything, they are good with whatever they have a whim to measure at any given time. Unfortunately, in attempting to simply re-create what they already have, they stifle the ability of their HR analytics' team to deliver strategically significant insights.

"Teacher's Pet"—Solving for Your Own Pet Issues

"Teacher's Pet" is quite similar to the preceding characteristic. The difference is that it is focused on furthering a specific agenda. Most commonly, you see this in the HR leader who supports analytics in order to "prove" or "validate" that their favorite pet project is yielding the promised results.

HR analytics can also be hijacked by the leader who is seeking to show others where there are deficiencies in the organization (rarely or never their own) or in other leaders. In this case, it is all about "analytics by vendetta," with the focus being on shining the light on a colleague's people issues, not only on providing compelling, enterprise-relevant insights about their people.

Either approach ("proving" the value of "pet" projects or "torpedoing" an adversary's project) is detrimental to the efforts of your workforce analytics initiative. How? Nothing kills the credibility of workforce analytics faster than it being perceived as an "arm" of a self-promoting leader.

"Penny Wise and..."—Refusing to Invest Strategically

This is most commonly observed with leaders who attempt to initiate analytics programs by making their team use inadequate technology. Itis not that the workforce analytics initiatives necessarily require significant investments. However, there is—in most cases—incremental investments, whether they are people or technology-related.

This is often most apparent in organizations where a senior HR leader will not support any incremental investments, requiring the workforce analytics leader to beg, borrow, or—god forbid—steal the resources necessary. The bottom line is that they do not have confidence in the value of the initiative and, hence, do not want to risk any of their own financial or political capital.

"Headcount Neutral"—Requiring Cuts in Other Areas to Fund Analytics

This is very similar to "Penny wise"; the primary difference being that the leaders who embrace "headcount neutrality," deliberately or otherwise, put analytics in a "no-win" situation, competing for limited resources (people, dollars, technology, etc.) with their peers (who are, like HR analytics, competing for limited resources and their own survival).

These leaders place their HR analytics initiatives in sort of a "Hobson's choice." Named after Thomas Hobson (a 16th-century British livery stable owner known for his practice of offering customers the choice of either taking the horse in the stall nearest to the door— as a means of rotating the use of the horse—or none at all), a "Hobson's choice" is a free choice in which only one option is offered. As a person may refuse to take that option, the choice is therefore between taking the option or not. In plain English, itis a form of "take it or leave it."

Leaders who use this approach may, erroneously, believe that they are being good stewards of their organization's budget. However, what they are, in fact, doing is pitting their HR analytics initiatives against all others seeking the same source of funding.

"Other Duties as Assigned"—Making Analytics a Leader's Part-time Role

In many cases, this is also related to a dynamic described above—the leader does not appreciate the potential value of their analytics investment (and are, in effect, looking to get something for nothing). The problem, in a nutshell, is that what they often get is just nothing. Or they get very little in the way of progress because they are not willing to allow a team member to focus their efforts on the opportunity.

Granted, this is not always bad, per se. In some cases, this approach can be a great way to start, in part, because it makes the RoI so attractive. Also, for the part-time analytics leader, he/she has very little pressure to produce , because the expectation to deliver is so low.

However, for those leaders who are truly committed to HR analytics and are desirous of timely, impactful results, this is rarely the best way to go but many will still choose to do so.

"Dumbing Down"—Assigning Analytics to Report to a "Less Analytically Inclined" Leader

Most commonly in these cases, HR analytics is assigned to report to a vice president of talent, organizational effectiveness, or some other function. In theory, it makes sense on some level; the assumption is that HR analytics is a "centers of expertise," as is staffing, compensation, benefits, and other functions.

Unfortunately, the assumption that HR analytics is just another "CoE" is flawed. It is a capability possessed by very few HR organizations (unlike staffing, compensation, benefits, etc.) and with good reason, it requires a specialized set of knowledge, skills, and abilities.

Trust me, it is a rare "less analytically inclined" HR leader who can effectively advocate for and support an HR analytics initiative of any size, scale, or complexity. I have tried it. I would never do it again. Life is too short. I will leave it at that.

"Know It All"—Believing You are the Person to "Sell" Analytics

An extension of the preceding "sin," "know it all" HR leaders (who are often also "less analytically inclined") take upon themselves the role of "selling" HR analytics to others within the HR organization and the company as a whole. Unfortunately, lacking a background in analytics, scientific methodology, or research methods, it is the rare non-analytics HR leader who is equipped to do so.

When this is paired with a "less analytically inclined" leader who also is insecure in allowing members of the HR analytics team to represent the work done by the analytics team to other leaders, these issues only become more apparent and put the efforts of the analytics team at risk, as they are being voiced by someone who cannot begin to form complete sentences with respect to the work being done, not to mention explaining the nuances of the projects undertaken.

Prologue

Hopefully, I have been able to shed light on some of the "sins" prevalent in the field of HR analytics. If, in looking in the mirror, you see a "sinner" staring back at you, there is only one true option: Repent! Recognize the error of your ways, seek to make right your wrongs, and put your feet on the path leading to what is good and proper. HR analytics initiatives, not plagued by these "sins," can provide strategically significant and sustainable competitive advantage. Do not allow yourself to become (or continue to be) ensnared in the errors of these sins.

Now, go forth and sin no more.

(*Source:* Mark Berry, Vice President, HR, CGB Enterprises Inc., Covington, LA, US.)

APPENDIX C

STARTING WITH WORKFORCE ANALYTICS? FIVE CONSIDERATIONS BEFORE TAKING THE LEAP

Interview with Bill Roberts, for Harvard Business Review Analytical Services by Stela Lupushor.

If you are starting on your journey to use analytics in the context of HR—congratulations! The timing could not be better. With analytics in HR becoming a popular topic, there are more skilled professionals who are interested in switching their specialization and who bring a wealth of knowledge and experiences to HR. All this is good, but where do you start?

1. **Hire "top guns".** This is a new area for HR and it requires a very different skillset than a typical HR professional will have. Consider individuals with degrees and experience in statistics, data science, computer science, I/O psychology, consulting. They can learn HR processes much faster than training a traditional HR professional on technical skills. Be prepared, they might not come cheap! This is an area where the "war for analytics talent" has been won by the "talent." But giving HR the ability to consult the business with facts and analytics-driven insights is priceless!

   Start with the business questions. There will be plenty of things in HR to focus analytics projects on, but the biggest value will come from linking the data about your workforce to business outcomes. What are the characteristics of employees that bring in a disproportionate amount of revenue, or have the most impact on customer satisfactions scores? How can you focus hiring and development activities on those characteristics? How can you tweak learning programs to bring employees to a productive level faster?

2. **Ruthlessly pursue the right problems.** An even more important question is, "Are we solving the right problem?" For example, predicting attrition risk is one of those perennial issues that many mature analytics functions attempt to solve. There are many predictive models that have been created over past decades (yes, decades). We have more sophisticated tools to perform analyses. We now have more data, a whole lot more of it—structured, unstructured, internal, and external. We can quickly assess the supply and demand for specific skills, which location—down to a city, where those skills are in great demand, which profiles our competitors are looking for, what are the characteristics of those who might be at risk, etc. We are talking beyond typical segmentation and getting to a very granular analysis of online behavior. But guess what? Little has changed. All this sophistication still does not change the fact that people leave. People will always leave. The question is whether one needs to spend time trying to prevent the inevitable or think about the problem through a different lens. The questions that can be asked of the data instead are more about how to get the most out of the employee while he/she is with the company.

3. **Data perfection might be optional. Being on the same page with stakeholders—mandatory!** There is nothing more damaging to an analytics team's reputation, especially at the early stages of building the analytical mind-set in HR, than poor data quality. People will discover that "Bob is missing from the report" and discredit the whole analysis as a result. With the increasing amount of data there will be more opportunities for error. Is 80% accuracy sufficient to make the right decision? Would you get more value from your analytics team having time to run another analysis versus going on a "finding Bob" expedition? The surest way to mitigate the concerns, however, is to agree with the stakeholders very early on about the expectations for accuracy, the analysis methodology, the type and completeness of data, the structure of the report, and types

of recommendations that will come out of it. It might take more time up-front. But it will possibly be the only thing that prevents the analysis from ending up in the "discard pile."

4. **Be a humanizing force.** HR professionals have a huge impact on the working environment of many. Analytics gives great insights and power. Take a step back and think of its impact. Put yourself in the shoes of those employees. Would the change make you personally feel comfortable? Would it allow you to realize your full potential? Would it inspire you? If you are hesitating to answer, you might not be solving the right problem. There is a human being with dreams and aspirations, behind every number in your analysis—a human, a social creature, who wants to belong, to connect, who wants someone to care, and to be treated with respect and dignity. Do your job such that you create an environment where you and other people can thrive. And use analytics for good; use it to tell the story of that human being, use it to humanize the workplace.

I would like to end with this thought. The rapid changes, onslaught of data, and analytic capabilities necessitate strong leadership, conviction, boldness to try non-conventional methods, to take risks, and ask the right questions. It also means that sometimes you do not know whether the path you are taking is the right one and the only way to know is to give it a try. Have the courage to try and do not forget to share the scars, bruises, and everything else you have learned with all of us!

(*Source:* Stela Lupushor, Vice President, HR Planning & Analytics, Fidelity Investments, NY, US.)

APPENDIX D

SMALL DATA CAN BE AS POWERFUL AS BIG DATA

As the Shakespearian quote goes "What's in a name?," one needs to look beyond name to get the meaning or essence of the object. Same is the case with EIN, which is equivalent of a personal name record (PNR) in the organizational context providing link to all kinds of demographic and work history data of the employee. That seems to be a simplistic way of looking at EIN without attempting to understand the powerful insights this number can provide into a working of an organization.

EIN is allocated to a full-time employee on joining upon the organization and in some organizations, all types of employees, such as full-time equivalent (FTE), contract, contingent, temporary, etc., have same continuous series number, whereas in some organizations EIN for FTEs is different than that for non-FTE employees. Irrespective of how it is being deployed, use of people analytics approach can throw up interesting insights hidden behind this number. Like any people analytic approach, EIN analysis can be applied to a specific organization to get required insights about workings of the organization. EIN as a tool is like EBITDA or EPS analysis which, if done properly, can provide a lot of information about any company working.

Let us take a case of a company to illustrate this. An employee, John joins in company X in June 2004 and is given an EIN as 19450. Company X was founded in 1995 and operates in the IT services sector. IT services sector typically has an attrition rate of 15%–20% per annum and business growth rate ranging from 10% to 20%. After few weeks of joining, John found that total employee headcount including all type of employees is 4,600. John worked in the company for 8 years and left in April 2012. At the time of leaving John found that latest EIN is 52157 and total headcount is 12,350. A quick analysis of EIN data for company X from 1995 to 2012 shows that:

1. From 1995 to 2004, company had hired 19,000+ on its rolls during the 9-years period and the actual headcount in June 2004 was 4,600.

2. From 2004 to 2012, company had hired 32,000+ employees during the 8-years period and the actual headcount in April 2012 was 12,000+.
3. And company, since its inception in 1995, had hired 52,000+ employees till 2012 but the actual headcount in April 2012 was 12,000+.

A quick interpretation of the above data shows that:

1. From 1995 to 2004, headcount churn was close to 5 times in 9 years.
2. From 2004 to 2012, churn was 2.5 times in 8 years.
3. And from inception till 2012, churn was 4 times in 17 years.

If the company A had grown within the growth rate range of 10%–20% and had an attrition rate in the range of 15%–20%, it would had have experienced a homeostatic state on the headcount front.

Nevertheless, using the data analytics approach, what insights does these data provide about the business and growth of company, people management approach of the company, culture, and more importantly a peep into the operating philosophy of the senior management? Let us try to derive some insights from this analysis by looking at the impact on business outcomes:

1. **Business and business growth quality:** Data analysis points out that
   - Company has witnessed fast growth at different time periods in 17 years of its existence.
   - Growth is not a stable one and has periods of high growth followed by a sharp drop in growth. This is evidenced by high volume hiring of 32,000 during the period 2004–12 whereas the actual survival is close to one-third.
   - That company lacks a focused business strategy with clarity on what business it is in and what business it is not in, similar to an "Indian *thalli*" (a large plate served with everything available to eat!) approach which has spread of all dishes, leaving the consumer confused. It points out

that company is unable to figure out where to invest and grow and where to get out.

- Company has been unable to develop core competence areas as a differentiator from similar companies in the industry as this would have enabled to maintain a steady growth in core areas without witnessing too much turbulence in employee headcount while allowing it, at the same time, elbow room to explore emerging areas.

2. **Culture of the company:** In the absence of data related to how many employees have the longest tenure in the company since its inception, it can still be concluded that culture will always be in a flux with the absence of a true culture acting as a glue for creating identity of the company. As churn ranges from a multiple of 2.5 to 5 over a period of 17 years, one can easily imagine challenges related to process implementation and continuity as well as creating a cultural identity for the company.
3. **Customer satisfaction:** With such a high employee churn rate and low tenure rates, customer service will suffer as service level agreement (SLA) is impacted due to constant deployment of new employees and thereby inability to deliver consistent quality service to customer. As a consequence, one can safely assume that company might be experiencing high customer churn also.
4. **Senior management quality:** As the data shows, 12,000 is the headcount in 2012, whereas 52,000 were hired since 1995, so it implies that company has witnessed complete replacement of employees four times in its life cycle so far barring few (assuming 5–10%) continuing over longer periods beyond 10 years tenure.
   a) This points to senior management's preference for mirror images of self at different levels that can have a longer tenure.
   b) Also it highlights deficiency of sound business and operational knowledge coupled with lack of leadership

skills in senior management as evidenced by the inability to build a sustainable and lasting organization (or institution).

5. **People management:** As in any IT services sector company, people are the key drivers and differentiators of business, and insights based on company X's data analysis shows that:
   a) Company believes in just-in-time hiring for growth as headcount maintained is linked to what business can sustain.
   b) Just-in-time hiring raises the overall employee costs as lateral hiring is always costlier than developing from entry level upwards, thereby providing less elbow room for employee investment or innovation.
   c) Company has pure "task-based" (or project based in IT parlance) approach towards talent rather than "people" or "individual" based. What this means is that as soon as the project or task is over, an employee loses its value unless he/she can be deployed for a similar task, if available. People- or individual-based approaches signify that organization values an individual beyond the skills for current task or project and is willing to help the individual to grow and develop over a longer period by skill development.
   d) Employee development and growth is purely a tick-mark approach as evidenced by the lack of company's interest to maintain a pool of people for projected or anticipated growth. Clearly, talent management will be restricted to task or work at hand with no planning for future.
   e) HR will be heavily transaction-focused as large volumes of hiring and onboarding and exit management will consume significant amount of HR team.
   f) Also just-in-time hiring has another unintended consequence of pulling resources from ongoing projects for deployment to new projects to prevent the revenue loss till the time new hire joins, which creates adversarial relationship between HR and line managers as the latter sees HR prowling for people for new projects.

6. **Employer Brand:** More than 40,000 people have passed in and out of the company doors. Thus, company has huge alumni outside at any point of time than the actual employee strength. Now these alumni might have worked for different periods of time while in the company, more likely joined as laterals, and had good and bad experiences at the company. Assuming only half of alumni talks good about the company while the other half shares negative things, still the number is huge for any company to sustain and build its employer brand to keep attracting quality talent.

Above narrative based on simple analysis of EIN data and looking beyond what EIN hides shows that data analytics, even if done with very small and simple dataset, can be source of powerful insights about what is happening inside the company. Typical HR person need not to apply sophisticated algorithms to people analytics for getting powerful insights. And if this EIN data is supplemented with more data, such as quality of hire, quality of performance ratings, manager and senior management churn rates, actual attrition rates, actual business growth rates and customer satisfaction, etc., more powerful insights can emerge on the state of affairs of a company.

(*Source:* Kuldeep Singh.)

APPENDIX E

ESTABLISHING ROI FOR TRAINING INVESTMENTS

It was April 2009. The global financial crisis had hit the world and countries across the globe with no exception were in some way or the other impacted. The mood in the corporate world was rather somber.

The organization ABC Private Limited is a manufacturing organization of renown. It manufactures auto components and has its sole manufacturing location situated in Central India. The company supplies its products to both original equipments (OEs) and the retail space (aftermarket) in the Indian domestic market. The company had no immediate plans to explore opportunities in the export markets.

The company was facing tough competition in the market place and was not able to grow as much as it would have desired to. The global recession had its impact and was taking a toll with customer orders on the wane. The capacities were lying idle and the company's huge investments in capacity expansion (of over 100 crores), with a presumption that customer orders would fully utilize plant capacities, was not happening as had been anticipated whilst planning the capex investments.

Also compounding this were its droping productivity and quality levels as well as spiraling fixed costs due to addition of manpower to man the additional capacities. Quality complaints from the customers were also on the rise. The senior management was truly a worried lot. Hitherto, the company had a large market share in the OE space and was garnering close to 35% of share of business (SOB) and had a healthy market share of 15% in the aftermarket space as well, with an overall compound annual growth rate of 16% over the last 5 years (FY03–FY07).

The market indicators were pointing to the organization losing its OE business as well as competition eating into its aftermarket space. The SOB in the OE space had shrunk to 31% and the after-market SOB to 11%. This was a huge dip and had the organization worrying and scramble for some solutions to fix this. Some key personnel from middle to senior levels too had put in their papers compounding the problem in hand.

The organization had started as a family-owned small scale industry in 1978 and had, over the years, grown to a mid-sized organization with a turnover of over ₹1400 crores. The company had professionalized over the years and the CEO and other senior team members were professionals hired from companies of repute.

The promoters had decided to step back from day-to-day management and had completely empowered the CEO. The CEO in fact got the full support of the promoters and the board as well since his induction into the organization 5 years ago.

The board met with the senior leadership team to discuss possible options to mitigate the problems that the company was facing. It was decided after long parleys that the need of the hour is to seek external consulting support.

The company decided to take this ahead and sought the support of a renowned global consulting firm to advice on its business strategy. The consulting firm did a detailed study of over 12 weeks and came out with its findings and recommendations. The key recommendations were to enhance the visibility through brand promotion, relook at its channel management strategy, its portfolio of offerings and supply chain management (SCM) strategy (to contain costs), enhance its focus on safety, and most importantly beef up skills and competencies of its human capital across all levels of the organization.

To elaborate, skills were more from an execution/work standpoint, whilst competencies were supervisory/managerial in nature.

Based on the advice of the strategy firm, a formal mapping of the key roles and evaluation of skill and competency levels were undertaken by a leading HR consulting organization. It was clear from the study that there was a yawning gap between desired level of skills and competencies (based on the strategic business intent) and the actual ground reality.

The CEO was apprised about the matter and decided to meet with his senior management team to address this skill and competency gap issue, which was seen as crucial to the very existence and growth of the organization. The CEO committed to invest at least

3% of the annual turnover in training each year and gave this assurance to the senior team when they met.

The senior management team met to discuss the execution of modus operandi and next steps.

The CHRO was anointed the project manager of the project aimed at driving the skills and competencies enhancement. This was christened "Parivartan," (transformation) since it was agreed and understood that this is not a skills development project but a larger project of change, requiring a paradigm shift in the very thought process of learning and application of knowledge. This also included ushering in knowledge management practices and tapping into the tacit knowledge of members gained over the years. It will be pertinent to note that attrition was hovering around 8% on an average over the last 5 years. Also, many employees had been with the organization for long and the average tenure of an employee was about 10 years.

With the flagging off of Parivartan, the die was cast for a multipronged approach to address all levels of the organization from a training and development perspective.

The organizational leadership decided that a synchronous training strategy and not a sequential one, is the need of the hour. There was also no time to lose and it was important to act. Identified senior leadership members were nominated for general management programs conducted by management institutes of repute in India. In fact, two high flyers, which were in the succession plan for the CEO's slot, were nominated to the Ivy League universities in the US for a long development program spanning three months. Some select senior members were also mentored by life coaches. The middle management team members were nominated for specific functional, developmental, and skills upgradation programs. The junior management team members were provided functional training as well as nominated for a development program aimed at honing their supervisory and decision-making skills. An e-learning portal was created and technical, functional, and management modules were made available to all employees across, in English, Hindi, and vernacular. This helped employees learn at leisure and use these learnings to do better at their work place.

Hitherto, the training was addressed more as a by-product of business outcomes. The paradigm shift now was that the training was no longer an activity that was just nice to have, but an important business driver that had to be invested in and nurtured assiduously.

The investments were steadily but surely beginning to pay off.

FY 13 saw a sea change in the approach as well as the attitudes of the members all across. The buoyancy was palpable even when the business plans for the fiscal were being drawn up. From an approach of "can we do it" the paradigm shifted to "we will do it." The organization created a slogan "Hum Honge Kamyaab" (we will succeed) and this created a lot of excitement and an adrenalin rush across the rank and file.

The investments in these training interventions over the last few years had paid rich dividends. The results of FY 14 were speaking for themselves. The top-line grew by almost 22%. The cost of employing expense to sales hovered steadily around 6%–7% over the last 3 years—a remarkable achievement. The sales per head count almost doubled. The OE market share and the AM SOB improved by 3% in both the segments.

From an operational perspective, the focus was on enhancing the profitability through prudent energy management, ergonomic plant layout design, easing of material flow, low-cost automation, and reduction in rejections through better adherence to defined manufacturing and quality processes. A thrust was given to drive total quality management (TQM), total productive maintenance (TPM), and lean manufacturing and an organizational productivity head was nominated to champion these initiatives with a committed cross-functional team, who were christened "change evangelists" to anchor and evangelize project Parivartan across the organization.

Safety was given paramount importance and safety training was prerequisite every six months for all employees CEO downwards. A formal safety certificate was required for the employee to work on the shop floor and this was to be renewed every six months after being duly certified by the safety head. A leading multinational firm was co-opted to advice on safety and work closely with the safety and operations team. The point to note is that safety was made an integral part of the organizational working credo across all functions (not just shop floor operations). Safety was not just a staff function playing an advisory role but an important strategic arm of the organization.

This thrust on safety ensured nil accidents and the company saw, very minimal near misses. The impact was that man-days lost on account of accidents came down by 25% over a period of 3 years. The organization, therefore, was saved considerably as there were no man-days lost due to absenteeism. The morale and motivation of the employees also took an upswing, as they were convinced that they were in a safe working environment and no harm would befall them or their families.

Through education and training of employees, on the need and benefits of energy conservation and the use of wind/solar power (where feasible), the specific energy consumption came down by about 5% YOY and this helped the company save about ₹12 crores per annum, a considerable sum. The impetus on TQM, TPM, and lean manufacturing saw rejection levels come down by about 10% over a 3-years period. Through prudent SCM processes and quality processes, the company was able to save about 2% in its material costs over a 3-years period and this amounted to about 8 crore per annum of savings. The savings, in a sense, more than compensated for the investment on training, and the greater intangible benefits were rise in employee morale, motivation, productivity, and overall organizational health.

The process of change was through constant education, employee involvement, using cross-functional teams to solve organizational issues together, suggestion scheme rewards, creation of a TQM club, and quality circles. The key was that these were driven by the employees themselves and were surely the cornerstone for the success of these interventions. Constant recognition and commensurate rewards helped shore up employee morale and motivation levels. A pointer to this is that the overall employee engagement index went up from 65 in 2010 to 74 in 2014.

Given the flurry of activities on the people development and training front, the attrition of mid-to-senior level employees too was not there and this helped create a stable working/strategic team in the organization. The reputation of the organization as an employer of choice also helped ABC attract lateral talent and added power to the talent pool of the organization.

It is also important to mention that the number of days per employee went up from 3 days a year to 6 days a year, a 100% increase over a 24-month period. The Kirkpatrick Model was used to measure training effectiveness using the four levels, namely reaction, learning, behavior, and results. There was a perceptible change that was visible in the behavior and this manifested itself through visible improvement outcomes in terms of the results.

The success and turnaround of this organization from a training and development perspective have induced many other manufacturing outfits in the near vicinity and also across the country, to follow suit. The belief that human resources are a differentiator, that no product or technology can ever be, has finally dawned. The power of human resources of ABC Company has positioned it on a strong pedestal and given this company an edge to be a market leader and also be an employer of choice for aspiring talent.

As the CEO Remarked, "The proof of the pudding lies in its eating."

The overall business outcomes were ample testimony to the benefits accrued through a concerted effort on the training and development on all fronts. The investment in terms of man-days on training doubled, there was a behavioral shift towards looking at the future with confidence, business outcomes in terms of enhanced top-line and bottom-line growth were clearly visible, safety indices were showing a surge for the better, and most importantly employee engagement indices had improved, indicating the fact that the overall health of the organization was positively impacted by the efforts ploughed into training and development by the organization over the last few years.

(*Source:* T.K. Srinath, Executive Vice President & CHRO, Vistaar Financial Services Pvt. Ltd., Bangalore.)

APPENDIX F

WHY PERCEPTION IS IMPORTANT FOR PEOPLE ANALYTICS

In an article in *The New York Times* in May 2015, Alex Peysakhovich and Seth Stephens-Davidowitz, data scientists with experience at Google and Facebook, discuss "How not to drown in numbers."

In the article, they describe how big data will get us so far, but it will never provide a full picture. With event data, we can understand what has happened and predict *what* is likely to happen in the future. With data about the individual for example demographic data, we can identify *who* it is likely to happen to or who will behave in this way in the future.

In some situations, just knowing what will happen and to whom might be enough. In marketing, it might be good enough to understand, "if I send this communication to these groups of customers I am likely to see X return." With employees this is unlikely to be true.

Many of the models we develop for clients have an exploratory data purpose to them. Clients are interested in knowing *how* the model identifies individuals. *What* are the factors that will most determine success or failure? If I do not give my sales person in China a promotion within the first 22 months in a role, are they likely to leave?

There are two great ways of dealing with this issue. Analysts can use their domain knowledge, ideally based on the knowledge of academic research, to understand *why* the effect that they are seeing could occur. Alternatively—or even better, as well—they can ask individuals *why* they have behaved as they have.

In *The New York Times* article, the authors describe how Facebook and Google do this to understand user behavior. If a user clicks the back button shortly after landing on a page in Facebook, they might be delivered a short question on *why* the page wasn't of interest. As analysts, we need this *why* to move from an insight to action.

THE NEED FOR PERCEPTION DATA

Collecting perception data is one form of data acquisition. Usually, as people analysts we find that the best way of improving our initial models is by including new data and not using better algorithms. Data acquisition is a strategy which is not frequently discussed in the popular discourse on people analytics, where people find magical insights from the vast amount of existing data, but it is a critical component for most experienced analysts.

Usually, these data need to be linked at the individual level to other data we have from our HR and business systems. When this is done, it can be used on everything from employee dashboards to creating predictive models. It provides insight which we otherwise would not have had.

TRADITIONAL SURVEYS HAVE ISSUES

HR has been capturing perception data for a long time. From early job satisfaction surveys to more recent employee engagement and from exit surveys to manager feedback it is rare to find a large HR function which is not using surveys at least once a year.

Unfortunately, the value of these surveys is usually low. Employees do not enjoy completing them. They are usually long, comprising of tens of Likert-type questions covering every possible aspect that the designers could identify and often many more that internal politics dictates should be included.

The results often are not terribly useful. Do we really care that some measure has moved by 2% since last year? Is a 7% difference when comparing two functions really important or is the result we are seeing due to the fact that one department mostly has long-tenured professionals whilst another has a young team, hired in the last 24 months? Many of the statistical techniques used depend on the assumptions that are frequently missing.

And whilst having 40, 50, or 60 questions might give an illusion of detailed information the uncomfortable truth is that itis usually less useful. In one experiment with the employee survey data of a large firm we removed 80% of the answers. We then used a recommendation algorithm to make predictions of what the missing answers were. We got almost 90% right. Employees answered in patterns.

THE JOY OF TEXT

One of the lessons that I learnt earlier was that executives love the open text answers to surveys. We can weave a bunch of charts into a narrative to show what is happening but one emotionally charged comment can easily swing the decision.

The problem with text of course is that it does not scale well. It is okay reading tens of comments but when you have tens of thousands of employees globally, responding in multiple languages, making sense of this data has been difficult or at least very expensive.

Fortunately, text analytics is now at a stage where it can be of assistance. There are two key tasks that analysts typically want to do with employees comments; we want to categorize them, that is, identify what proportion are about each topic and in what context they are being discussed, and we want to score them, for example, rate how happy or sad they seem.

If we can accurately do this, we can transform the survey. A typical engagement asks a small number of questions to determine a level of engagement and a large number of questions through which the analyst hopes to identify the factors that drive this engagement.

Let us take the example of a recent set of survey data which we looked at. Using an unsupervised learning approach, we were able to identify 54 separate topics—both the subject such as "career opportunities" and the context "shortage of career opportunities." Many of these entities would be expected by a good researcher but others, for example "the parking situation", would be highly unusual to find on an employee survey.

This survey had asked two open text questions:

- If you could do one thing to improve your working life at "company," what would it be?
- What is the best thing about working for "company"?

Both questions not only are asking for topics but also have a ranking or importance aspect to them. This is difficult to get via a traditional survey where there are technical issues to the ranking of a large number of features.

Of course a largish proportion of individuals mention several topics for each question. We, therefore, can look at co-occurrence between topics—which topics are most likely to appear together. Even only with single topic responses to each question, we are able to identify how people answer the two questions in relation to each other and other more traditional questions such as an engagement score.

If we link the perception data to the demographic data or event data, we are able to use algorithms to spot groups of employees most likely to mention each topic. We can start to develop rich stories about a multitude of employee perceptions.

At an aggregate, creating and analyzing the metadata associated with the comments in this manner provide the ability to understand trends and patterns individual text comments which frequently communicate nuances that algorithms are unlikely to identify.

As Ben Shneiderman famously noted in his information seeking mantra, "Overview first, zoom and filter, then details-on-demand," users need to have the ability to drill down to the base information, in this case the actual comments. Good interactive data visualization can provide this capability and the pattern-seeking algorithms can be used to guide users' attention to the important groups to make the "zoom and filter" more effective.

There are several other places where people analysts have access to large quantities of text data. Generically, the approaches are similar—preprocess the data, score, or categorize it and then use the metadata as you would otherwise, especially count data. There are numerous packages and libraries available that make many of the key tasks easier such as the tm package in R. There are also several application program interfaces which provide various aspects of the text workflow.

People analytics arguably suffers at the moment from inflated and often unrealistic expectations. In many instances, this is because the audience expects it to reveal more than just the probabilistic patterns. With perception data we can move one step further towards genuine insight, developing an understanding of why our models might be behaving in the way that they do.

(*Source:* Andrew Marritt, Founder, Organization View GmbH, Zurich, Switzerland.)

APPENDIX G

CASE STUDY FOR TALENT ACQUISITION

An Australian EPC company has revenues in excess of $5 billion and employs more than 30,000 people. This company needed to hire 150 plus specialist engineers to bolster their Middle Eastern/North African/Indian engineering services capabilities. Niche skills required include cross-country pipeline design, undersea cabling, and offshore rig establishment. On releasing an advertisement, the company received 19,200 applications. With their existing processes and bandwidth, it would have taken them four months and cost over a million dollars to successfully complete the process. Using context-based search and analytics, they were able to accomplish the entire process in 45 days at 40% of the estimated cost.

USAGE CONTEXT-BASED SEARCH AND MATCH

We search for something on the Internet all the time. The search engine takes the phrases we have entered and then compares it against the documents that have the same exact phrase. However, the outcome we get is not sorted just on the basis of frequency of the appearance of these keywords. The algorithm also searches for documents that have been accessed by most people so that it throws up the most relevant matches right upfront.

Resume screening, is a search activity as well. There are keywords that a hiring manager is looking for. It could be,

- Years of experience,
- Skillset,
- Nature of projects worked on,
- Management experience,
- Location, and
- Quality of companies worked with.

Often the screening process takes time as the search is done manually, resume by resume. To some extent, this can be accelerated by searching for the keywords. However, the benefits are only incremental as the screener still needs to open each resume and then read through it.

Spire Innovations is a Bengaluru-based technology company focusing on contextual search and intelligence. The company has created the context for effective talent acquisition by creating a context cloud for thousands of jobs. Once the hiring specifications of the company are finalized, the company runs its context search to arrive at a shortlist that is based on the demand for the jobs a company is looking for. The effectiveness of this process can be identified from the following visual.

In the first round of screening, 35% of applications were matched. This is not different from a manual process but it took just 48 hours. This was further pruned by 24% using the context matching. The context was created by the company identifying specific competitors within the industry.

Subsequently, the list was winnowed to just 370 most eligible candidates, from whom 287 appeared for the interviews and 209 were made offers for employment. Using the technology, there was

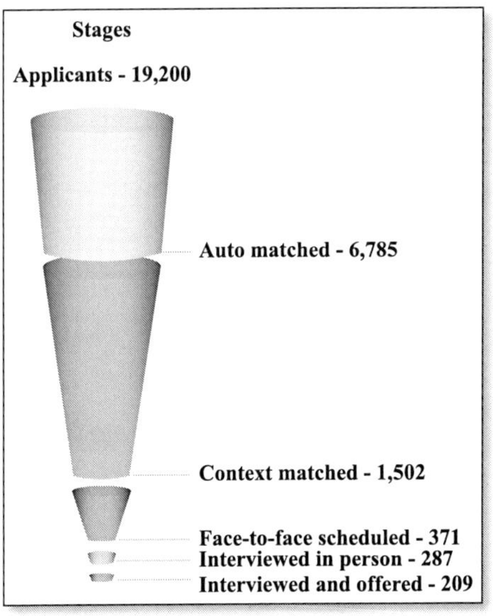

Source: Spire Innovations Inc.

more than 80% improvement in the effort needed for recruiter and for panelists.

There are several steps within the talent acquisition process which are ripe for the use of technology as this illustration shows. However, where is analytics in this?

Spire Innovations have also created the dashboard for reviewing the process to improve the talent acquisition process. This is represented in the enclosed graphs.

Let us look at the first of the graphs. The first graph shows the percentages of resumes from different companies that have made the first cut and the second. For companies A, D, and F, the gap between the two is less when compared to the other three. This gives an indication of the suitability of profiles from such companies that help in fine-tuning the effort.

The second graph compares the company's compensation with that being stated by candidates from different companies. Other things being equal, this gives an independent validation of competition salaries as well as the gap.

Third graph is around the notice periods stated for different companies. Plotting and reviewing this helps a company to consider this key input for selection. If one needs 10 people in a

Figure G.1 (a) Candidate Skill Matching

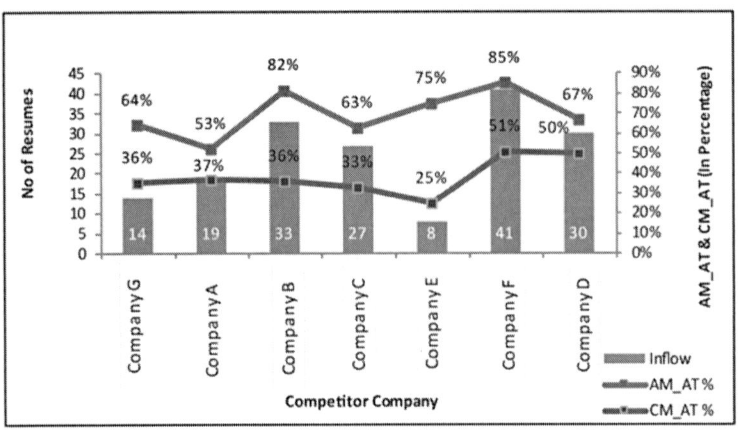

Figure G.1 (b) Competitive Compensation Intelligence

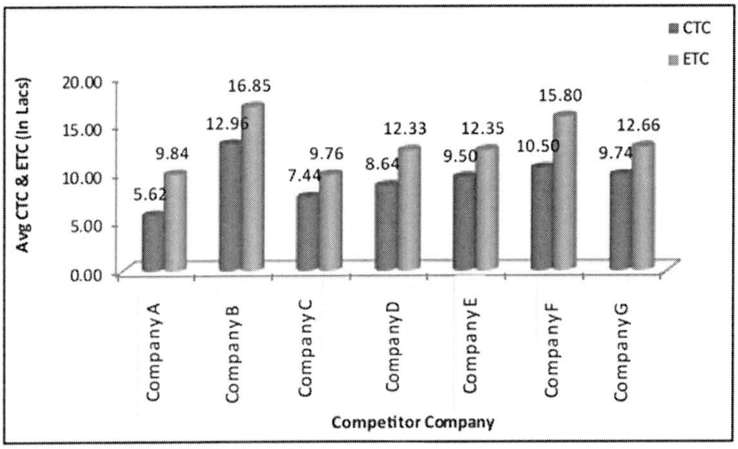

Figure G.1 (c) Notice Period Distribution of Interviewees

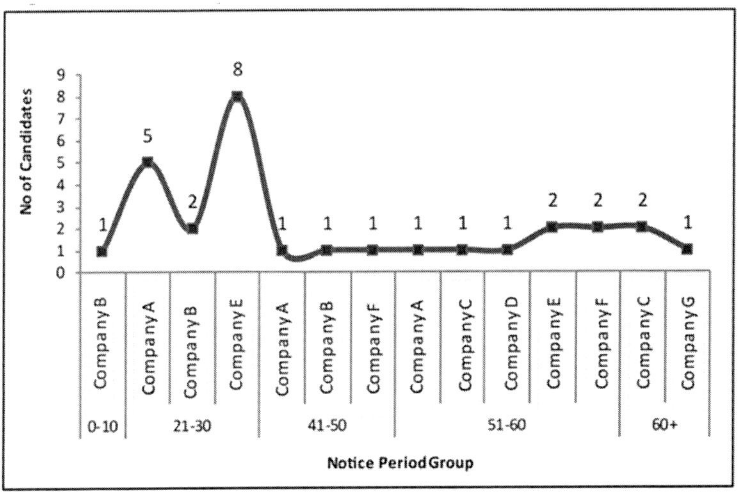

Figure G.1 (d) Interview-to-select Conversions

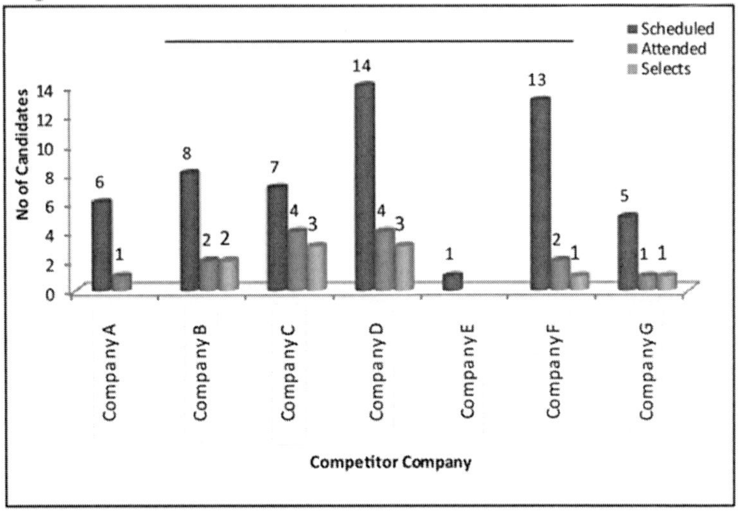

month's time, it makes little sense to make offers to employees from companies that have a 3-month notice period.

The fourth graph presents the company-wise statistics on the recruiting measures:

- By plotting the candidates who were called for interview to those who appeared, one is able to get a measure of comparative brand versus that company.
- By plotting the interview to offer rate, one gets an indication of quality of talent available from that company.
- Finally, by plotting the offer to join rate, one gets the strength of comparative positioning and likelihood of success from hiring from different companies.

These measures are identified and sometimes tracked by companies. However, they do not have the desired impact, unlike this example, as the following steps are not taken:

1. The questions are looked at in terms of "how many" and "how soon." "Where from" is not looked at as an input for

strategizing the talent acquisition strategy. Often, recruiters discern patterns, but lack the analytical language to articulate the same.

2. The measures are stacked wrongly. In this example, measures, such as cycle time, turnout rates, etc., are mapped against unique positions against companies. This again helps the process to be adaptive based on patterns identified. On the other hand, often companies measure these across positions or arrive at one particular number for the entire company. So, a measure like "we have a 65% offer conversion rate" does not help, when one is looking to hire for a specific position. The numbers vary widely across the board and unless these are tagged correctly, one might not be able to predict the outcome of actions.
3. Looking at an available talent as a marketplace where the company competes for resources using its value proposition with other competitors. The ability to attract talent from competitors is a very good indication of whether the positioning is effective or not. A company-centric inside-out view is important, but a market-centric outside-in view is crucial for perspective as well as dynamism in HR policies.

(*Source:* Spire Technologies.)

APPENDIX H

CASE STUDY FOR BUILDING A BUSINESS CASE FOR EMPLOYEE RETENTION[1]

Infosys Limited is a global leader in consulting, technology, outsourcing, and next generation services. The company has revenues in excess of $9 billion and employs close to 200,000 people across the globe. The company has one of the largest training facilities in the world in Mysore, India. To facilitate ongoing growth requirements, the company hires thousands of fresh engineers from across India and the world. The fresh engineers undergo their three-month orientation to programming, soft skills, and computer technology in Mysore.

Context

The company handles a challenging process of arriving at balancing the following:

- Business needs for fresh engineers: This forecast is nearly 18 months ahead, but reviewed on a continuous basis, so that most trainees can be allocated to projects on completing their training.
- Skill requirements: The company trains fresh engineers in several technology streams from Mainframe to. Net, Java, etc. The allocation to skills has to be synchronized to the skill requirements from the business.
- Allocation to locations: The software development headcount in Infosys is distributed across 11 cities. The demand–supply matrix has another variable in terms of utilization numbers from each location.

[1] The data provided in this case study about Infosys is for data representation purposes only. It is not to be republished in any form without the consent of authorized persons from Infosys Limited.

The allocation of employees to the skill is based purely on business demands. At the same time, the company used to consider the employee's choices of location before making the allocation.

In 2012, the company analyzed and found that the fresh engineer attrition was having an impact on the business. The company undertook a six sigma process to measure the reasons for this attrition and reduce the same.

ROOT CAUSE ANALYSIS

With available information, the company performed an analysis on the causes for this attrition. The following reasons were identified.

1. Lack of alignment between the Infosys locations and hiring locations. The company has larger centers in places, such as Bengaluru, Hyderabad, and Chennai. The centers in locations, such as Chandigarh, Gurgaon, etc., are relatively smaller. The hiring numbers from different geographies needed to integrate with the relative headcount ratios, keeping diversity in mind.
2. Low awareness of demand-supply challenges. The trainees were not really aware of how the demand for locations was arrived at. Without this awareness, once allocated they demanded transfer on the allocation being made.
3. Disconnect between actual demand and employee preference. As per the existing process, the trainees needed to make five choices from among the existing locations. This gave them a feeling that they would be allocated to at least one of these locations. In reality, the demand may be in five other locations only. This made the trainees disillusioned with the process.
4. Inadequate communications on the allocation process. The trainees are fresh off college. Just doing a single communication and mailers to them were insufficient, as they were also transitioning to the processes of a corporate career for the first time.

Objectives

The following are the actual measures and goals set by the company.

S. no	Measure	Actual	Objective
1	Percentage of top three preferences met	73	82
2	Percentage of top preference met	47	57
3	Employee satisfaction with the process	44	60

ACTIONS TAKEN

In line with the root cause analysis, the following actions were taken:

1. Repeated communication on the allocation process. The trainees were given an initial overview as well as a mid-course refresher on the allocation process. FAQs and SOPs were shared on portals.
2. Transparency into the list of available vacancies. The number of vacancies available in each location was shared with the employees. This increased their trust in the process, as they were no longer giving preferences based on just their wishes.
3. Simplification of the preferences. Instead of five, trainees needed to just identify their top three choices. The process was initiated on the basis of demands 1 month before the final allocation. This was revisited 15 days later, with the most current set of demands. Trainees were allowed to change their choices accordingly.
4. Creation of an algorithm to prioritize allocations. It is possible that 100 trainees may want to be in Bengaluru, while only 60 slots were available. An automated spreadsheet was created to prioritize in such cases based on the first preference as well as the performance during training. In other words, a

superior performance during training is the best enabler of getting a location of choice.

5. Involve all stakeholders on a continuous basis. Regular updates were shared with the location and BU HR partners. The numbers were shared and process was reviewed with all stakeholders, namely corporate planning, talent planning managers, HR, Global Education Center allocation team, etc. These meetings helped surface the improvement opportunities.

RESULTS

In the quarter before the new process was rolled out, the attrition was 2.74%. The next batch was 4500 strong.

Batch Size:	4,516
Expected attrition at 2.74% =	124
Actual attrition:	59
Attrition percentage:	1.3%

The company also performed creditably against the objectives it had set.

S.no	Measure	Target	Achievement
1	Percentage of top three preferences met	82	80
2	Percentage of top preference met	57	63
3	Employee satisfaction with the process	60	58

The pilot showed a positive outcome. Subsequently, the changes were institutionalized.

BUSINESS BENEFITS

What were the business benefits deriving from this exercise?

Training is expensive, as there are not only payroll costs incurred but also costs incurred in terms of infrastructure, training costs, transportation costs, etc. These worked out to around $5,000 per person. When a trained employee leaves, this becomes a sunk cost.

The new process helped reduce allocation-related attrition by 65 (124–59).

Straight off, this was a saving of 65 × 5,000 = $325,000.

However, there are more benefits as well, from reducing attrition. If a trainee stays on with the company, there is a 70% chance of him/her getting absorbed into a billable project. The company potentially loses that revenue.

It is assumed that it would take six months to find a replacement when a trainee leaves. The opportunity cost of reduced attrition then becomes one of the revenues enabled. In this process, how much did the company benefit from retention?

Taking a conservative estimate, let us take that they are billed $3,000 per month. Then the billing loss if 65 more people quit would be

$$65 \times 0.7 \times 3{,}000 \times 6 = \$819{,}000.$$

The business value from the initiative then is of two parts

1. Savings on investment: $325,000
2. Opportunity retained: $819,000

SUMMARY

This concise case study illustrates the power of reviewing metrics, setting numerical goals for a program and then establishing tangible RoI. Many HR processes can benefit from such an approach.

(*Source:* Infosys)

APPENDIX I

USING STATISTICS TO ARRIVE AT ENGAGEMENT DRIVERS[1]

App Annie is a company focused on delivering powerful market data and insights that allow companies to succeed in the app economy. They are no stranger to how analytics can help people and companies make better decisions. Their free business analytics dashboard aggregates app store, advertising, and usage data for a single view into an app or app portfolio's key metrics. Their app market data provides powerful insight into the market and competition including store intelligence to view download and revenue data, usage intelligence to understand an app's usage, reach, and retention, and audience intelligence to view user demographics and cross-app adoption.

Founded in 2008 in Beijing, they are now headquartered in San Francisco with 400 plus employees across 15 global offices (in four different continents). Denise Lyle is the Global People Programs Senior Manager at App Annie (part of the Human Resources team), responsible for managing the HR related programs that help App Annie grow and scale. Their strategy in building out these programs involves the use of people analytics on the Culture Amp platform. Lyle says that the need for analytics is great as they are a high-growth global company. In her words, "We are definitely dealing with a lot of moving parts at the same time in different corners of the world."

As a global organization, App Annie's values reflect the spirit of the company and its employees, and it strives to live up to them in everything it does. Whether it is "making it happen" on a tight deadline, having a festive happy hour after a product launch to "empower individuals and celebrate achievements," or working across its global offices with the talented people that make up its "many cultures, one team," App Annie's values can be found at the root of all of its decisions.

When App Annie employees were asked which value they personally identified with. Lyle says that about half of the

---

[1] Learn more at www.appannie.com

company said "Many cultures, one team" which she attributes to the fact that, "we certainly do have many cultures here, but there is this sense of 'We are all in it together.' We all share something culturally even though we may have this ethnic or geographical difference."

THE CHALLENGE

App Annie's major challenge was that growing fast made it difficult to drive the right behaviors to achieve the expected outcomes, and their internal and external brand was suffering, explains John Chu, Vice President of People at App Annie. Also like many large companies, especially those with a distributed team, they needed to ensure their employees continued to be engaged; they have grown from 45 employees in 2012 to over 450 employees in 2016. App Annie's first iteration of trying to understand employee sentiment was a brief engagement survey and series of culture focus groups, led by local HR leaders, across the company. These were small group discussions on the culture of the company with key focus on identifying App Annie's core values. While this provided the HR team with some data, they wanted to dig further to find out more about engagement in their employee base.

During this time, App Annie received some negative reviews on the recruiting website Glassdoor. This issue was later determined to be caused by a fragmented culture and shift in expectations as the App Annie headquarters was moved from San Francisco to Beijing. Lyle says quite frankly,

> [W]e don't want negative reviews on Glassdoor for two reasons. Primarily, we don't want people to feel that way, we don't want them to have a poor employee experience at App Annie. Secondarily it also harms recruiting efforts and our employer brand. If we're not providing employees with a way to give us feedback directly, other than this extremely public forum, something's wrong.

Looking back on this time Lyle says, "We just wanted to know what was going on. We thought we knew, but the outputs were telling us some of what we knew but not everything. We needed to know what was happening with our people."

THE SOLUTION

App Annie decided to use Culture Amp, the world's first real-time People Analytics platform, to collect and analyze data from engagement surveys. In her own words, Lyle says, "We use Culture Amp to help us figure out what's going on, gauge employee sentiment, see what's working, what's not. Because we are growing so fast it's really important that we're agile and we iterate quickly." One instance in which the ability to iterate quickly shows itself is in App Annie's practice of setting quarterly goals to keep them moving at a pace to meet their annual goals. This allows them to shift priorities and "focus on what matters most or what needs most attention using Culture Amp analytics," says Lyle.

App Annie's survey methodology is to take two engagement surveys on an annual basis. One main, 50 question survey in Q4 followed by a 15–25 question "pulse survey" in Q2. Their end-of-the-year survey acts as their baseline with a wide range of questions to inform key areas for planning and action while the pulse survey gives feedback on the actions that have been taken, provides index information, and potentially identifies timely issues. High-level results are shared at an all-hands meeting one month after the survey closes and planned action is shared the following month after multiple executive team strategy meetings. Onboarding and Exit surveys are implemented on an ongoing basis.

Where Culture Amp really helps the HR team is in revealing the drivers of engagement, which help interpret the results into tailored actions. The statistics behind the driver analysis helps the HR team at App Annie accelerate the typically lengthy duration of analysis to understand what to address and take action faster. Drivers of engagement are a Kendall tau-c correlation analysis that identifies statistical dependence in ordinal data. Rather than focusing simply on high or low scores, it relies on correlative statistics to identify which topics would have the largest impact on engagement and business outcomes. Lyle says specifically, drivers "provide rich insight for us because they show us what matters most to our employees and where we should focus our efforts to make the biggest impact on engagement."

Culture Amp helped App Annie learn their overall drivers of engagement and allowed them to drill down to drivers in each region:

> This is insightful for us because what is working well in some regions may not be working as well in others, and we can target some of our action plans geographically. For example, we had a surprising result that our employees in APAC were more engaged with our leadership, like communicating the vision of the company, than our employees in the headquarters in San Francisco. That was an interesting data point because you would think that where leaders are located, there would be stronger engagement but we actually saw the opposite. This showed us where to dig a little bit further to understand some root causes.

Additionally, survey items in the leadership factor show a high Kendall tau-c coefficient, ranging from 0.34 to 0.52; signaling these topics relate to business outcomes like productivity and as App Annie has evolved their people analytics methodology Lyle's attitude towards surveys changed as well. She says,

> I think what's most important with gathering survey data, and Steven Huang (Strategist, Data and Insights at Culture Amp) taught me this, is data, insights, and analysis are helpful. But what's really important is how you use the data to plan and take action. It's vital to communicate with your employees along the way.

After their most recent annual engagement survey, App Annie held a global meeting with their senior management group to discuss the results. Each leader received access to specific parts of the survey (divided by three regions: Europe, America, APAC and their department) to review beforehand. They were asked to arrive prepared to discuss some of their hypotheses on engagement based on the survey data, along with a plan of action. Lyle says, "We spent a few hours in breakout sessions facilitated by our HR leaders, looking at specific data and then coming up with action plans by department and by region. Once action plans were created, we communicated back to the employees."

BUSINESS RESULT

Chu says one of the biggest benefits of using Culture Amp is that the results have helped to "inform and validate leadership decisions to change multiple organization structures and move forward with a larger investment in strengthening manager effectiveness". It also allowed the HR team to get executive buy-in for people programs at App Annie. As Lyle says,

> Having data that is valuable to the executive team is really key in making any sort of progress with action planning. Otherwise it is just an HR initiative. It's a very tight window of opportunity right out of the gate to demonstrate data that has strong insights, that is valuable, that is easy for an executive to understand and digest.

A top driver of engagement at App Annie is the leader communicating a motivating vision about the company (Kendall tau-c coefficient of 0.52). Based on their most recent survey results, Lyle says they are on the lower side, but there is action planning taking place to bring those scores up. App Annie plans on sharing their company vision more openly, more frequently, and getting it in front of the employees at company meetings. Specifically, this feedback spurred the creation of their two-part annual survey methodology and skips level one-on-ones. So, in addition to executives and managers having one-on-ones with their direct reports, they are encouraged to have conversations with the employees of their direct reports.

Skip-level meetings can be the best way to learn about your team and a wise investment of your management time for these reasons. First, leaders can gain insight into what is going on with their teams and their day-to-day work. Second, they can assess how managers are doing by checking in with their employees. Lyle says,

> [I]t's also an opportunity for leaders to provide transparency—hitting directly on that issue of communicating a vision that's motivating. It enables leaders to get real-time feedback about what the company is doing, what we should and shouldn't be doing, and getting the employees perspective.

They are also encouraging check-in meetings with the HR team and traditional manager one-on-ones.

Using Culture Amp has allowed App Annie to collect valuable data on their people and allows them to make better decisions to scale their company. Lyle says,

> As the People Operations team in a fast growing organization, we have to use the analytics in order to plan, iterate, grow. Insights and analytics are key to the growth of our company and making sure we are moving in the right direction. We certainly know we are moving fast, we just need to make sure we are focusing our efforts in the right place—we use analytics to do that.

(*Source:* Steven Huang, Strategist, Data & Insights, Culture Amp, San Francisco, California, US.

Alexis Croswell, Associate Marketing Manager, Culture Amp, San Francisco, California, US.)

APPENDIX J

MAKING THE CASE FOR PREDICTIVE ATTRITION RISK MODELING: A ROADMAP FOR THE FUTURE

G.D. Graham, E. Olesen, and R. Dutta

As organizations continue to move up the "people analytics maturity curve," the capability and appeal of using advanced statistical modeling techniques to predict who is likely to leave and why is becoming more prevalent. However, creating statistical models to predict attrition risk is not enough. Two critical issues prevent organizations from harnessing maximum value from these efforts. First, you cannot sacrifice on robustness of your models. This may seem obvious but often organizations overestimate the validity of their data, and in doing so inevitably compromise the integrity and utility of their predictive models. When adopting predictive analytics, many organizations make the mistake of oversimplifying the process by running bivariate correlations on a handful of HRIS data fields, often focusing on a single data source, or performing simple psychometric assessments. Unless the organization adopts a more "complete" stance by gathering data from different sources, internal or external, and then validate their model predictions against actual results, credibility, and value delivered by these models will remain questionable.

The second issue is equally important and perhaps even more challenging: organizations must actually *do something* with the results from these models. They need to find a way to integrate results from their predictive modeling efforts into management of talent workflow and start to address the "so what?" question that arises once the models are built. Actions derived from predictive models can have impact on change management, hiring strategies, workforce planning, risk management, and IT integration. This brings a wealth of new challenges, but neglecting to act on results eliminates any possibility of getting real return on investment of predictive modeling.

Although more and more organizations are investing in predictive attrition risk modeling, very few organizations have totally and seamlessly integrated their results into their talent and workforce management practices. That said many organizations are at least starting that journey—whether it is improving data governance to use for a predictive effort, or conducing pilot studies on targeted populations. Other organizations, like the case study presented in this chapter, are further along on the journey and have validated attrition risk models over several years and begun action planning based on results. The following chapter provides guidance around optimizing a predictive analytics program and a real-life example of an organization currently capitalizing on the potential of predictive attrition risk modeling.

STEP 1. ENSURING THE MODEL(S) IS/ARE ROBUST

When embarking on the predictive analytics journey, it is important to remember the tenet of "garbage in, garbage out." In other words, while logical processes may be robust, the outputs of predictive models are only as good as their data inputs and/or methodological approach. Therefore, any actions or initiatives that stem from those models will only be effective if the models themselves are reliable and that includes not just statistical validity measures like area under the curve or Kolmogorov–Smirnov(KS)value but actual behavior of employees compared against predictions. If organizations truly want to use predictive modeling to affect change, then the model(s) must be rooted in sound data, techniques, and methods. Ensuring model robustness is also key to building credibility in the model and confidence from business leaders, both of which will be critical in building the business case for change.

Start small. Rather than creating an attrition risk model for the entire organization, it is advisable to focus initial efforts on a specific pilot population, such as a business unit, job role, or location where attrition is an issue. While the selected group will still need to be large enough to generate reliable results, focusing on a targeted population is not only more manageable from a data governance perspective but can also give more precise insights into the attrition risk factors affecting that particular group. Even once the pilot population has been selected, HR leaders should also think critically about other criteria for inclusion. For example, a client-facing organization might want to exclude internal support teams. Additionally, part-time employees or those that have been with the organization for less than a year typically leave for different reasons, and therefore may also need to be excluded from the pilot study.

Even within a pilot sample, certain subgroups may act differently when it comes to attrition. For example, within a key role, junior staff may attrite at a different rate than more senior staff. In some cases, these differences are great enough to warrant separate models. Prior to modeling, practitioners should statistically investigate differences between groups in attrition risk variance to determine if multiple models should be deployed to explain different segments of the pilot population.

Only use reliable data. In gathering data for predictive modeling, it can be tempting to use any information or metric that is readily available. However, data that is not systematically and reliably collected can result in erroneous findings. Data that is either not cleanly available or not reliable should be omitted but also tabled as a data governance objective for the future.

Collate multiple sources. Data is also more valuable when it is gathered from different sources across the organization. Using a single source of data to test your hypotheses not only limits the statistical viability of your dataset but also provides a narrow set of predictors for testing your hypothesis. In addition to the standard information found on a typical HRIS platform, analysts should think creatively about other sources that can be leveraged from both inside and outside the organization and those decisions should ideally be guided by a hypotheses framework, rather than arbitrary data hunting. Within the organization, access other databases such as learning management, performance ratings, and employee surveys. Outside the organization, macroeconomic, socioeconomic, social media, and benchmarking data can also supplement your list of predictive input data.

Look beyond bivariate relationships. The end goal of an attrition risk model is not to identify any and all factors that correlate with turnover. Simply reporting the factors that correlate with attrition will result in a list of correlates that may not have any causal linkage with attrition behavior. Instead, attrition risk modeling should use a combination of statistical criteria and organizational knowledge to expose the predictors of attrition that are most impactful. This not only makes findings and results more manageable in terms of reporting but also provides insight into the specific levers to pull in order to affect changes in turnover rates.

Verify against actual attrition. Rather than immediately acting on pilot model results, organizations can do much to ensure the validity of their model by letting it "play out" for a while and then compare the model-generated attrition predictions against actual attrition behavior. Just as inaction can detract from the utility of predictive analytics, premature action implemented before a final model is solidified can be equally harmful. Therefore after conducting a pilot study, many organizations spend six months to a year simply observing the model and then determining the percentage of voluntary leavers that were correctly identified as "high risk."

Refine as needed. As the organization continues to change, the model should continually be refined to remain valid and useful. This could mean that new data has become available that should be tested, or existing data should be re-operationalized in a more meaningful way. Additionally organizational initiatives, population turnover, and even socioeconomic factors could render certain predictors more or less impactful in characterizing attrition. Therefore models should be continuously evaluated in terms of validity and refined as necessary.

STEP 2. INTEGRATING MODEL RESULTS INTO ORGANIZATIONAL TALENT WORKFLOW

Once model results have been validated and refined, HR can begin to take actions to mitigate attrition. First, findings from attrition risk modeling should be integrated into the organization's retention strategy wherever possible. This means identifying the *actionable* factors in the model that are causing employees to stay, and capitalizing on them in various aspects of the employee experience. For example, if training hours is associated with lower attrition, HR's learning and development sector can find ways to make training more accessible, useful, and prolific among employees. In the same vein, HR can identify actionable factors that increase attrition risk, and implement ways to mitigate them. If career stagnation has been shown to increase attrition initiatives such as cross-job training, coaching, and reward structures can all be avenues for improving retention.

In terms of talent management, results from an attrition risk model can be a key piece of information for leaders. Using robust statistical algorithms, attrition risk modeling can predict the likelihood of attrition for all employees in the organization, and classify "high risk" leavers as necessary. This list of probable leavers can be mapped against the list of top talent that leaders generate during an annual talent assessment. Taking the outputs of attrition risk modeling one step further to identify not just the potential loss but potential *regrettable* loss can help leaders plan their talent management strategies accordingly.

Attrition risk findings can also inform selection strategies. While some predictors of attrition, such as educational background or previous experience, may not be actionable in terms of the current employee population, they can be targeted in recruiting, assessment, and selection. In doing so, organizations can weed out candidates with high-risk characteristics and focus on those with characteristics consistent with longevity in the organization.

Finally, HR, and IT sectors will need to work together to answer the question: How can we integrate attrition risk findings into our technology infrastructure? To begin, dashboards and other visualization tools are useful for monitoring significant predictors and attrition patterns. Many organizations start this effort by creating a stand-alone attrition risk dashboard, and work towards incorporating it into the overall HR dashboard. IT can also enhance data governance structures to create easy access to modeling data. Currently, a significant amount of manual work goes into pulling, merging, compiling, and computing modeling data, but in the future the more sophisticated organizations will be able to do all of this at the click of a button. Few, if any, organizations currently have this capability and current "black box" approaches sold by some software vendors are not robust enough. But along the predictive analytics journey the demand will ideally be for a system (rather than a team of individuals) that can run models on an ongoing basis and continually provide results to managers and leaders of an organization.

CASE STUDY: BOOZ ALLEN HAMILTON[1]

Over the past 5 years, Booz Allen Hamilton (BAH), a large professional services firm based in the US, has worked with PricewaterhouseCoopers (PwC) People Analytics (Saratoga) practice to build, refine, and act on attrition risk models as part of their larger HR strategy. Within the company, attrition rates had been high for some time but leaders had few tangible results on which to base their retention strategies. As a professional services firm, BAH recognized that people were their main "product," so any investment made to mitigate unwanted attrition is likely to have a substantial return. Additionally, the company had a reputation for being tech-savvy in many of their own offerings, and wanted to apply that same scientific rigor to solving their "people problem." Predictive analytics—particularly, attrition risk modeling—was identified as something that would be both useful and a differentiator for BAH in the talent management marketplace.

THE ROADMAP TO DATE: YEARS 1–3

In the first year of their attrition risk modeling effort, BAH identified the need to create three models—one for each of their three business units. This decision was based not only on the statistical finding that attrition rates differed between the units but

---

[1] Booz Allen Hamilton provides management and technology consulting and engineering services to a range of public sector organizations, private corporations, government agencies, and not-for-profit companies. With offices and clients around the world, BAH provides expertise and insight in consulting, analytics, technology, cybersecurity, engineering, innovation, and more.

also the practical realization that any actions or efforts stemming from the results would most likely be implemented at the business unit level. After the models were built, BAH focused primarily on disseminating results to senior leaders and educating them on the potential utility of the findings. This focus on gaining leader buy-in not only prevented HR from implementing actions premature but also helped strengthen the business case and support for attrition risk modeling across senior leadership. The rollout of findings largely consisted of education on the purposes of the model and discussions around particular variables. Specifically, HR leaders continually expressed that the model was intended to identify the factors that affected attrition above and beyond all else, rather than simply identify any and all contributors to turnover. Discussions also centered on concerns from leaders, such as ensuring that results were only distributed to only the high-level managers and protecting the privacy of employees identified as "high risk." Beyond this education of high-level leaders, no other tangible actions were taken other than simply observing the model over the next year.

The second year brought refinements to the model as well as an increased interest from leadership and a more useful communication of results. Due to HR's large-scale educational efforts in the prior year, leaders who saw results last year began to ask for updated findings, while leaders who did not see the results asked to be included in the current year's rollout. This brought the challenge of educating a new segment of leaders and opening up the model to more critique, but it also meant the demand for attrition risk modeling was growing within the organization especially because the predictions made in the previous iteration were increasingly coming out to be true. In assessing the accuracy of the first year prediction, BAH saw that most employees who had been classified as "high risk" actually left the organization in the following year, while very few "low risk" employees left. To accommodate the demand and make results more useful, the second year results included a rank order of elevated risk employees based on their model-generated probability score. This helped leaders prioritize who they wanted to target in their retention strategies. HR leaders also created a toolkit to assist leaders in using the information.

The toolkit contained the findings themselves, information on how to interpret the findings, and a preliminary "action guide" that leveraged information found in current best practice periodicals. It also contained guidance and questions for managers to use in conducting "stay interviews." Managers were encouraged to integrate these questions into their already existing one-on-one cadence with direct reports, with a focus on those employees identified as "high risk."

BAH has recently completed its third annual iteration of attrition risk model. This past year, BAH implemented changes to the model itself, the communication of findings, and their strategic retention actions. To start, the model was expanded to a larger population within the organization. This decision was based not only in confidence of the existing model's robustness but also in demand from other leaders whose business units had not been included in prior models. The request signified a shift from "push" to "pull" in terms of how information was distributed to the organization's decision-makers. Leaders were now directly asking for annual attrition modeling results. HR and executives were continually having discussions around attrition, and in turn were seeking out as much information as possible. Attrition risk modeling results had come to be viewed as a critical piece of that information.

To further aid in the dissemination of information, HR partnered with IT to create a Tableau-based dashboard visualization of attrition risk results. In prior years, results were given in static Microsoft Excel files containing a list of high-risk employees and heat maps that identified pockets of high risk across the organization. With the deployment of an attrition risk dashboard, the findings could be disseminated more efficiently and included many of the details that leaders had previously been asking for, including segmentation and filtering capabilities. Other HRIS information was also integrated into the dashboard that provided more information about high-risk employees which would be a "regrettable loss" (e.g., top talent, high tenure or time in level, recently promoted, highly billable, etc.). This information further helped leaders prioritize who they needed to address in their retention strategies. At the completion of the third year, BAH maintains that it is still too early for enterprise-level action based on modeling results. However, they noted that there has been a tangible shift in focus when it comes to acting on attrition risk models in which BAH leaders went from addressing teams of high-risk employees to addressing all teams in the organization and the high-risk employees within those teams.

ROADMAP FOR THE FUTURE

As the results of the attrition risk models continue to effectively inform retention strategies BAH plans to implement other predictive studies that address a variety of organizational issues. First, with the support of PwC People Analytics, they are preparing to conduct an analysis to predict the quality of hire among current and potential employees. The first step in that process will be to identify a primary key role that will be critical for growth in the future. For example, the role of software engineer is seen as a key position and consists of about 1,600 employees across the organization. By targeting a particular role rather than a family of jobs, BAH is hoping to generate a specific quality of hire profile rather than a more generic characterization of a "good" employee. The end goal of a quality of hire model would be to identify the characteristics that make someone successful at BAH and ultimately translate that into a hiring "checklist" that can be used when evaluating potential candidates. However, this model brings its own set of challenges. For one, the outcome variable—quality of hire—is not as easily defined as attrition. Leaders and HR practitioners would need to think critically about what constitutes a "high-quality hire," and how those characteristics can be measured and operationalized. Additionally, much like leader education was the initial focus of the attrition risk model, significant efforts would need to be made to orient leaders to a qualitatively different predictive model. Fortunately, the progress made in educating leaders on the utility of predictive attrition modeling will provide a solid foundation for easily and efficiently getting leaders up to speed.

Another potential avenue for predictive analytics is a study around why candidates reject hire offers from BAH. The interest in this model was sparked by an uptick in this metric, but again provides a unique set of challenges for HR to address. To date, the most critical challenges are surrounding both the quantity and quality of existing data. Not only is there a paucity of data being collected in this area by BAH but the data that does exist is largely derived from self-report and is therefore less reliable than more objective metrics. Nevertheless, as BAH continues to expand and integrate its predictive analytics capabilities, leaders will be more willing and able to take on such challenges in an effort to create data-based actions and strategies.

Full integration of multiple predictive tools is also a long-term goal for BAH. By marrying results from models around attrition, quality of hire, declined offers, and more predictive analytics can inform the entire workforce planning process. Retention strategies, selection processes, career development practices, visualization tools, and other aspects of talent management can all be rooted in a series of robust statistical findings and data-driven decision-making. This will provide BAH, and other organizations willing to embark on this journey, with a more concrete foundation on which to build their leading practices and a greater return on investment from their workforce and workforce planning initiatives.

Finally, the ultimate goal of any analytics investment is to eventually integrate analytics into all business decisions. Right now, BAH, like many other organizations, uses data in most if not all business decisions. For example, basic decision-making around recruitment and selection needs can be informed by simple data such as the number of new hires in last month. But to make more long-term strategic plans and decisions, organizations will need more than just straightforward data—they will need the insights and knowledge that can only be generated by more complex analytics. Right now, BAH is applying these predictive methods to the beginning and end of the employee life cycle with the quality of hire and attrition risk modeling, respectively. But what about all of the aspects of the employee life cycle that fall in between? Just as there is currently no part of the life cycle that does not have data associated with it, a robust analytics program will eventually ensure that predictive modeling and analytics touch each phase of the employee lifecycle as well. In doing so, a comprehensive analytics program can elevate data-driven business decisions into robust strategic initiatives rooted in rigorous analytical insights.

Gia Graham, Ph.D., PwC People Analytics

Gia Graham is a Senior Associate with PwC in the people analytics practice. Her work consists of various analytic initiatives such as metrics and benchmarking, conjoint analysis, workforce and customer surveys, and predictive modeling. Prior to joining PwC, Gia worked at the US Army Research Institute for the Behavioral and Social Sciences as a research fellow and research scientist. Gia earned her PhD in Industrial/Organizational Psychology from George Mason University in 2013.

Eric Olesen, Booz Allen Hamilton

Eric s a Senior Associate with Booz Allen Hamilton and leads their Workforce Analytics function. He has over 15 years experience in the fields of Applied Statistics and Predictive Analytics in the areas of Human Capital, Quantitative Market Research, and Survey Methodology. Eric received his bachelor degree in Psychology and Business Administration from Wayne State University and holds a Master of Science in Industrial/Organizational Psychology from the University of Akron.

Ranjan Dutta, PhD, PwC People Analytics

Ranjan is a Director at PwC's LLP with over 15 years of experience in management consulting, workforce analytics, statistical modeling, and behavioral economics. He leads the predictive analytics practice at PwC People Analytics (Saratoga). Ranjan has provided advisory services to senior executives all over the world spanning multiple industry sectors and functional domains. He is a thought leader in the area of people analytics and has been variously interviewed/ quoted by prominent media outlets, such as *CFO.com*, *HR Magazine*, HBR Analytic Services, *HR Executive*, *CNN/Money*, *Wall Street Journal*, Bloomberg BNA.

APPENDIX K

DISCOVERING TEAM COHESIVENESS AND INFLUENCERS USING ORGANIZATION NETWORK ANALYSIS

One of India's leading financial services companies was seized of a challenge. Should it continue to fill its ranks by hiring from outside for middle management roles? Or should it groom talent from within, by hiring at entry levels? This is a problem faced universally by organizations.

Growing from within creates a strong culture, but needs patience and a mature approach to deliver results. Employees need to grow into roles and get promoted. Need-based external hiring is swift at the outset, but in the long run it takes far more effort to onboard and integrates employees from different organizations. Long-term retention becomes another challenge.

While the problem is common, the organization innovated by using the emerging technique of organization network analysis.

PRINCIPLES

Organizations are not what their formal structure denotes. Let us look at a social network metaphor. In social networks, the stories can emanate from anywhere and gain likes. Influencers in social networks are not necessarily the biggest stars but ones with a very original point of view. It helps to be a celebrity.

Similarly, work and goals cascade down a formal organization structure. Increasingly, organizations resemble a network and the successful ones are far more cohesive than those which are not. The informal and uncharted organization wields as much influence or more, than the formal.

Mapping information flow helps us in recreating the informal organization. Correlating the cohesion of the informal organization with the percentage of in-house/lateral talent would establish the case to groom from within or otherwise.

PROBLEM STATEMENT

The company had moved from a "buy just in time talent" to "make talent in-house." However, the success rate for this strategy varied across different business entities. Some of them attributed a talent shortage to account for their region's mediocre performance. The company wanted to:

- Identify what the enabling conditions for the success of the strategy are.
- Identify who can be tapped to ensure that the program is a success.
- Assess the long-term viability of the strategy.

The company worked with i-Cube, a company specializing in organization network analysis using their proprietary tool OWEN.

Approach

The company ran a survey across its HR organization. The brief survey required the participants to answer questions across areas, such as mentorship, innovation, career, etc. In the survey, there were specific questions for employees to enlist who in their peer group is:

- Someone who they interact with for helping out with their daily issues,
- Someone who they look upto as mentors, and
- Someone who is their role model and whose inputs they value for career growth.

That someone can be their manager but also a peer or a manager in a different group. Based on their inputs, the informal organization was created. The following insights emerged.

1. *Uniformly distributed networks perform better*

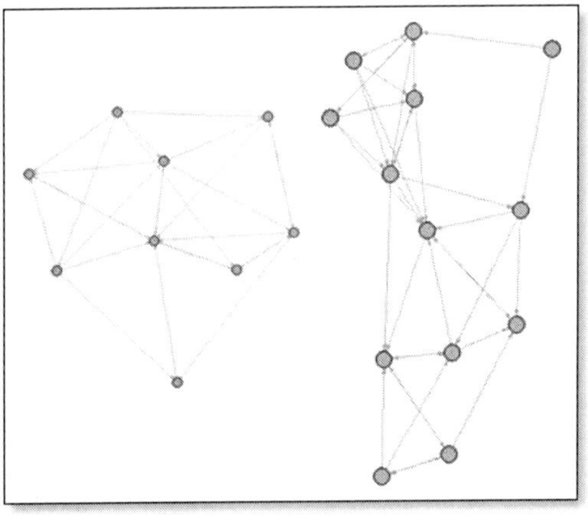

Let us look at the two entities. Each point corresponds to an individual and the connections are based on the survey inputs. The one on the left shows a more fluid structure with a greater degree of interconnects. On the other hand, the structure on the right has fewer nodes through which the information flows and there are outliers, who are not connected to anyone. This correlated with the performance of respective organizations.

It was also found that the closeness of a leader to his/her team (as measured by the average distance in nodes for all team members from the leader) also influenced the performance positively.

2. *Cohesive teams perform better*

Cohesiveness of the team can be represented using the following two measures:

1. Team density: Let us assume that there is a 20-member team. Let us consider two scenarios. One, where only 5 members are identified as "go-to" people by the team. The second, where 15 out of 20 people are mutually identified as "go-to" people. Team density in the first case is 5/20 = 0.25, while in the second case it is 15/20 = 0.75. A higher team density indicates greater collaboration levels within the team.

2. Team average path: To begin with, each team member is just a point on a plot. Then, based on the survey feedback, connections are established between points. Some points have several lines passing through them, indicating an influential role. How many degrees of separation are there on average for every team member? A team with an average path of 1.2 is far more cohesive, than the one with 2.1 for instance.

The organization's survey showed the following trends. These clearly established that there is a correlation between cohesiveness and performance.

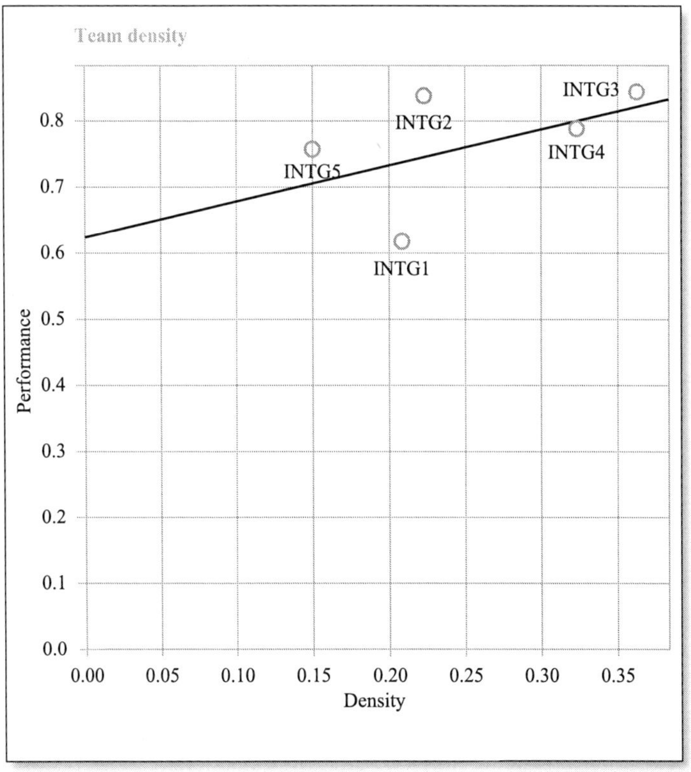

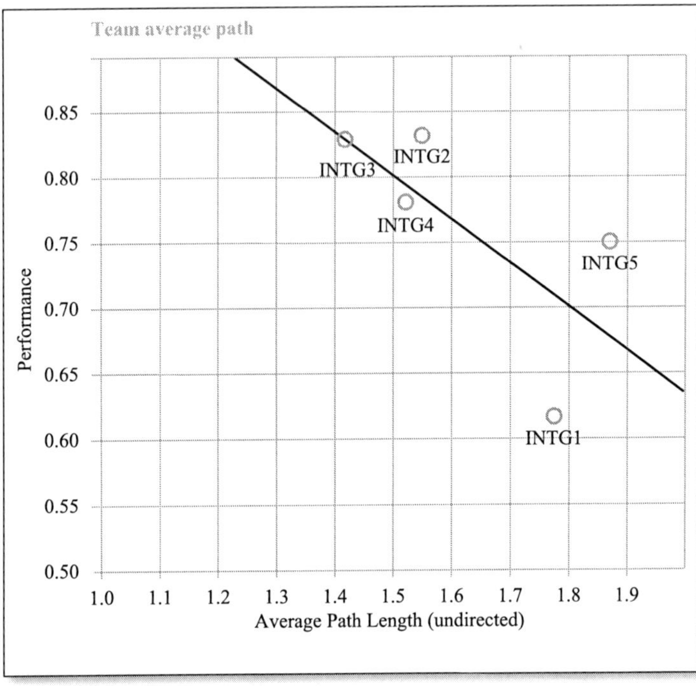

3. *Junior team members can wield disproportionate influence*

Once the linkages are plotted, we can identify the influencers by their connectedness. "Connectedness" is indicated by the number of times a certain node (person) appears in the shortest path between two other nodes. A well connected person will have a higher score of connectedness, than a lower one.

The study identified several team members, who wielded considerable influence.

SUMMARY

By using the organizational network analysis, the company was able to identify the factors that can make or break the HR programs, independent of the merits of the program. In a loose network, the leader's formal power and his/her opinion holds sway. If the person

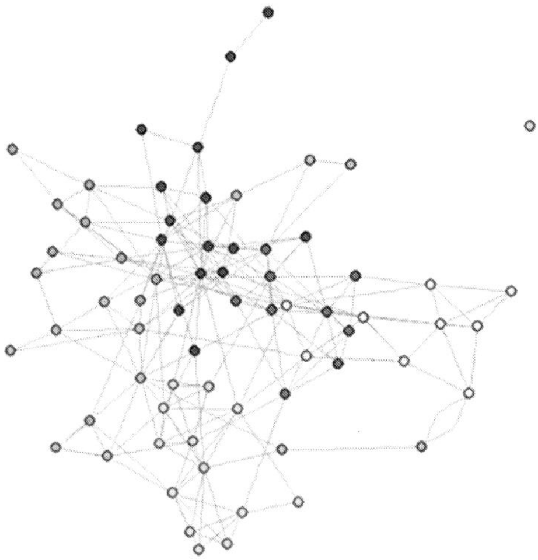

is in favor of lateral hiring, then lateral hiring works. However, in a more cohesive team with distributed influence, there are greater interactions and the team arrives at the best decision based on the team's view. HR can leverage this by sharing the business case not just with the formal organization, but by reaching out to the influencers also.

Network analysis offers us a powerful way of measuring and visualizing the strength of teams. With future going towards holacracy from bureaucracy such analytical tools are expected to play a big role.

This case study is on the basis of inputs provided by M/s I-cube, using their OWEN framework.

(*Source:* I-cube)

References

Adler, Seymour, & Golan, Jacob. (1981). Lateness as a withdrawal behavior. *Journal of Applied Psychology* (October), *66*(5), 544–554.

Baird, L. & Meshoulam, I. (1988). Managing two fits of strategic human resource management. *Academy of Management Review*, *13*, 116–128.

Barney, J. (1991). Firm resources and competitive advantage. *Journal of Management, 17*(1), 99–120.

Bersin, J. (2016). Is software better at managing people than you are? *Fortune*.

Bersin, J., O'Leonard, K., & Wang-Audia, W. (2013). *High impact talent analytics: Building a world class analytics and measurement function*. Oakland, CA: Bersin by Deloitte. Retrieved July 18, 2016, from http://marketing.bersin.com/rs/bersin/images/hita100113sg.pdf

Cantrell, S., Benton, J.M., Laudal, T., & Thomas, R.J. (2006). Measuring the value of human capital investments: The SAP case. *Strategy & Leadership, 34*(2), 50.

Cascio, Wayne F. & Boudreau, John. (2011). *Investing in people: Financial impact of human resource initiatives*. New Jersey: Pearson Education.

CedarCrestone. (2014). *Going global with HR technologies—2014: CedarCrestone 2013–2014 HR systems survey*. Alpharetta, GA: Sierra–Cedar.

Coco, Cedric T., Jamison, Fiona, & Black, Heather. (2011). Connecting people investments and business outcomes at Lowe's, *HR People + Strategy* , *34*(2).

ConAgra Foods. (2010). Conagra foods recognized for its innovative leadership development programs. Retrieved June 16, 2016, from http://www.conagrafoods.com/investor-relations/news-ConAgra-Foods-Recognized-for-Its-Innovative-Leadership-Development-Programs-1486696

Coolen, Patrick & IJsselstein, Auke. (2015). A practitioner's view on HR Analytics. Retrieved July 18, 2016, from https://www.linkedin.com/pulse/practitioners-view-hr-analytics-patrick-coolen

Crush, Peter. (2009, March). Engagement surveys: Gallup and best companies face criticism. *HR magazine*.

Davenport, Thomas H., Harris, Jeane, & Shapiro, Jeremy. (2010). Competing on talent analytics. *Harvard Business Review*.

Drucker, P.F. (1954). *The practice of management*. New York: Harper & Row.

Fitz-enz., J. (1978). The measurement imperative. *Personnel Journal, 54*(4).

Friedman, T. (2014, February). How to get a job at Google. *New York Times*.

Gallup. (2012). *State of the workforce report*. Washington, DC: Gallup Inc.

Garvin, D.A., Wagonfel, A.B., & Kind, L. (2013). *Google's project oxygen: Do managers matter* (Case 313–110). Boston, MA: Harvard Business School.

Gates, S. (2002). *Value at work: The risks and opportunities of human capital measurement and reporting*. New York: The Conference Board.

Gates, S. (2008). *Strategic human capital measures: Orientation, accountability and communication*. New York: The Conference Board.

Gebicke, S., & Magid, S. (2012). *Lessons from around the world: Benchmarking performance in defense*. MoG_Benchmarking, McKinsey & Company.

GoogleEDU (2012, July 5). School's in session at Google. *The Wall Street Journal*. Retrieved June 22, 2016, from http://www.wsj.com/articles/SB10001424052702303410404577466852658514144

Harrison, David A., Newman, Daniel A., & Roth, Philip L. (2006). How important are job attitudes? Meta analytic comparisons of integrative behavioral outcomes and time sequences. *Academy of Management Journal, 49*(2), 305–325

Hausknecht, J. (2013, December). They are watching you at work. *The Atlantic*.

Huselid, M.A. (1995). The impact of human resource management practices turnover, productivity and corporate financial performance. *Academy of Management Journal, 38*(3), 635–672.

Kirkpatrick, D.L. (1959a). Techniques for evaluating training programs. *Journal of American Society of Training Directors, 13*(11), 3–9.

Kirkpatrick, D.L. (1959b). Techniques for evaluating training programs: Part 2—Learning. *Journal of American Society of Training Directors, 13*(12), 21–26.

Kirkpatrick, D.L. (1960a). Techniques for evaluating training programs: Part 3—Behavior. *Journal of American Society of Training Directors, 14*(1), 13–18.

Kirkpatrick, D.L. (1960b). Techniques for evaluating training programs: Part 4—Results. *Journal of American Society of Training Directors, 14*(2), 28–32.

Kowske, B. (2012). *Employee engagement: Market review, buyer's guide, provider profiles*. Oakland, CA: Bersin by Deloitte.

Laney, D. (2001). *3D data management: Controlling data volume, velocity, and variety*. Stamford, CT: META Group Inc.

LaValle, S., Lesser, E., Shockley, R., Hopkins, M.S., & Kruschwitz, N. (2011). Big data, analytics and path form insights to value. *MIT Sloan Management Review*, 52(2).

Lavoie, A. (2014). Measure these 5 talent metrics for greater success in hiring and managing employees. *Entrepreneur*. Retrieved July 18, 2016,from https://www.entrepreneur.com/article/239117

Lewis, M. (2003). *Moneyball: The art of winning an unfair game*. New York, NY: W. W. Norton & Company.

Lombardi, M., & Laurano, M. (2012). *Human capital management trends*. Boston, MA: Aberdeen Group.

Macy, John (2015). HR will never be strategic. Retrieved July 22, 2016 from https://www.linkedin.com/pulse/hr-never-strategic-john-macy?trk=mp-reader-card

Mavrinac, S., & Siesfeld, T. (1998). *Measures that matter: An exploratory investigation of investor's information needs and value priorities*. London: Ernst & Young Center for Business Innovation.

Michaels, E., Handfield-Jones, H., & Axelrod, B. (1997). *War for talent*. New York, NY: McKinsey & Company.

Neilson, G., & Wulf, J. (2012, April). How many direct reports? *Harvard Business Review*.

Organ, Dennis. (1988). Organization citizenship behavior, the good soldier syndrome. Lexington, MA: Lexington Books

Palmer, S. (2010). *Making the business case for learning and development: 5 steps for success*. Chapel Hill, NC: UNC Kenan–Flagler Business School.

Pease, G., Beresford, B., & Walker, L. (2014). *Developing human capital: Using analytics to plan and optimize your learning and development investments.* Hoboken, NJ: Wiley.

Penrose, E. T. (1959). *The theory of the growth of the firm*. New York: John Wiley.

Phillips, J. J. (1996a). How much is the training worth? *Training and Development*, *50*(4), 20–24.

PwC Saratoga. (2014). *Trends in workforce analytics: Capturing the latest benchmark results from US human capital effectiveness report*. New York: PwC. Retrieved June 16, 2016, from http://www.pwc.com/en_US/us/hr-management/publications/assets/pwc-trends-in-workforce-analytics.pdf

Rucci, Anthony J., Kirn, Steven P., & Quinn, Richard P. (1998). The employee–customer–profit chain at Sears. *Harvard Business Review* (January–February).

Schneider, C. (2006, February). The new human capital metrics. *CFO*.

Shobha, V. (2015, July 31). Sridhar Vembu, the code breaker. *OPEN*.

Sun Microsystems. (2014). Vestrics—Client success stories. Retrieved November 15, 2015, from http://www.vestrics.com/client-success-stories.html

Training Industry Inc. (2016). *Size of the training Industry*. Raleigh, NC: author. Retrieved June 16, 2016, from https://www.trainingindustry.com/wiki/entries/size-of-training-industry.aspx

Vickers, M. (2010). *The crummy state of talent management metrics (and what to do about it)*.i4cp. Retrieved July 23, 2016, from http://www.

i4cp.com/trendwatchers/2010/06/02/the-crummy-state-of-talent-management-metrics-and-what-to-do-about-it

Waterman, R. H., Peters, T. J., & Phillips, J. R. (1980). Structure is not organization. *Business Horizons*, *23*(3), 14–26.

Index

About the Authors

Ramesh Soundararajan is an HR professional with 25 years of experience as a practitioner and consultant. An electrical engineer from National Institute of Technology (NIT), Kozhikode, Ramesh completed his master's in personnel management and industrial relations from Xavier School of Management (XLRI), Jamshedpur.

Crompton Greaves, TVS Whirlpool, Infosys Technologies (more than a decade), and Sasken Communications are the prominent companies he has worked with. Presently he is the founding partner of Culstran LLP, a firm focused on consulting corporates in the areas of culture, strategy, and analytics. He has worked as a location head of HR, head of a CoE, as well as the head of the function. He has consulted with clients in India as well as in the USA.

In all his roles, he has pioneered an analytical approach to reviewing information, integrating insights from across different functions to help the function put its best foot forward. The approach encompasses all HR domains such as performance management, learning and development, and talent acquisition and retention. His blog on analytics, "HR3by2", is widely referred to. He is working with large corporations from developing analytics competency in HR to designing interactive dashboards. He also works with start-ups in the HR analytics space. He is a trained assessor using the PCMM and CII HR models.

Dr Kuldeep Singh is Director, HR, at Capgemini, Bangalore. He has 20+ years of experience in HR having worked in manufacturing and IT sector. He has held various positions such as corporate head (HR), strategic HR advisor, global head (OD), etc., for organizations with headcount size from 4,500 to 67,000+. His last position was corporate head (HR) and strategic HR advisor for UST Global Inc. Prior to UST Global, he has worked at Infosys as senior manager and head Performance Management System (PMS), spearheading PMS and Organization Development (OD) interventions globally.

Before his corporate career, he worked as an associate professor (HR) at IIM Indore. He has specialized in HR/people analytics and conducted open workshops on HR analytics with IIMs at metro locations and in-house workshops for business partner HR teams of a tier-I Indian technology services company. His publications on HR analytics on social media, and in HR magazines and leading business newspapers have been globally acclaimed. He is fortified with HR and business analytics certifications from Wharton and UC Berkeley and a PhD in HR from XLRI.